The Mysteries of the Head and Heart Explained

Also from Westphalia Press
westphaliapress.org

The Mysteries of the Head and Heart Explained

A Look at Phrenology and Mesmerism

by J. Stanley Grimes

WESTPHALIA PRESS
An Imprint of Policy Studies Organization

Westphalia Press
An imprint of Policy Studies Organization
1527 New Hampshire Ave., NW
Washington, D.C. 20036
info@ipsonet.org

ISBN-13: 978-1-63391-594-7
ISBN-10: 1-63391-594-8

Cover design by Jeffrey Barnes:
jbarnesbook.design

Daniel Gutierrez-Sandoval, Executive Director
PSO and Westphalia Press

Updated material and comments on this edition
can be found at the Westphalia Press website:
www.westphaliapress.org

A VISION SEEING MEDIUM.

"I see a beautiful rainbow, and beyond, beneath the arch, I see the spirit land, and I hear the spirits sing."

THE

MYSTERIES

OF THE

HEAD AND THE HEART

EXPLAINED:

INCLUDING

AN IMPROVED SYSTEM OF PHRENOLOGY: A NEW THEORY OF
THE EMOTIONS, AND AN EXPLANATION OF THE MYSTE-
RIES OF MESMERISM, TRANCE, MIND-READING,
AND THE SPIRIT DELUSION.

ILLUSTRATED BY UPWARDS OF ONE HUNDRED ENGRAVINGS.

By J. STANLEY GRIMES.

SEVENTH EDITION.

———————

CHICAGO:
R. R. DONNELLEY & SONS COMPANY.
1897.

INTRODUCTORY.

THIS Volume contains a summary of the results of more than sixty years of study and experience concerning Mental Phenomena. Part First consists of what the author and his friends regard as a greatly improved system of Phrenology. Part Second contains an entirely new account of the relations of the body and mind to each other, including several discoveries concerning the Physiology of the Emotions, and their beneficial effects upon the heart and other vital organs. Part Third is devoted to an application of the principles previously explained, to solve the mysteries that have hitherto surrounded the phenomena of Trance, Mesmerism, and Spiritism.

If any of my readers, on seeing that my whole superstructure is founded upon phrenology, are inclined to reject it on that account, with the remark that they do not believe in phrenology, my reply is that I ask no one to believe in it. Science is not a matter of belief, but of positive knowledge. If it cannot be demonstrated to be true beyond all doubt, it does not deserve to be regarded as a science at all. No one is expected to believe in chemistry, in geology, or in astronomy. When Galileo, by means of his newly invented telescope, discovered that Jupiter had four moons, some of his opponents declared that they did not believe it. Very well, said Galileo, I do not ask you to believe, I only ask you to look through this small tube and see them for yourselves; but instead of looking they arrested and punished him.

Now I assert, from abundant experience, that no person can fairly examine phrenology for a single day, under the guidance of a competent examiner, without finding satisfactory evidence that its main features are in accordance with nature. Let me suggest a few tests: 1. Find a man with a very low, wide, short head, and he will, upon acquaintance, in *all* cases, prove to be extremely selfish, and indifferent to the interests and wants of his fellow men. 2. Find another, whose head is very high and long and narrow, and he will prove to be deficient in selfishness; he will be prone to neglect his own affairs and attend to those of others. 3. Find a man whose head is high in front and low at the upper back part, and he will be found to be deficient in firmness of purpose; on the contrary, one who is low in front and high at the back of the head, in the region of Firmness, will manifest decision and stability of character. 4. Find one who is very prominent in the lower part of the forehead and narrow and retreating in the reflective region, and he will prove to be a mere imitator, and incapable of invention.

The history of the commencement of this science is exceedingly instructive. Francis Joseph Gall, the founder of phrenology, was born in Suabia, in Germany, in 1757. At the age of nine, as he himself states, he was placed, with another boy, under the tuition of an uncle, and while with him was often reprimanded for his inability to compete with his companion in learning by rote, although in other respects he greatly excelled him. The two boys were subsequently sent to school at Basle, where thirty boys attended, several of whom committed to memory with such facility, that, although they stood in the eighth or tenth place in other exercises, in this they rose to the highest. Two of the thirty even excelled Gall's first companion; and he was struck at the coincidence of all of them having eyes so prominent as to have given rise to the nickname of bull's eyes. He was subsequently transferred to another school, and again lost his place by inability to compete with other boys at verbal recitation; and here, too, he observed the projecting eyes of those who excelled him in this exercise. At a later period he again suffered defeat in the same way at the college of Strasburgh, and by youths whose eyes exhibited the same kind of prominence. Here was the beginning of phrenological discovery. He now entered upon the study of medicine. This, of all professions, was best calculated to aid him in his new researches, not only by outward observations in connection with mental manifestations, but also in extending his researches to the brain itself, by examination after death.

The first written notice of Dr. Gall's enquiries concerning the head, appeared in a familiar letter to Baron Retzer, which was inserted in a German periodical, in December, 1798. Two years previous he had given private lectures upon the subject at Vienna. Some of his hearers made public notices of his doctrines, which ultimately drew from the Austrian government an edict that such lectures must cease, his doctrines being considered dangerous to religion. Gall then removed to Paris, where he remained until his death, which occurred in 1828. It is an interesting and remarkable fact, that while Gall was in Paris, it was, temporarily at least, the residence of a greater number of the fathers of science than ever honored any other city of the world during an equal time. Among these were Cuvier, the father of systematic paleontology, with his celebrated pupils, Beaumont and Agassiz; Lamark, the father of the doctrine of evolution; Franklin, the inventor of the lightning-rod, and the discoverer of the electric nature of lightning; Rumford, the father of the doctrine of the co-relation of force; Bichat, the father of modern physiology; Laplace, the author of the nebular hypothesis; Mesmer, the father of the practice of artificial trance; Lavoiseur, one of the fathers of chemistry; and Champolion, the father of Egyptology, and the first decipherer of hieroglyphics.

All the sciences which may be said to have had their birth near the beginning of the present century, have been more cultivated and improved, and more readily adopted, than phrenology. The reasons are not difficult to discover. The other sciences had no rival systems to supplant as phrenology had.

A metaphysical system of mental philosophy was taught in every superior school in christendom — a science of mind with the *organs* of mind left out. This metaphysical system lay at the foundation of the theological doctrines of all the sects, To teach that the mind is dependent upon material organs, and subject to physiological laws, they regarded as equivalent to teaching materialism and fatalism; in other words, rank heresy and infidelity. Gall and Spurzheim not only had to encounter the mental philosophy of the schools, but the theology of the churches. A more formidable opposition cannot be imagined. The consequence is that phrenology has been taboed and excluded from all regular schools and colleges, and forced to make its way not only without their assistance, but in spite of all their opposing influences.

This book is an attempt to advance phrenology, and bestow

upon it the dignity of a systematic science, by showing that it is inseparably connected with physiology; that when any emotion of the mind is excited, the head and the heart act in unison to effect the purpose of the will. I have furthermore endeavored to demonstrate that this new system of phreno-physiology furnishes the only reasonable explanation of the phenomena of trance Mesmerism and Spiritism.

As these pages will doubtless be perused by many who are but slightly acquainted with the history and details of the subjects treated, it is due to them, to my predecessors, and to myself, that I should designate the principal innovations that I have made both in Physiology and in Phrenology, and thus enable the reader to distinguish the new from the old:

I. Gall and Spurzheim discovered all the phrene organs now generally recognized, except Alimentiveness, which was discovered by Dr. Hoppe, of Copenhagen, and Vitativeness, which was first suggested by Vimont, of France. He and Andrew Combe thought that it was situated too far from the outside of the head to be made the subject of examination during life. But I found that persons whose heads were full immediately under Destructiveness, so as to crowd the ears outward, were remarkably apprehensive of personal injuries and of sickness, and were unnecessarily anxious about their health. I regard it as the propensity to preserve the constitution and health, rather than the life, and have, therefore, named it *Sanativeness*, from the Latin *sanatus*, soundness or healthiness.

II. Gall made no classification of the organs, and proposed no new philosophy of the mind. In his published catalogues he mingled the Intellectual, Ipseal and Social organs together with very little discrimination. His proceedings were purely empirical. He found Destructiveness large in the heads of murderers, and he therefore called it the organ of murder; he denominated Acquisitiveness theft; Secretiveness lying, and Submissiveness religion. Spurzheim possessed a more analytical and methodical mind; he pointed out the fact that the Intellectuals are all grouped together in the forehead, and that they are all perceptives except the two highest, which are reflectives. The other organs he denominated affective faculties, or feelings. He observed that the organs in the lower parts of the brain are manifested by animals even more decidedly than by man; he therefore denominated them animal propensities, while the higher organs of the brain, being much more strongly manifested by man, he named them Moral Sentiments. I regard this last division as unfortunate. There is no place where a line can be drawn so that all above it may be regarded as peculiarly human or moral, and all below it animal. Besides, the higher organs are just as much *propensities* as the lower, and some of the lower — those, for example, that relate to friendship and love — are accompanied with quite as much of *sentiment* as any of the higher.

Spurzheim confounded the Social and Ipseal propensities together; he classed Amativeness and Adhesiveness with Destructiveness and Acquisitiveness; Cautiousness with Benevolence, and Hope with Firmness. Mr. George Combe, and all the other European and American Phrenologists, have adopted a similar incongruous arrangement in all their works.

III. The reader will perceive that I have made an important change in the classification and arrangement of the organs, by recognizing all as Ipseal or Social propensities that are not Intellectuals, and regarding feelings or emotions as mere temporary states of mind and body *produced by* excited propensities.

IV. I have also taken the liberty to change the names of some of the organs when I conceived that they were calculated to mislead inexperienced students. *Conscientiousness* I have

NOTE.—Dr. Wm. Carpenter, the most distinguished and able physiologist of Europe, has lately published a volume of upwards of seven hundred pages on Mental Physiology, in which, I am sorry to say, he does great injustice to his own reputation. It cannot be said that he is an anti-phrenologist, although he ignores the doctrines of Gall and Spurzheim, for he introduces in its place a phrenology of his own, which he seems to regard with great complacency. He places the lower mental faculties in the forehead, the higher in the posterior lobes, and the emotions and the sensorium among the sub-cerebral ganglia. The brain he regards as the organ of all the mental faculties excepting *the will*. This is independent of the body, and has no particular local habitation. It is a kind of lobby member of the mental congress. It however exerts a kind of regulating influence over the body and mind in a manner which he does not explain. Dr. Carpenter does not cite any authority to fortify his unphysiological assumptions, except that of Cardinal Manning. Now, although I have great respect for the opinions of the learned Cardinal in matters relating to the Catholic church, I beg leave, with all deference, to suggest that physiology is not properly within his jurisdiction, and I may therefore be permitted to question his infallibility when treating of this subject. It is evident that Dr. Carpenter derived his notions concerning the will from the old theological, rather than from the modern medical schools.

changed to Equitableness or Justice. The organ in question does not alone produce honesty nor the feeling known among Christian people as Conscientiousness; Reverence, and proper moral and religious training are necessary to produce those desirable states of the mind. The state of mind called Mirthfulness depends upon large Hopefulness, small Cautiousness and good health. I regard the *organ* (miscalled Mirthfulness) as the propensity to try experiments, and wit as one of its sportive manifestations when combined with a keen intellect. The organ that has been called Marvelousness, Wonder, Supernaturality and Spirituality, I regard as the propensity to believe the testimony and assertions of others. The names that have been given to this propensity indicate only its excesses and not its proper and normal manifestations. As for the candidate and doubtful organs, at the base of the brain, I wish it distinctly understood that I only propose them for investigation, and not for acceptance without further evidence in their favor.

V. In 1845 I first published the conclusion, at which I had arrived some time previous, that the oblongata is the seat of the consciousness of all mental impressions. Since then I find that several European and American authors have adopted the idea.

VI. I first insisted upon a distinction being made between the dormant faculties and the states of mind that they produce when excited.

VII. The fact that the emotions powerfully influence the vital organs has always been known, and Gall was the first to suggest that the sympathetic nerve was the channel of this influence; but I have attempted to show that the emotional influence is a useful and functional one, and that it is of a preliminary character.

VIII. In studying the relations of the voluntary and involuntary functions to each other, I have ascertained that the accents of speech are related to pulsation, and the pauses to the respiratory movements, and that both are almost entirely involuntary.

IX. I have demonstrated that what is called spirit trance, or Mesmeric sleep, depends upon the excessive action of the depressing propensities, especially of Submissiveness.

It has never before been taught that those propensities which increase the voluntary exertions increase the circulation to sustain the exertions, and that, on the contrary, those propensities which restrain the voluntary exertions restrain the circulation also. Before this law was known it was impossible to understand the causes of trance, the phenomena of Mesmerism, and the mental manifestations of the spiritists.

Several very able writers — Maudsley, Spencer, Bain, Carpenter, Tuke — have, within a short time, written with great learning and ability concerning the relations of the mind and body, without adding much to our knowledge of the subject. The reason is evident. They overlooked or ignored the only principles upon which their problems can be solved.

This book does not contain a mere theoretical essay; it is adapted to the wants of those who wish to make themselves acquainted with both the principles and the practice of Phrenology and Mesmerism, including the development of the so-called spirit mediums.

Any person of common abilities who will carefully study these pages can learn to go into any community, and in a few days develop several writing, ghost and vision-seeing, table-tipping and speaking mediums, and at the same time so vary his experiments as to convince all reasonable and unprejudiced persons that all the honest manifestations proceed from the unbalanced and dreaming brains of the mediums and the credencive imaginations of their patrons.

For the information of those who wish to consult other authors upon phrenology, I will state that "Combe's System," together with this volume, contains substantially all that is at present known upon the subject.

CHICAGO, May, 1897.

TABLE OF CONTENTS.

PART FIRST — THE HEAD.

PART SECOND—THE HEART.

PART THIRD.

THE HEAD AND HEART UNBALANCED.

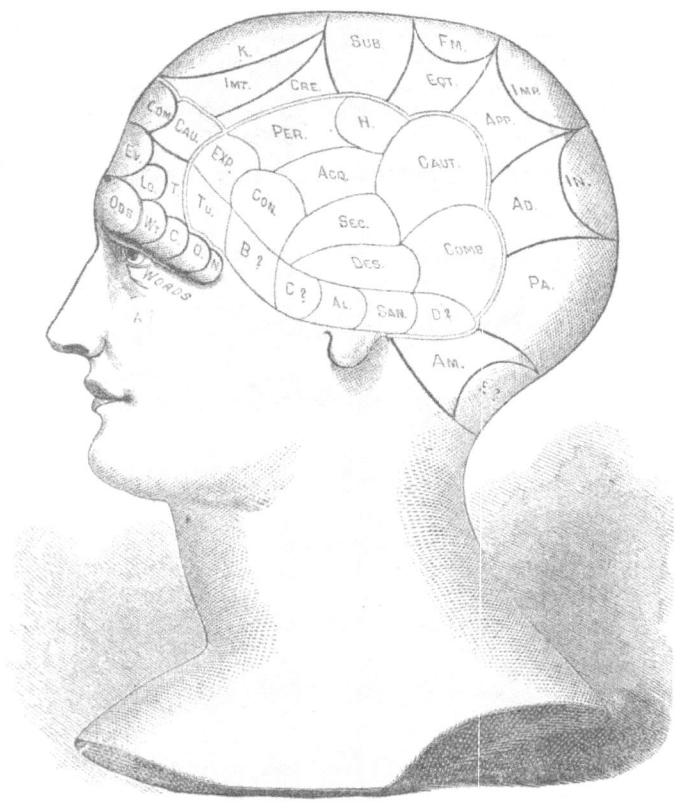

Figure 1.

EXPLANATION OF THE BUST.

The three classes of organs are separated from each other by double lines. The Intellectuals are in the forehead; the Ipseals or self-relative propensities on the side; and the Social propensities occupy the posterior and upper parts of the head.

INTELLECTUALS.

PERCEPTIVES.

REFLECTIVES.

IPSEAL OR SELF-RELATIVE PROPENSITIES.

SOCIAL PROPENSITIES.

DOMESTIC GROUP.

GOVERNING GROUP.

CONFORMING GROUP.

SCALE OF NUMBERS.

The sizes of organs are usually represented by numbers — one being the lowest, seven the highest, and four the average or mean. According to this scale, if a head is perfectly balanced every organ will be marked four. If any organ is marked more than four it has more than an average share of influence in the mind, and if marked less than four it has less than an average share of influence. It is a great mistake to suppose that many high numbers indicate a superior character. The nearer all the organs come to being marked four the more perfect is the character. When a head is well proportioned, a large and active brain indicates superiority.

MYSTERIES

HEAD AND HEART.

PART FIRST—THE HEAD.

CLASSIFICATION AND ARRANGEMENT OF THE PHRENE ORGANS.

THE first proceeding which is necessary in the creation of a new science is the collection of its crude materials — its facts; the next is to make a correct classification. Those things that are in many essential particulars alike should be put into a class by themselves. A science scarcely deserves the name until this task has been performed by its devotees. While the classification is imperfect the student is in continual danger of confounding together things that are unlike, and separating other things that nature has associated together. Dr. Gall laid the foundations of phrenology by discovering twenty-seven phrene organs; but he made no classification. His partner, Spurzheim, pointed out the fact that the intellectual organs constitute a distinct class, and that they differ in function from the emotional faculties. This distinction was

previously recognized by metaphysicians, but Spurzheim demonstrated that the intellectual organs are
grouped together by themselves in the anterior lobe
of the cerebrum, while the emotional faculties occupy
the rest of the brain. Spurzheim also distinguished
the two highest intellectual organs from the others,
and denominated them reflectives, while the others are
perceptives. No one has questioned the propriety of
this subdivision.

Dr. Gall observed that the organs at the base of the
brain are more peculiarly animal than the higher, and
Spurzheim drew a line between what he considered the
animal propensities and the higher faculties; there is
no such line in nature. This was the condition of the
science when Spurzheim died in Boston in 1832, at
which time I began the study of the subject. In 1838
I published a new system of phrenology, the principal
novelty of which consisted in the natural classification
and arrangement of the propensities or emotional
faculties. I demonstrated that they consist of two
great classes — the Ipseal and the Social; that one
class is evidently designed to prompt the individual
to preserve himself and advance his own personal
interests, without reference to the wants or wishes of
others; the other class is designed to multiply and preserve the species, and bind them together into societies.

The importance of this division cannot be over
valued. The moment we admit that nature has put
in one group all the propensities that relate to the
individual, and in another all those that relate to
society, we are forced to acknowledge that no one can
form a correct idea of the functions of the organs who
ignores this division. Any one who pretends to teach

phrenology, and rejects or neglects this division, d s
injustice to himself, to his pupils, and to the science.

The Ipseal class occupies the side of the head, and
has its base in the middle lobe of the brain. The
social class has its base at the posterior part of the
brain, and extends along the middle line to the upper
part of the forehead.

The lower part of the brain has always been divided
by anatomists into three lobes — the anterior, the
middle, and the posterior. It is interesting now to
learn the meaning of this natural division. The Intel-

lectual class occupies the anterior
lobe, the Ipseal the middle, and
the Social the posterior.

It is also a curious and interesting fact that the *body* may be
divided into three departments.
The anterior (including the hands
and face) may be regarded as the
Intellectual department; the middle (including the digestive and
respiratory organs) are Ipseal;
and the posterior (including the
reproductive organs) are Social.
This relation becomes more striking and obvious when we consider
that the lowest organs of the
posterior of the brain are related
in function to the lowest parts of
the body, the lowest middle organs of the brain are related to
the middle parts of the body, and
the lowest anterior parts of the

Fig. 2.

brain to the hands and face, the anterior parts of the body. In other words, the anterior of both the body and the brain (D, Fig. 2) relate to the Intellect, the middle of the body and brain (I, Fig. 2) to the Ipseal functions, and the posterior of the body and brain (S, Fig. 2) the Social functions. But important as this division is, the succession or superaddition of the organs of each class is, if possible, still more so. I know of nothing in any science more remarkable.

If Gall and Spurzheim, when they first promulgated phrenology, had pointed out this classification and succession of the organs, they would certainly have been accused of mapping the head and arranging the organs to adapt them to the requirements of a previously formed theory. But the truth is that neither of these philosophers suspected that the organs which they discovered were susceptible of such an arrangement. If any additional argument were needed to establish the truth of phrenology, it is furnished by the fact that after Gall and Spurzheim were both dead, the crude materials which they brought to light are found to be capable of being formed into such a wonderfully harmonious system.

Let us review each of the three classes separately, and observe the manner in which the higher organs are superadded to those immediately below them:

ARRANGEMENT AND RELATIVE POSITIONS OF THE INTELLECTUAL ORGANS.

The lowest intellectual organs are those situated near where the nose joins the forehead, at the base of the anterior lobe, near the middle line. The organs that cluster around this basilar central point have the peculiarity that they relate to what may be denominated the *individual* qualities of things, while the other intellectual organs represent their *relative* qualities. Thus, form, size, weight, color, place, sound and motion may be possessed by a single object without any necessary reference to any other; but order, number, comparison and causality imply several things and their relations to each other. The lowest animals may observe the individual qualities of things, but only the higher minds can fully understand their relations.

ARRANGEMENT AND RELATIVE POSITIONS OF THE IPSEALS.

The Ipseals are developed in five ranges or stories, one above the other. 1. The corporeal range relates to the bodily wants. Only two of them, Alimentive-ness and Sanativeness, have been fully established, though there must be several others in their vicinity that are yet to be discovered. There can be no doubt that all the corporeal organs of the Ipseal class that are undiscovered are near the two that are known. No sensible person would think of looking for them anywhere else. 2. Above the corporeal are the belligerent organs. The struggle for existence resulting from the necessity of obtaining food requires those organs. 3. Above the belligerent are the prudential organs, which are rendered necessary by the previous existence of animals possessing the belligerent organs. 4. The Industrial organs relate to the necessity of providing shelter and food for a coming winter. 5. The Improving range crowns this class and produces ingenuity, ornament and enterprise. There is nothing in the functions of the organs of these five ranges that implies even the existence of society, or that tends to qualify their possessor for its enjoyments; they all relate to self. If they benefit society it is because the social organs are large enough to dominate over them and force them into subordination.

ARRANGEMENT AND RELATIVE POSITIONS OF THE SOCIALS.

The lowest animals manifest the lowest social faculty; the next higher manifest some degree of the parental instinct; the attachment to particular places, and the tendency of the young to remain under the protection of a parent, implies a still higher social development; the gregarious instinct which binds several families together for mutual protection, and forces them to acknowledge one or more for leaders, is a still further advance, for it introduces general government and subordination. Imperativeness, Approbativeness, Firmness and Justice, as well as Obedience, Kindness and Imitativeness, will naturally be needed and developed under these circumstances; they will be more and more developed as the community becomes more numerous and intelligent. The societies of bees, ants and beavers are illustrations of the fact that social institutions are not the results of human reason; they proceed from instinctive propensities which are possessed in different degrees by different classes of animals.

The order of arrangement and succession of the social organs in the human brain is the very order in which society must necessarily have required them.

It should be particularly remarked that the social organs lowest in position are lowest in rank, and those in the mesial or middle line of the head are lower than the others adjoining. According to this rule, Amativeness is No. 1, Parentiveness 2, Inhabitiveness 3, Adhesiveness 4, Imperativeness 5, Approbativeness 6, Firmness 7, Justice 8, Submissiveness 9, Kindness 10, Imitativeness 11, and Credenciveness 12. The last is the highest in rank. Of all the social propensities, Credenciveness is the most peculiarly human; it is the propensity to receive communications, and is. therefore the basis of tradition, history, religion and literature. Take these away and man would be a brute. Before the natural classification was understood, this important faculty was known as Wonder and Marvelousness, and its extraordinary influence upon human affairs was not understood. Imitativeness was also regarded as a mere mimicking and dramatic faculty; whereas it is a powerful social element, and an important moral faculty. We imitate those whom we most reverence and admire: our mother tongue, our manners and fashions, and most of our work is learned by imitation. It is the basis of sympathy. The social character and influence of this important faculty has been overlooked on account of the erroneous classification which has been adopted. Even the propensity of Kindness or Benevolence has been but half understood. The truth is it tends to conciliate strangers and persons in whom we have but a general interest. The lower any social propensity is in rank the more limited is its sphere. The domestic socials relate only to the family, but Kindness relates to all creatures that can appreciate it. It is an interesting fact that Causality, the highest Intel

lectual, Perfectiveness (Ideality), the highest Ideal,
and Credenciveness the highest Social, come together
at the upper lateral part of the forehead where the
heads of the lowest savages are most deficient.

FUNCTIONS OF PHRENE ORGANS.

THE INTELLECTUALS.

PERCEPTIVES.

OBSERVATION OR INDIVIDUALITY.

"You see, indeed, but perceive not."—Isaiah.

The faculty of observing the most obvious things in a cursory and general manner. Dr. Gall called it, very appropriately, "the spirit of observation." Practically, it is undoubtedly true that persons large at this part and small in the other organs above and each side of it, are very observing, though they may not understand what they observe, but I doubt this being a single faculty. It is probable that several of the lowest perceptives are very small, and

Fig. 3.

are crowded together here. Combined with Eventuality, it gives the memory of facts and transactions. Those who have it small are in the habit of passing things in which they have no particular interest without noticing them. If such persons have the Reflectives large, they are prone to be too metaphysical, and though possessed of good reasoning faculties, they reason erroneously, because they have acquired but an imperfect knowledge of the facts.

(13)

While I admit that persons who are large here are more practical and observing than those who are small, I am not convinced that there is a distinct faculty of the mind such as that which Spurzheim and Combe have defined under the name of Individuality. Combe says, "Individuals in whom it is large experience delight in becoming acquainted with objects, without reference to their uses or active or passive qualities." Again he says, "It gives the notion of the existence of substance, and forms that class of ideas represented by names when used without an objective, as *man, rock, tree.*" I cannot admit that we ever have an idea of any substance without reference to its qualities. Every substance has a form and a size, and we cannot even imagine its existence without these qualities.

FLAVOR.

"Who taught the nations of the field and wood
To shun their poison and to choose their food."—*Pope.*

Independent of phrenological observation, we have quite as good reason for believing that there is in the brain an organ for perceiving flavor (including odor and savor), as in admitting an organ of color that is related to sight, or an organ of weight, related to the sense of touch. In 1838, I called the attention of phrenologists to the fact that persons whose faces are prominent in that part Fig. 4.   that is immediately under the eye and near the nose, possess an unusual power of discrimination in regard to the odor and savor of food and drink. It seems to me that there is a part of the brain, just behind the convolution of the organ of words, that may give prominence to the bones under the eye, for the same reason that the word organ gives prominence to the eye itself.

This faculty, says Dunglison, is capable of being largely developed by cultivation. The spirit-taster to extensive commercial establishments exhibits the truth of this in a striking manner. He has, of course, in his vocation, not only to taste numerous samples but to appreciate the age, strength, flavor and other qualities of each; yet the practiced individual is rarely wrong in his discrimination. Some persons can tell by the taste whether birds, put upon the table, are domesticated or wild, male or female. Dr. Kitchener, indeed, asserts that many epicures are capable of saying in what precise stretch of the Thames the salmon on the table has been caught.

Fig. 5.   Fig. 6.

Figure 5 is Apollo, the Grecian classical ideal of the highest civilization and refinement, contrasted with Figure 6, a somewhat exaggerated representation of the negro face. No one would hesitate long in deciding which of the two to prefer for the kitchen department.

FORM.

" I knew him at a glance! My father is not altered;
   The form that stands before me, falsifies
   No feature of the image that hath lived
   So long within me."—*Coleridge.*

The faculty of judging concerning forms and remembering them. Dr. Gall named it the sense of persons. When large it gives width between the eyes.

Spurzheim thinks that ideas of roughness and smoothness depend on Form. It is principally by means of Form that animals are capable of distinguishing one object from another. A large development of this organ also accounts for the extraordinary power which some persons possess, of remembering faces; Cuvier, the celebrated Naturalist, could remember for years, the forms of animals which he had seen, and could draw them from memory with great accuracy. The talent for drawing is almost entirely dependent on this organ. When Language and Form are not in proportion to each other, persons can remember the names and not the faces, or vice versa, of their acquaintances. I knew a gentleman in Auburn, New York, who called into a store to see an acquaintance, but not finding him in, inquired of the clerk—" Is Mr.—Mr.—Mr.—r—r—you know who I mean,—is he in?" "Oh yes," said the clerk, "I know who you mean; it is Mr.—Mr.—Mr.—r—r—No! he is not in,"—and they parted in mutual embarrassment. Dr. Gall relates of himself, that he could not recollect a person who dined by his side, if in the afternoon he met him in the street. Dr. D., of Ann Arbor, Michigan, assured me, that it was to him a frequent source of embarrassment, that persons would come up to him, and claim to be his intimate acquaintances, and he was ashamed to say he did not know that he had ever seen them before.

Authors who have it large are prone to describe the configuration of the objects which they introduce, and in their works of fiction,

" Imagination bodies forth the forms of things unknown."

SIZE.

" A boundless sea forevermore,
Without a bottom or a shore."—*Watts*.

Raphael — Fig. 7.   Richard Baxter — Fig. 8.

The faculty of measuring distances and magnitudes by the glance of the eye. It is one of the organs required in perspective drawing, and in judging of proportion. It is large, and Form also, in Milton, and he frequently manifests them in his writings. A good instance is his description of sin and death:

Figure 7, the brow of Raphael, one of the greatest of artists in regard to form and outline. Observe the width of the part where the nose and forehead join; this indicates a large development of the organ of Size. The organ of Form is also very large in Raphael, and is indicated by the uncommon space between the eye and the nose.

Figure 8 is the brow of the Rev. Richard Baxter, a celebrated and pious metaphysical divine, who regarded all the uses of this world and its enjoyments as "stale, flat and unprofitable," compared with the glories of the things that are invisible.

"The one seemed woman to the waist, and fair,
 But ended foul in many a scaly fold,
 Voluminous and vast.   *   *   *   *
 *   *   *   *   The other shape,
 If shape it might be called — that shape had none
 Distinguishable in member, joint or limb,
 Or substance might be called that shadow seemed,
 For each seemed either.

Again, he describes Satan:

" As far removed from God and light of heaven,
 As from the centre thrice to the utmost pole.
 *   *   *   *   *   *   *   *
 Prone on the flood, extending long and large,
 Lay floating many a rood.
 *   *   *   *   *   *   *   *
 Collecting all his might, dilated stood,
 Like Teneriffe or Atlas, unremoved ;
 His stature reached the sky, and on his crest
 Sat horror plumed."

Nearly all poets have the organ that produces
exageration (Credenciveness) large, and there is nuth-
ing that they exagerate more frequently than magnitudes.

WEIGHT.

"And earth, self-balanced, on her centre hung."—*Milton.*

Fig. 9.

This is the perception of
weight, and the sense of force
and resistance.   Animals that
are very low in the scale manifest this faculty with as much
skill as the most profound philosopher.   The cater-
pillar travels to the end of a limb, and extends itself
as far as it can reach, and if it finds nothing to rest
upon returns the way it came, but never loses its
balance.

The nymphs of water moths, commonly called *cod-bait*, cover themselves with pieces of wood or gravel. It is necessary that they should keep in equilibrium with the water, and when they are too light they add to themselves a piece of gravel, and when too heavy a piece of wood.

I have uniformly found this organ large in those mechanics and artists whose success depends upon their faculty of bringing force to bear with skill, precision and delicacy. It is large upon authors who describe, in a natural manner, the effect of force.

> "And hark! The river, bursting every mound,
> Down the vale thunders; and with wasteful sway
> Uproots the groves, and rolls the shattered rocks away."
>
> —*Beattie.*

The organ, when large, gives depth and an overhanging appearance to the brow near the nose, as seen in the brow of Washington (Fig. 9). Watt, Brunell, and other great practical engineers, have the same development. I have seen many persons who could sing well, but could not touch the piano with proper delicacy and skill. Men have the organ much larger than women, and though women are the better vocalists, and a hundred women to one man learn the use of the piano, the best performers upon that instrument are men. Machinists, blacksmiths, railroad engine drivers, coachmen, and all men engaged in employments requiring them to exert, to guide or to regulate force, require this faculty.

LOCALITY OR DIRECTION.

"There is a power whose care
　Teaches thy way along that pathless coast,
　The desert and illimitable air,
　Lone wandering but not lost."—*Bryant to a water-fowl*

Americus Vespucius — Fig. 10.

This may be defined to be the perception of the direction of objects. It is largely developed in the heads of all celebrated navigators, travelers and geographers. Migratory animals manifest it in a much greater degree than man. It is very large in James Fennimore Cooper, and his "Pilot," and other nautical works, afford admirable illustrations of it. His hero is represented as steering the vessel among rocks and shoals, through a thousand dangers that seem each moment to increase in magnitude; but with a firm and decided voice, and a calm spirit, he gives each necessary order, as with a skillful hand he guides the noble ship in safety.

The head of Americus illustrates several peculiar traits. His forehead indicates a very observing, practical, orderly character. His large neck, and strongly marked face indicate energy and strength. The back of the head indicates powerful domestic affections; but the upper back part of the head shows a great deficiency of self-will and firmness of purpose.

WORDS OR LANGUAGE.

"With words of learned length and thundering sound,
Amazed the gazing rustics ranged around."—*Goldsmith.*

Fig. 11.

This organ does not give the *love* of talking, nor does this alone bestow the gift of speaking with fluency. Those who have it large, remember and use unusual words, such as they have seen in books, and which are mostly used only by literary and professional characters. Those who have it small are forced to use common expressions which have become familiar by habit. They cannot readily acquire a literary and classical style, nor do they easily learn a foreign or a dead language. This faculty is much more easily cultivated in early youth than afterwards. It is very important for parents and teachers to understand this, especially in those cases in which the organ is small in children who are otherwise intellectual. Mathematics are learned more readily when the mind is more mature, but language is best acquired in childhood, by imitation and habit. The organ crowds the eye downward and outward when large.

Fig. 11. This is the face and head of a gentleman with whom I am well acquainted. He keeps a hotel, and is an excellent landlord in every respect but one; he can recollect the names of scarcely any of his guests. A wag tells an amusing story of him that one day, after dinner, he forgot his own name, and went out and looked at his sign to refresh his memory. But, in another respect, his memory is extraordinary. He can recollect and describe what he has had for dinner each day for several weeks. Observe his deep sunken eye and the prominence of the bone beneath.

Language is the perception of the manifestations of mind. The mental process is concealed from observation beneath the silent and mystic convolutions of the brain. Not so the manifestations of mind — the contractions of the muscles, producing voice, and the motions of the limbs and features; these enable animals to indicate their thoughts and feelings in such a manner that other animals, possessing the same organization, readily understand them. Animals do not, like men, connect by a process of reasoning the motions and sounds or other signs of ideas with the ideas themselves in which the signs originate; but they are endowed with an instinctive perception which is perfectly adapted to certain animal motions and sounds, so that, as soon as they are born, they can understand the signs of the mother inviting them to feed or warning them of danger. This view of Language is in agreement with its location at the base of the brain, near the root of Observation. It must certainly be possessed by all animals that have any communication with their own species, or attend to the wants of their young. Those phrenologists, therefore, who consider Language peculiar to man, and rank it next in dignity to the reflective faculties, cannot be well acquainted with the natural history of animals, and they must also have overlooked the situation of the organ in the brain.

Man uses artificial language for the same reason that he uses artificial clothes, tools, and a thousand other things which his superior reasoning power has enabled him to invent. Having invented an artificial language, it is the organ under consideration which enables him to learn it with facility and remember it with ease. It is plain that it requires more judgment to understand artificial than natural language, as the one is directly adapted to our faculty of Language, and the other is adapted to our faculty of Language *combined* with the reflecting powers that invented it. This is the reason why animals and some idiots cannot learn artificial language, although they readily understand natural language; the latter requires no effort of reflection, whereas the former originated in human invention, and can be understood only by human judgment.

It is astonishing with what facility some writers and speakers pour forth a flood of indefinite words upon a subject which might be expressed in a few short sentences. On the other hand, we see individuals whose gigantic intellects survey at a single glance the whole circle of the sciences, and yet in a sudden emergency cannot find language to express themselves intelligibly upon the most familiar and ordinary topics. But a distinction must be understood between a facility of conception and a facility of expression. This will be explained under Comparison.

COLOR.

" A thousand odors rise,
Breathed up from blossoms of a thousand dyes."—*Bryant.*

Titian —Fig. 12.

The faculty of perceiving nice shades, tints and hues of color. Painters usually have it large; but in ordinary persons it cannot be pronounced

Figure 12, the brow of Titian, the celebrated painter, who excelled in the coloring of his pictures. Observe how his brow arches in the middle, where the organ is located.

upon with confidence. When very deficient persons do not notice the colors of flowers nor of dresses, and they often fail to distinguish one color or one shade from another.

ORDER.

Fig. 13.

The faculty of noticing the succession and arrangement of things in nature, in business, or in art. When large the person is neat and orderly without intending to be so, or even being conscious of it. When small there is a tendency to neglect the proper arrangement of things. It requires great care and perseverance to acquire orderly habits if they are not natural.

The mechanical animals manifest Order in a most remarkable manner. Who has not admired the regularity with which the spider arranges the thread of his web, the bee the cells of his honeycomb, or the bird the materials of her nest?

Those who have the organ very large, are apt, unconsciously, to arrange in order whatever material objects occupy their attention. A retail merchant, for instance, has his attention (his Observation,) continually occupied with the numerous articles that constitute his stock; and, if he has order very large, he will instinctively and unconsciously arrange and keep them in order; yet he may neglect his garden or his library, because his attention is directed to another subject of all-absorbing interest; as soon, however, as his mind is relieved from business, and he has leisure to attend to his garden or his library, he will manifest the same degree of order there that he previously did in his store. This will explain the apparent anomaly which some persons present, who are remarkably orderly in some things and neglectful in others. I know some students who are very neat and orderly in regard to their papers and books, but careless of their personal appearance, while others are careless of every thing but their dress; this is all easily explained by the relative development of Intellect and Approbativeness, and the circumstances which have directed their attention to different subjects.

Good clerks and accountants have this large; and it is of the greatest importance to merchants, especially if they have it small themselves, to select assistants who have it large. It is also large in women, and they are proverbial for their habits of putting things "to rights."

Order must not be confounded with *system*, which is the result of reflection. I know many individuals who are very systematic — they plan well, but they need an assistant continually at their elbows to execute their plans in an orderly manner. I know others, who are remarkable for order, but are totally incapable of conceiving a complicated and systematic plan.

NUMBER.

" The stars are numberless, resplendent, set
As symbols of the countless, countless years
That make eternity.—*Hillhouse.*

This is the faculty of arithmetical calculation; combined with order it gives book-keeping talent. When large it bestows readiness in counting and reckoning; combined with reflection it gives mathematical ability. When deficient, it is difficult to excel

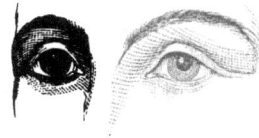

in any business constantly requiring it; if not very small it can be cultivated, so that this deficiency will not be severely felt.

Lagrange — Fig. 14.

" The special function of this faculty seems to be to give the conception of numbers and their relations, including arithmetic, algebra and logarythms, but geometry does not belong to it."— *Combe.*

I would here respectfully point out an error into which some good phrenologists have fallen, in supposing that Order should be preceded by Number, in the arrangement of these organs. Mr. Combe, 397th page, says: "Order supposes a plurality of objects, but one may have ideas about a number of things, and their qualities, without considering them in any order whatever." And he accordingly ranks Number before Order. Spurzheim also says: "The idea of order supposes plurality, but number may exist without order." Now I acknowledge that there cannot be order without number; but it does not follow that we must *perceive* number before we perceive order.

Let me ask what *can* there be without number; do not the five senses, and Observation — does not the organ of Color, adapted as it is to the seven primary colors, suppose the existence of plurality? Does not our very existence, " suppose a plurality of objects," previously existing?

Figure 14   The brow of Lagrange. He had both order and number large. We seldom find number large and order small. When number is large it causes the brow to extend outward toward the ear.

But Mr. Combe says: "We may have ideas about a number of things without considering them in any order whatever." I reply, so may the animals, that are destitute of both Order and Number; but all animals do not have ideas of several things of the same appearance at once; they certainly have ideas of a number of things, but not *as numbers*. I once knew an idiot, who, although he could not count ten, yet, out of his father's flock of fifty sheep, if one was missing, he was always the first to discover it; for he knew every one of them by some peculiar mark; and he had names for them expressive of their peculiarities, such as crook-horn, smut-face, etc.; but he could not distinguish the difference between a lot of thirteen eggs and another lot of a dozen. Again I reply, we may also have ideas about the order of things, without having any idea of their number. This same idiot, who could not count ten, was yet extremely fond of order. Dr. Spurzheim mentions that the Sauvage de l'Avignon at Paris, though an idiot in a very high degree, cannot bear to see a chair, or any other object, out of its place. He also saw, in Edinburgh, a girl who in many respects was idiotic, but in whom the love of order was very active. She avoided her brother's apartment in consequence of the confusion that prevailed in it.

The lower animals manifest order in the most perfect and astonishing manner, but they manifest number very imperfectly. Spurzheim says: "I am not certain whether this faculty (Number,) exists in animals." Combe also remarks: "It seems difficult to determine whether the faculty exists in the lower animals or not." This fact alone would seem to decide the question of precedence in favor of Order. Another important fact is, that in ordinary transactions we always use order before number. When we wish to count a number of articles, we arrange them in some order, that we may perform the operation with greater facility; for if the articles are in confusion, we find it next to impossible to count them. These two organs are of the greatest importance to merchants. Those who have the organ of Number large, can compute, without using the slate, with a rapidity and accuracy which to others is incomprehensible. This faculty does not give the ability to solve difficult arithmetical problems; it only gives the power to perform with rapidity and accuracy any operation in addition, subtraction, multiplication or division; but it must be combined with higher powers to produce skill in the higher and more difficult branches of mathematics. Zerah Colburn, the youth who astonished the world with this talent, was but an ordinary mathematician; and accordingly his organ of Number was very large, but Causality moderate. Both Order and Number are large in the bust of Washington, and his whole life was in harmony with this fact. In the papers in his own hand-writing which he has left behind, though very voluminous, every *i* is dotted, every *t* crossed, and scarce a blot to be found upon them. His accounts were kept in the most regular manner, and perfectly correct.

This organ is large in the bust of Alexander Hamilton, and in Lagrange, the greatest of French mathematicians.

EVENTUALITY.

"Sit at the feet of history — through the night
Of years the steps of virtue she shall trace,
And show the earlier ages."—*Bryant.*

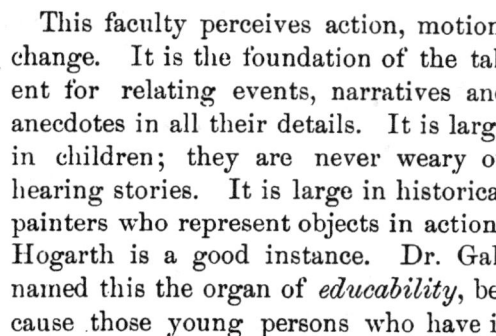

This faculty perceives action, motion, change. It is the foundation of the talent for relating events, narratives and anecdotes in all their details. It is large in children; they are never weary of hearing stories. It is large in historical painters who represent objects in action; Hogarth is a good instance. Dr. Gall named this the organ of *educability*, because those young persons who have it large acquire general information easily.

Pitt — Fig. 15.

He also thought, with Camper and Lavater, that animals are tamable in proportion to the fullness of this part. It is certain that tame and tamable animals are fuller in the center of the forehead than wild, untamable ones; but I suspect that the conforming social organs of Kindness and Submissiveness produce the greater part of the fullness in these animals.

Figure 15. The forehead of Pitt is remarkable. The organ of Observation (D) is small; Comparison (C) is only average, but Eventuality (E) is very prominent.

TIME.

" To-morrow, and to-morrow, and to-morrow
Creeps in this petty pace from day to day,
To the last syllable of recorded time."—*Shakspeare.*

Spurzheim proposed this organ, but practical phrenologists are not yet satisfied that it is correctly located. It is still merely a candidate which may yet be rejected. **Mr. Combe** remarks that " the power

of conceiving time, and of remembering circum
stances connected by no link but the relation in which
they stand to each other in chronology, and also the
power of observing time in performing music, is very
different in different individuals." This organ cannot
be considered as established. It is located between
Eventuality and Tunefulness.

REFLECTIVES.

COMPARISON.

" Look at this picture and at this."—Shakspeare.

Moore—Fig. 16

This is the faculty of comparing things
and ideas, assorting them, and distinguishing the like from the unlike. It perceives
differences, resemblances, analogies and contrasts. It gives the talent for classification
in science, and for illustration by comparison in speech and in literature. It gives
birth to allegories, parables, metaphors and
other figures of speech. It gives to business men quick practical judgment. They
compare the matter before them with what

Figure 16. The forehead of Moore, the Irish poet, represents
a large class of persons of all professions who are remarkable
for quickness and acuteness of understanding, and skill in illustration and expression, but who are not distinguished for the
variety and extent of their learning. Comparison (c), and Observation (D) are large, while Eventuality (E) is depressed. This
forehead is greatly in contrast with that of Pitt.

they have previously known, and thus judge according to experience. When small the judgment is slow, and the person seems stupid. When he talks he fails to state and illustrate his ideas clearly or popularly, he is unfit for a place where immediate decision is required.

Almost every object or subject which can occupy the mind belongs to a class to which it bears more or less analogy; and it is the function of this faculty to compare all our perceptions together, and perceive their resemblances and differences, and the classes to which they belong. It harmonizes all our perceptions and perceives the agreement among them. If a new object is presented to us, Comparison immediately compares all that we know concerning it with every thing else within our recollection, in order to know to what class it belongs; for instance, if a new phrenological organ is discovered in the brain, this faculty would compare it with the organs already known and discover whether it belongs to the Ipseal, Social or Intellectual class.

If all the perceptives below Comparison are large, and this organ is also large, the individual will possess great power of discrimination — will be capable of making nice distinctions, or conceiving striking contrasts. When he is explaining any difficult subject he will illustrate it by comparison; he will discover analogies between things which to the common observer appear totally dissimilar; his language will abound with figures of speech brought together from all quarters of the explored universe; from the heathen mythology, the history of individuals, of nations, of animals, and vegetables — science, literature and the arts—every thing under the sun will be pressed into his service to adorn, amplify, or illustrate his productions.

The talent for public speaking is very dependent upon this faculty. After a plain and simple statement of the case has been made, many speakers find a great difficulty in dwelling longer upon the subject; even though Language may be large, they find it difficult to continue their remarks from a want of interesting matter which is related to the question.   Let now a speaker with large Comparison rise, and he immediate.y begins to present the subject in a new light, and to refer to analogous cases; or, if he knows no such cases, he supposes some to suit his purpose; and, if he is artful, he will suppose cases in which the audience feel a deep interest, thus enlisting their feelings warmly upon a subject which before was a matter of indifference to them.

CAUSALITY.

" Observe how system into system runs."—*Pope.*

This is the faculty of perceiving the causes and effects — the natural connections and dependencies of things and facts — tracing things and events back, step by step, to their origin, and forward to their consequences.   It is the principal but not the only element in profound reasoning.   Combined with Observation it gives philosophical talent; combined with Number it bestows mathematical ability.   It is dependent for facts upon the perceptives, and if they are deficient in development or cultivation, this faculty arrives at erroneous conclusions.   When very small the reasoning is superficial, and the person is only capable of practicing what superior minds have originated.

Gibbon — Fig. 17.

That cause which immediately precedes an effect is called the *immediate cause*, and all the other links in the chain of causation are *remote causes*. So also those effects which immediately follow a cause are called *immediate effects*, and all others are *remote effects;* it is the function of the faculty of Causality to perceive the relations among phenomena which constitute cause and effect.

It perceives the dependence of one *thing* upon another, of one *event.* upon another, or of one phenomena of any kind upon some other. Thus it perceives the dependence of the rivers upon their tributary streams; the dependence of the streams upon the springs; of the springs upon the rains; of the rains upon the clouds; of the clouds upon evaporation; of evaporation upon heat; of heat upon the sun, and the dependence of all these phenomena upon the laws of gravitation.

It perceives the dependence of known things and facts upon those that are unknown — thus Columbus perceived the dependence of one side of the earth

Figure 17. The head of Gibbon, the philosophical historian of the causes of the decline and fall of the Roman empire, affords a good illustration of this organ. Below Causality, Tunefulness and Order appear to be small, and above it Credenciveness is quite deficient. The position of the eye indicates a good development of the organ of Words. He was a splendid writer, ornate and profound, but skeptical.

which was known, upon the other which was unknown; Cuvier perceived the dependence of the forms of animal's bones upon their dispositions and habits, and thus was enabled to ascertain the nature of the unknown animal by inspecting the fossil remains of a single bone. Gall discovered the dependence of certain powers of mind upon certain portions of the brain.

Causality perceives that many strange phenomena which superstitious minds have ascribed to supernatural powers depend upon natural causes.

In mathematics, a certain number or quantity being known, this faculty perceives the necessary existence of other numbers or quantities. Combined with Comparison and Observation, it invents and originates improvements in the arts. We observe the operations of nature, and discover the causes upon which they depend; we observe the operations of art, and compare them with those of nature, and by adopting the natural process we improve the effect.

Sir H. Davy's safety lamp originated in his observing that a metalic net prevented the passage of flame by cooling it, while it allowed the passage of light; observing also that in coal mines fatal explosions were frequently caused by the flame of the lamps communicating with the gas, his Comparison perceived the analogy between the two cases, and his Causality enabled him to remove the cause of the explosion while he retained the cause of light, by constructing a lamp surrounded with fine metalic net work.

All useful inventions must originate in observation; but it is necessary to compare the facts which have been observed, and also perceive their connections and dependences. The knowledge of facts alone would not distinguish man from other animals; and on the other hand, however profound the reflections, they are useless unless based upon correct observations. I have seen many visionary characters who were continually dreaming of improvements, and who really seemed to manifest much originality of mind, but could never bring any of their plans into successful operation; the reason is, they were deficient in that practical talent which depends on the lower range of perceptives; had these organs been large, they would have been able to perceive the practical facts necessary to the execution of their plans; or else to discover some facts which rendered them impracticable. The dependence of the upper organs upon the lower, and the great importance of attending to the proportions which the different parts of the forehead bear to each other, cannot be too much insisted on; but it needs no further explanation in this place.

It is common for those who have but a moderate degree of Causality to think that there must be some mistake in their case, because, they will tell you, they are habitually inquiring into the cause of every thing. I reply, so do children, so do all except idiots; but it does not follow that Causality must be large. The difference between a large Causality and a small one is that the latter is satisfied with knowing *immediate* causes, but the former traces out *remote* causes;— the large organ delights in tracing a *long* chain of causes and effects, and perceiving the connection and dependence of a great number of links, — the small organ only delights in tracing a few links, and can easily comprehend their connection and dependence; but

they are satisfied with this, and do not voluntarily
and habitually proceed further. If circumstances
compel them to urge their Causality to its utmost, it
soon becomes an irksome task; and if thrown into
competition with a large Causality they are easily
overpowered.

IPSEAL OR SELF-RELATIVE PROPENSITIES.

CORPOREAL RANGE.

RELATED TO THE PRESERVATION OF THE BODY.

ALIMENTIVENESS.

"Give us this day our daily bread."—*Lord's Prayer.*

Paine — Fig. 18.

The propensity to obtain food and attend to it habitually, even to the neglect of all other pleasures. This propensity, like all others that are dependent upon the body for their excitement, varies in its activity as the condition of the body varies. When very small, especially in the young, the constitution is seldom strong. The organ, when large, gives width to the head just before the ears, as in Thomas Paine.

This is the propensity to take food and drink. The new born infant, the most helpless of all creatures, without any previous teaching, makes the requisite exertions to obtain aliment, and it is evidently impel-

(37)

led to do so by a power inherent in its nature. This propensity is absolutely necessary to animals even in the first hours of existence; and they manifest it then in as much perfection as they do after years of experience. Many instances are on record in which this propensity has been diseased, while the others were in health. Plutarch relates that Brutus, after the death of Cæsar, when advancing to the attack of a city, was seized with such an irresistible desire to eat, that he was obliged to halt three days to recover. Medical books contain numerous reports of cases which establish beyond all doubt the existence of this propensity, and all authors now agree in referring it to the brain. Dr. Andrew Combe, physician to the King of Belgium, in his admirable work on the Physiology of Digestion, makes the following appropriate remarks:

"The sensation of hunger is commonly referred to the stomach, and that of thirst to the upper part of the throat and back of the mouth; and correctly enough to this extent, that a certain condition of the stomach and throat tends to produce them. But, in reality, the sensations themselves, like all other mental affections and emotions, have their seat in the brain, to which a sense of the condition of the stomach is conveyed through the medium of the nerves.

"The relation thus shown to subsist between the stomach and the brain, enables us, in some measure, to understand the influence which mental emotion and earnest intellectual occupation exert over the appetite. A man in perfect health, sitting down to table with an excellent appetite, receives a letter announcing an unexpected calamity, and instantly turns away with loathing from the food which, a moment before, he was prepared to eat with relish; while another, who, under the fear of some misfortune, comes to table indifferent about food, will eat with great zest on his ' mind being relieved,' as the phrase goes, by the receipt of pleasing intelligence. In such cases no one will imagine that the calamity destroys the appetite otherwise than through the medium of the brain. Sometimes the feeling of loathing and disgust is so intense as not only to destroy appetite, but to induce sickness and vomiting — a result which depends so closely on the state of the brain that it is often induced even by mechanical injuries of that organ.

" The most common source, however, of the errors into which we are apt to fall in taking appetite as our only guide, is unquestionably the *confounding of appetite with taste*, and continuing to eat for the gratification of the latter, long after the former is satisfied. In fact the whole science of a skillful cook is expended in producing this *willing* mistake on our part; and he is considered decidedly the best *artiste* whose dishes shall recommend themselves most irresistibly to the callous palate of the gourmand, and excite on it such a sensation as shall at least remind him of the enviable excellence of a natural appetite. If we were willing to limit the office of taste to its proper sphere, and to cease eating when appetite expressed content, indigestion would be a much rarer occurrence in civilized communities than it is observed to be.

" Viewed, then, in its proper light, appetite is to be regarded as kindly implanted in our nature for the express end of proportioning the supply of nourishment to the wants of the system; and if ever it misleads us, the fault is not in its unfitness for its object, but in the artificial training which it receives at our own hands. When we attend to its real dictates, we eat moderately, and at such intervals of time as the previous exercise and other circumstances render necessary; and in so doing we reap a reward in the daily enjoyment of the pleasure which attends the gratification of healthy appetite. But if we err, either by neglecting the timely warning which it gives, or by eating more than the system requires, mischief is sure to follow."

SANATIVENESS OR VITATIVENESS.

" Infirmity doth still neglect all office
  Whereunto our health is bound: we are not ourselves
  When nature, being oppressed, commands the mind
  To suffer with the body."—*Shakespare.*

This is the propensity to preserve the constitution from injury. No faculty is more universally or more plainly manifested. Were it not for this, animals, and even men, would sacrifice their limbs and their lives without making an effort to save them. I think the organ is smaller in women than in men, and this accounts for the apparent firmness with which they endure pain. They do not suffer from it as intensely, and can, therefore, bear it with more patience and sub-missiveness than men.

I find, as a general rule, this organ is larger the more vigorous and robust the constitution. It is larger in the carniverous than in the herbiverous animals. It is larger in children than in adults. It would, however, be obviously unphilosophical to name it the organ of pain, as this is only the disagreeable affection of a propensity, the proper gratification of which yields the opposite feeling, which is denominated *bodily ease.* The proper inquiry is, what was the design of the Creator in bestowing this propensity? And this naturally brings us to the conclusion that it is the organ of Sanitiveness, or·the propensity to protect and preserve the integrity of the bodily constitution, to prevent disease, injury and destruction. Children and animals, ignorant of this design, make use of it instinctively when roused by the feeling of pain which it produces when disagreeably affected. If these views of pain are correct, the opinion of the poet, that the beetle which we tread upon,

"In corporal suffering, finds
A pang as great as when a giant dies,"

may be again revived, notwithstanding the belief of physiologists that the pain which an animal suffers is in proportion to the number and development of his sensitive nerves.

CANDIDATE ORGANS.

In the engraved bust it will be observed that there are five places indicated by the five first letters of the alphabet, and that each has an interrogation mark before it, implying that the function of the part is questionable. Theoretical considerations and analogy seem to render it certain that all the faculties which these candidate organs are supposed to represent really exist in the brain; but it by no means follows that their locations have been discovered. Even if one observer should succeed in discovering the actual location of an organ, it would probably require half a century to obtain the assent of the other phrenologists. A phreno-ethnological society is greatly needed to collect, compare and discuss the observa-

tions that are now being made all over the world, and
to produce unanimity of opinion concerning the results of their researches.

There are very serious difficulties in the way of
determining the functions of organs at the base of
the brain. 1. Their positions are such that they produce but little effect upon the prominences of the skull
in places where it can be examined. This objection
would, at first, seem to be insurmountable. But every
practical phrenologist knows that the development of
the organ of *Words* is one of the most easily examined and determined, yet the cerebral organ itself is
situated directly over the eyeball, and its development
is only indicated by the fact that it crowds the eye
downward and outward. So also the organ of Number is very small, and lies beneath the bone at the
outer part of the brow, so that it would at first seem
impracticable to determine its development; indeed
it really does require great care and considerable experience, yet if we compare half a dozen merely literary
men with the same number of successful financiers or
traders, the difference will be obvious and convincing.

Alimentiveness and Sanativeness would seem to be
liable to the same objection, and they doubtless are
difficult to determine, yet all phrenologists are agreed
concerning them.

In a work that I published in 1838 I remarked that
persons whose faces are prominent at the place marked A? in the engraved bust, excelled in judging concerning the qualities of food and drink, and I named
it Chemicality, or *Flavor*. The correctness of my
observation was generally admitted, but it was supposed that the prominence merely indicated that the

external organs of smell were greatly developed, and not that the greater or less development of the brain produced the difference.

In the same work I proposed an organ of the propensity of *Pneumativeness* (marked c? in the bust), related to breathing and ventilation, situated immediately before Alimentiveness.

In another work, published in 1857, I stated that I had observed that persons who were broad in that part of the head just under Constructiveness (see the engraved bust B?), manifested a propensity of Thermativeness — that is, they were living thermometers — their houses, their clothing and their conduct showed that they acted habitually with reference to the climate and the changes of the weather. It is large in the Esquimaux and small in Negroes.

In the same work I mentioned an observation that persons largely developed behind the ear, just under Combativeness, manifested a propensity which may be called *Excretiveness*. They seemed to delight in talking about excrementive subjects, to which refined people only allude as a matter of necessity. In asylums for the insane I have found several patients whose principal monomania was upon this subject.

The organ marked E? in the engraved bust seems to be related, in some way, to locomotion. This has been indicated, not so much by the observations of phrenologists as by the experiments of physiologists. I suspect that it is the propensity to maintain *Equilibrium*. It occupies the central part of the cerebellum, while the lateral parts are related to Amativeness.

I am also confident that there is an organ of the corporeal range related to sleep — *Somniferousness* —

but I have thus far been unable to locate it to my own satisfaction. The only observation of any value that I have been able to make in regard to this propensity, is the fact that persons who are very narrow through the head, in the corporeal range, sleep but little, and have weak constitutions. This is especially true of precocious children.

BELLIGERENT RANGE.
RELATED TO AGGRESSIVE AND OFFENSIVE OPERATIONS.

DESTRUCTIVENESS.
" Rise, Peter, kill and eat."—*Acts*.

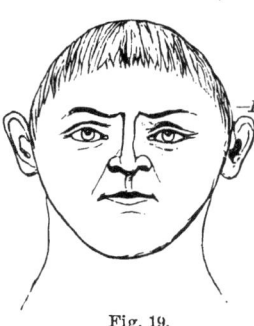

Fig. 19.

When this organ was first announced it was called the organ of Murder, and a thrill of horror was excited at the very suggestion that the Creator had bestowed upon all mankind a propensity which characterizes tigers and murderers. Dr. Gall himself, when he first noticed the resemblance between the

Figure 19. A boy named Armstrong murdered a girl in a very shocking manner, without any motive that could be discovered. For this offense he was confined in the Auburn State Prison. His head was so peculiar that I requested an artist to sketch an outline of his head. His Destructiveness (D, Fig. 19) is remarkably large; so also is Sanativeness; it is this organ that crowds his ears outward. In confirmation of this organ the overseer remarked that although the boy was cruel and malicious to others, he was very much afraid of corporal punishment. The organ of Alimentiveness was (just before the ear) also large.

heads of murderers and carniverous animals, recoiled from the conclusion to which it naturally seemed to tend. He says, " I revolted from this idea, but when my only business was to observe and to state the results of my observations, I acknowledged no other law than truth. It was afterwards ascertained to be in man the propensity of destruction in general, which when properly governed is absolutely necessary to the preservation of human existence."

Bitter, caustic, and severe language, in which is included cursing, swearing and scolding, is referable to this propensity. Some persons when weak in body or restrained by circumstances,

"Speak daggers, but use none."

Many persons commit cruel deeds in whom Destructiveness is small, for the reason that they are under the influence of some other passion which uses Destructiveness merely as a means. Some of the most bloody and revolting crimes recorded in history were committed under the influence of Conscientiousness when misled by superstition. St. Paul verily thought that he did God service by shedding the blood of the saints. Martyrs, in all ages, have been the victims of ignorance rather than of cruelty. I know many excellent men, with large Destructiveness, who are severe only when severity is a virtue; their frowns are terrible only to the wicked, and under their protection the weak and oppressed feel confident of safety.

COMBATIVENESS.

" I dare do all that doth become a man,
Who dares do more is none."—*Shakspeare.*

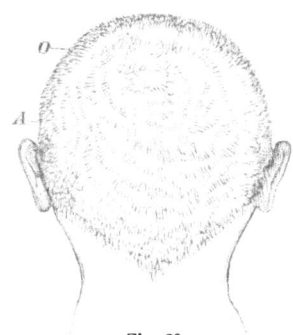

Fig. 20.

The propensity to oppose, contend and endeavor to overcome by superior strength, intellectual ability or social influence. When very large it renders a person pugnacious, quarrelsome and fond of disputes. When small, the person is averse to contention, even for the sake of justice and truth, if it can possibly be avoided.

The design of this propensity is to overthrow the obstacles which are in the way of enjoyment. It differs from Destructiveness in being satisfied with victory, and does not crush a fallen foe. It only inspires with courage to

" Strike till the last *armed* foe expires."

The feeling which it produces is *courage;* — the acts which follow the feeling are called hostile, brave, fierce, impetuous, hasty; while those of Destructiveness are cruel, malicious, revengeful. The object of Combativeness is conquest, but Destructiveness demands extermination. Some of the most bloodthirsty monsters in the world have been contemptible cowards — such were Robespierre and Nero; on the other hand some of the bravest men have in peace been the most

Figure 20 gives a good idea of a head, viewed from behind, in which Combativeness (A) is large, and Cautiousness (o) is small. Such persons are " sudden and quick in quarrel."

kind and gentle. There is also a great difference in animals in this respect; the bull, the ram and the hamster, though not destructive animals, frequently manifest a large degree of Combativeness in combination with the Social propensities. Combativeness borders upon Amativeness, Parentiveness and Adhesiveness; and when the enjoyment of these Socials is opposed, Combativeness is excited to battle in their behalf.

> "The wren, the most diminutive of birds,
> Will fight for her young in the nest against the owl."

Combativeness also inspires with feelings of opposition which vents itself in disputes; and, combined with a large intellect, produces literary and political controversies. Luther, Cobbett, J. Q. Adams, and Brougham are instances of this kind of manifestation. Combined with a very large organ of Equity, it disposes to moral controversies, such as relate to temperance, abolition, moral reform, etc. I know several individuals who, having embraced a doubtful or controverted doctrine, seem to take the greatest satisfaction in arguing the point, even when they do not expect to throw any light on the subject. They wish to gain victory, not converts — to confound, but not to convince. If at the same time Secretiveness is large, they love to puzzle and entrap their opponents, by getting their assent to propositions without their foreseeing the consequences; but when Secretiveness and Cautiousness are small, and Conscientiousness large, they contend openly, loudly, fiercely, and seem actuated by the spirit of Hamlet, when he exclaimed to Laertes:

> "Why, I will fight with him upon this theme,
> Until my eyelids will no longer wag."

This organ is large in all men who have distinguished themselves by great personal bravery. It is very large in the portrait of the chevalier Paul Jones, who refused to surrender, although his ship was sinking, and threatened to shoot the first man who proposed to ask for quarter.

It is more active in the males than females of all animals; and among some species the natural instruments of war or defense which they possess, such as horns, or tusks, are much more perfect in the males.

PRUDENTIAL RANGE.
RELATED TO SHREWDNESS, FORESIGHT AND DISTANT DANGER.

SECRETIVENESS.

" Look like the innocent flower;
But be the serpent under it."—*Shakspeare.*

The propensity to act indirectly or secretly; to conceal from opponents and even from friends the real truth in regard to motives and designs until a favorable opportunity occurs for displaying them. When very large and uncontrolled, it gives a tendency to deceitfulness in dealing with both friends and enemies; when small, it renders a person too open, frank and unsuspecting, and leads to self-betrayals and difficulties which might have been avoided by a little secretive management and justifiable shrewdness.

Suspicion is a disagreeable feeling which depends principally upon this propensity. Those who have it large are inclined to suspect that all appearances of good-will are deceitful; that professions are hollow and insincere; and that there is in every one a disposition to sacrifice the interests of others to the advantage of self. How far the

Fig. 21.

schemes which originate in Secretiveness shall be successful, depends very much upon the intellect; we accordingly have knaves of every degree of intelligence; some lay their stratagems so foolishly that they cannot possibly escape detection; their very faces are so indellibly stamped with the natural language of this propensity, that every one is thereby put upon his guard. But there are men whose large Secretiveness is so combined with intellectual and other powers, and who are so thoroughly acquainted with human nature, that it is almost impossible for any eye, but that of Omniscience, to discover their deep and comprehensive designs. Shakspeare has drawn a most perfect illustration of this kind of character in his Iago, and also Richard the Third, who says to himself:

> "Why, I can smile, and murder while I smile,
> And cry content to that which grieves my heart,

Figure 21 gives an idea of the width of the forehead produced by Constructiveness, Acquisitiveness and Secretiveness. Acquisitiveness is located at (c); Constructiveness a little below and in front of (c), and Secretiveness a little behind Constructiveness. In order to determine the development of Secretiveness, stand in front of the subject and fix upon Constructiveness; then observe whether the head continues to swell behind it.

And wet my cheeks with artificial tears,
And frame my face to all occasions."

I have seen very dishonest men, who had small Secretiveness and large intellect and Cautiousness; they
generally pride themselves upon their cunning and
ability to deceive; but they deceive themselves most
— they mistake caution for secrecy — and talent for
cunning. They are apt to overlook some secret means
of detection, or they forget to conceal something, or
unconsciously allow some expression to escape them
which leads to their exposure. They are unable to
compete successfully with those who have equal intellect and more Secretiveness. I have always found this
organ large on successful rogues; it enables them to
assume the appearance of honesty by suppressing the
expression of their real feelings.

It is large in most of the celebrated European politicians; in Talleyrand, Metternich, and in Pozzo di
Borgo, and enabled them to rise from obscurity and
exert a powerful influence upon the destinies of half
the civilized world. Such men possess a profound
and almost intuitive knowledge of human nature in
its secret operations. Artifice, in order to impose
upon them, must be most perfect; a single movement
of the eye or features, or the least equivocation of
voice or manner, is sufficient to excite their suspicion
and set them upon their watch.

The fact that Secretiveness is so much used, or
rather abused by rogues, renders a good development
of it the more necessary to the friends of justice, to
enable them to detect the machinations of the wicked.
Mr. Hays, the celebrated high constable of New York
city, had it very large, and was consequently capable

of conceiving the probable course which a villain would be likely to pursue in a particular case, and of suggesting plans and stratagems to circumvent and bring him to justice. It generally happens that petty scoundrels have small intellect and Equitableness, and large Secretiveness. They are cunning but not wise; an officer, therefore, who has Secretiveness equally large, with an intellect much larger, has greatly the advantage of them, and frequently astonishes both them and the public also by his superior sagacity. I know several merchants who have failed in business for no other reason than because they were too deficient in Secretiveness to suspect the selfishness and treachery of pretended friends. Honest themselves — frank, open, and confident — they cannot understand the feelings which actuate those who have an organization of a contrary kind. Experience only teaches them wisdom and prudence, but not cunning — to avoid knaves, not to outwit them.

CAUTIOUSNESS.

> " First fear, his hand its skill to try,
> Amid the chords bewildered laid,
> And back recoiled, he knew not why,
> Even at the sound himself had made."—*Collins.*

This is the propensity to avoid danger. The operations of the Lower Ipseals, which I have already described, is such as to produce a necessity for this propensity. Animals, in their eagerness to enjoy air and food and ease — and in their violent struggles to rend their prey, or to overthrow the obstacles to enjoyment, necessarily run into innumerable dangers, which this is designed to make them avoid. The great utility of this propensity is demonstrated by the consequences which may be sometimes observed to arise from its deficiency, or from the other propensities when unrestrained by its influence.   Goaded by Alimentiveness,

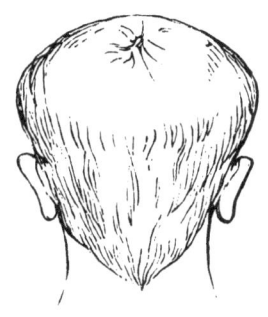

Large Cautiousness and small Combativeness — Fig. 22.

Large Combativeness and small Cautiousness — Fig. 22.

we sometimes see animals perfectly reckless of danger The hamster, mastiff and game-cock, in their eagerness for contention, seem to overlook the superiority of their opponents, and thus they sometimes unconsciously devote themselves to inevitable destruction. Other animals are prevented from doing the same by Cautiousness.   I have seen whole families in which this organ was very small; and the number of their scars, caused by scalds, burns, carelessness in the use of edge-tools, upsetting of carriages, and unnecessary quarrels, bore ample testimony to the importance of this wise provision.   One of them was a fisherman, who once went in a boat to Providence, without taking any provisions with him, and a storm keeping him several days at sea, he like to have starved; he afterwards facetiously declared that he would never trust to Providence for provisions again.   Some people are always meeting with *accidents;* they can scarcely go a journey without bringing back an account of some misfortune which has befallen them; nor can they engage in any business without meeting with uncommon losses; or carry out any enterprise when carefulness is requisite, without some disaster, which they attribute to any thing but the true cause. When such persons are deficient in the lower perceptives they are very phrenologically denominated *blunderheads*.

When Dr. Gall discovered this organ, he called it *Foresight* — because he first found it large in several individuals who were disposed to hesitate, doubt, and look forward prudently to consequences, before they said or did any thing irrevocably; but Spurzheim perceived that this was the effect of the propensity under consideration, combined with intellect, and he therefore changed the name to Cautiousness. Most of the herbiverous animals manifest it in a high degree; they have nothing to gain by destroying other animals; and except in self-defense, or in defense of their young, they never contend with other species of animals. Their mode of life, and their means of obtaining food, are peaceable. The males of herbivorous animals sometimes contend fiercely with other males of their own species; but this is only at certain seasons, when acting under great excitement from the activity of their social propensities; but they will fly in terror from the attack of a carniverous animal not one-tenth their size, and which they might crush at a single blow. Cautiousness was not intended to help animals out of difficulty, but to keep them out. Those very animals which are the most desirous to avoid danger, and which exert themselves the most vigorously to keep out of harm's way, submit with the most quietness to the infliction when it is present; whereas those which are the most reckless in their attempts to injure others, for their own gratification, make the greatest ado when a personal injury is inflicted upon themselves. Cautiousness, then, needs more intellect than the lower Ipseals; or, rather, it is related to *higher* intellectual powers; and the philosophical student of Phrenology will perceive that the higher organs of each class, in their very nature, presuppose the existence of the higher organs of the other classes. Without keeping this principle in mind, we shall be liable to take a too limited view of the functions of the superior powers; they are all more *general* in their effects — they take a wider range and exert a modifying influence upon those below them. This will be the more obvious when I have explained all the superior propensities, and it will be perceived that the nature of all the powers becomes more and more general as we rise in the scale.

INDUSTRIAL RANGE.
RELATED TO WORK, BUSINESS AND PROPERTY.
CONSTRUCTIVENESS

" I will pull down my barn and build greater."—*Luke*.

Propensity to work with the hands; to engage in manual mechanical operations. It gives only the *disposition* to work mechanically. The skill and ingenuity depend upon the Intellect and experience. When large, the person, even if indolent, prefers manual mechanical labor to any other employment.

Women, with this organ large, take pleasure in common house-work, even when they are under no necessity of doing it. When small, although the person is fond of exercise, and not indolent, he has an aversion to regular mechanical business; he prefers some other kind of employment. It is frequently small in engineers and other persons who excel in invention, and in directing the labors of others by superior intellect and knowledge, but who take no pleasure in working with their hands in a routine manner which requires only common ability.

So intimate is the relation between this propensity and the lower perceptives, that some Phrenologists have considered it as partaking of the nature of an intellectual faculty, and have denominated it *semi-intellectual;* but it is very easy to demonstrate that it is in no degree intellectual; however largely developed it may be, it never bestows mechanical *talent,* unless the perceptives are large. In this respect it resembles every other propensity, and gives its possessor a *feeling* of pleasure, which, in common language, is called a fondness of mechanics — a taste for architecture — a love for construction, etc. — and those who have it large have a great proneness to be engaged in mechanical operations, such as are in harmony with their other powers. How far an individual will be successful in his mechanical performances, depends altogether upon his intellect; but how much pleasure will be experienced in construction, depends upon Constructiveness. I know some persons who are excellent artists, with small Constructiveness; and others who are miserable bunglers with this organ uncommonly developed.

I have seen many persons with large Constructiveness aud large reflectives, and moderate perceptives;
they generally excel in mechanical contrivances, but
fail in practice. They will sometimes make good
general superintendents, and can *judge* well of the
nature and expediency of operations which they cannot perform. They make better masters than jour-
neymen. Again, there are some men who, although
first rate workmen, cannot proceed a step beyond their
instructions. They can work by imitation or by rules
which others lay down; but the moment they are left
to their own judgment, without any precedent, or
model, or overseer, they are in a maze of perplexity.
Under these circumstances they are frequently directed
by the judgment of a person who is totally ignorant
of the use of the instruments, and who could never
have equalled in practice the laborer whom he directs.
With large Perfectiveness this propensity gives a fondness for the fine arts and constructions of the improved
and ornamental kind.

ACQUISITIVENESS.

" And there will I bestow all my fruits and my goods."—*Luke*.

The propensity to acquire property — to attend to
pecuniary business. It gives a love of mercantile
pursuits; when very large it renders one unwilling
to follow any profession or calling that is not lucra-
tive.

When small the person continually sacrifices his
pecuniary interests to his love of pleasure, of art, of
literature, of social distinction, or of philanthrophy.
If this organ and Cautiousness are both small, the
result is improvidence, and the tendency is to extreme

poverty. On the contrary, if Cautiousness is large and Hope small, there is a tendency to penuriousness and a want of enterprise.

Dr. B. Franklin — Fig. 24.

It is remarkable that all the animals that acquire property first make use of their Constructiveness to prepare a proper store in which to deposit and preserve it for future use. The beaver, for instance, first makes use of his Constructiveness to gnaw down trees and build a convenient hut, and *afterwards* acquires bark to gratify his Alimentiveness during winter. The

Figure 24. Dr. Franklin's head is, in several respects, a good illustration of Phrenology. The dotted line indicates the position of Acquisitiveness, which was large; the height of his forehead, in the middle line, indicates large Kindness, and the prominence of his eye and the bagging appearance of the flesh beneath it, indicate the organ of Words large; all of which agree with his well known history.

rat also, that notoriously thievish animal, first prepares
a nest, or hiding place, by gnawing and digging in a
manner nearly as ingenious as the beaver, and then
begins to acquire provisions for winter. The same is
true of nearly all the rodentia. It is interesting thus
to trace the connection between the propensities of Alimentiveness, Constructiveness and Acquisitiveness,
and at the same time to observe the manner in which
they are chained together in the brain.

Man differs from other animals by the all-grasping
nature of his Acquisitiveness; he is not content to
preserve the bounties of nature for future comfort
merely — for food or clothing — the whole material
world is searched for things either of natural or artificial value; every ocean and river, every mountain
and mine is stripped of its treasures; the lives of
animals are sacrificed without number and without
mercy, not only to furnish food, clothing, light and
medicine, but even for mere ornament or show. Living animals also are acquired and reduced to labor to
increase his wealth. Not content with this, he often
assumes possession of his fellow men, and disposes of
them for the gratification of his misdirected Acquisitiveness. Even his own health and personal comfort
are frequently sacrificed to save property which he
can never enjoy — which he only desires to *possess* —
and does not expect to use to increase his happiness
and comfort.

Some with a very large Acquisitiveness are perfectly honest and noble in their dealings; they would
not, for the wealth of all the world, sacrifice the great
principles of morality, but they endeavor to gain
property by every honorable means in their power;

they rise early and sit up late; they are very industrious and attentive to all their pecuniary affairs;
place a high value upon their time; allow nothing
belonging to them, or left in their charge, to be wasted
or injured through neglect; they not only acquire but
preserve with great care; keep a watchful eye upon
their agents, and insist upon having every item accounted for; — while they are ready to pay every far-
thing that may justly be charged against them, they
in return insist upon all that is due to themselves;
they frequently give with great liberality to the poor
and to the support of useful institutions — but they are
careful not to give *all* — and they feel greatly shocked
and offended to learn that their gift has been appro-
priated without regard to economy; they love to
repeat the prudent maxims of Franklin, and show the
young " the way to wealth "; they take great pleasure
in seeing their property accumulating; they never lose
an opportunity to make a good bargain, and in the
language of Burns,

> " To catch dame fortune's favoring smile,
>   Assiduous wait upon her,
> And gather gear by every wile
>   That's justified by honor."

I have generally found Order and Number larger
on those with predominant Acquisitiveness than those
who have it small; probably this is owing to the fact
that these organs generally act together; large Number is necessary to calculate loss and gain with facility,
and Order to arrange the acquisitions in such a manner as to preserve them to the greatest advantage. I
know several merchants who have failed because they
neglected their book accounts, and in them all I found

small Order and Number. When large Acquisitiveness is combined with a large intellect, the reflectives
predominating, and Cautiousness medium, with Hopefulness large, then business will be likely to be done
on a large scale — the plans will be comprehensive
and complicated, yet systematic and reasonable. The
loss or gain will be such as to produce the most important results; sometimes affecting whole nations by
a single transaction, and even changing the policy of
the most powerful governments. But when Acquisitiveness is combined with a small Hopefulness and a
very large Cautiousness, the transactions are of the
most limited kind; a sure retail business is preferred,
and capital, instead of being employed to extend the
business, is lent on bond and mortgage. All the operations are small, the risk is little, the profits are
small, the expenses are moderate — everything is contracted within the narrowest bounds. In some extreme cases of *voluntary littleness*, the character is
strongly marked in the personal appearance. Alimentiveness is made to suffer; the lean, gaunt body is
contracted within threadbare garments, which are too
small in all directions; the snivelled features sharp-
ened to a point; the upper lip drawn toward the
nose, exposes the incisive teeth; the fingers crooked
to resemble claws; the body bent forward, and the
whole figure and expression resembling a rat in a sitting posture.

IMPROVING RANGE.

RELATED TO CIVILIZATION, INVENTION, THE FINE ARTS AND ENTERPRISE;
AND NOT TO THE IMMEDIATE ANIMAL NECESSITIES.

TUNEFULNESS.

Music — a spell whose magic might
Can raise the storm of passions high,
Or curb their fury at its height
And bid the raging tempest die. — *J. S. G.*

Dr. Gall declared that he had observed that great musicians are full just over the organ of Order (T), as seen at Fig. 25. in the head of Handel. I have failed to

Handel, Musician — Fig. 25.

confirm his observations on this point, but I have noticed that order and number are generally large on musical composers, though not on mere performers. This is what might be expected, since music as a science is founded upon mathematical principles.

May it not be that Gall mistook the peculiar development of those two organs for a supposed organ of Tunefulness? It is a remarkable fact that besides man birds are the only singing animals, and but a few species of them possess the faculty. They are also the only animals that have the faculty of imitating human speech.

Spurzheim and other prenologists have placed Tunefullness among the perceptive faculties, but it has every quality of a propensity. It does not *perceive* sound, for that is the function of the intellectual organ of Words or Language, for words are mere sounds. In some persons Tunefulness amounts to a passion. If then it is a blind propensity — what is its position in relation to the other propensities? Is it an Ipseal or a Social? What is its utility in the animal or mental economy? In answer to these questions I can offer nothing better than an hypothesis, which I shall abandon with pleasure when something better is offered. Although few animals sing, nearly all vertebrates make use of vocal sound, as a means of expressing their emotions and desires. There is, therefore, in all probability, a distinct organ of a *propensity* which may be denominated *Vocalitiveness*. In man, and in a few remarkably social birds, this propensity becomes modified, and receives a super-addition which constitutes the propensity of Tunefulness. A person may possess a strong propensity to make music without the perceptive ability and vocal or mechanical skill to perform it; and on the other hand one may have a perfectly correct perception of pitch, melody and harmony without any propensity to become a performer.

If this view of Tunefulness is correct, I am justified in placing it in the improving range of Ipseal propensities, as an exceptional and superior faculty, worthy to associate with wit, poetry and cheerfulness. The intimate relation of Tunefulness to Vocalitiveness — if we may assume the existence of the last named propensity — is indicated by the fact that music gives the most perfect expression to our emotions, passions and desires. Indeed Tunefulness may be defined as the emotions set to music.

EXPERIMENTIVENESS — WIT — MIRTHFUL-NESS.

" A heaven of invention." — *Shakspeare.*

Gall, who discovered this organ, named it *Wit.* He made no attempt at a philosophical analysis of the faculty, but contented himself by saying that it was the distinguishing trait in certain very witty authors. Spurzheim committed a grave mistake in changing the name to Mirthfulness. In my first work I suggested that it should be called Playfulness. But after many years of experience I became fully satisfied that the word Experimentiveness expresses its real function precisely. When exercised sportively by literary characters it manifests itself by producing witty expressions, but I conceive that its primitive function is to produce novel modes of proceeding when the old methods fail; it leads to mechanical, chemical and philosophical experiments and inventions, and all kinds of departures from old, routine habits and modes of action. It is, therefore, the natural antagonist of mere instinct, and of thoughtless imitation, and prompts its possessor to endeavor to discover the means by which he can vary his conduct and adapt himself to new circumstances. Combined with a large intellect it leads to scientific discoveries. If this organ is large and the intellect deficient, the individual will be continually trying foolish experiments, and attempting impossible inventions. Combined with large social organs it produces a love of news, of social variety, and a dread of monotony of all kind.

Many of the mental operations that have been attributed to imagination really depend upon the exercise of this propensity. The word imagination literally signifies image forming. When the intellect is stim-

Fig. 26.

ulated by Experimentiveness into a state of activity, it calls to mind all the facts and argu- ments relating to the subject and endeavors to perceive the best course to pursue under the circumstances. This so- ber reasoning process is not properly speaking imagina- tion, so long as it is confined to apparent realities, and deals in known facts and their logical relations; but when the intellect steps beyond these boundaries, enters the regions of conjecture, and begins to form hypotheses or mental experiments, it comes within the proper jurisdiction of the Imagination. The Intellect then enjoys unbounded licence; it is no longer held in check by the stern authority of truth; it passes beyond probability, revels without restraint amid the most incredible wonders, and even dares to scale the dizzy heights of the impossible. The character of the imaginative creations depends upon the other propensi- ties that are excited at the same time; Destructiveness imagines scenes of blood and carnage; Imperative- ness imagines itself governing subjugated nations; Reverence imagines a heavenly millenium; and Benev- olence the end of all human suffering.

If a person has Constructiveness active he will im-

Fig. 26. Represents Tunefulness (T) and Order very small, and Experimentiveness immediately above them so very large as to amount to a deformity.

agine mechanical inventions; if he has Acquisitive ness large he may invent schemes for enriching himself; if he is socially or politically ambitious he will form plans and resort to stratagems by means of which to rise above his rivals; if he has literary genius he may invent poems or romances, and soar into what Shakspeare calls a " heaven of invention."

The sense of the ludicrous is probably one of the incidental modes in which this propensity manifests itself playfully, by giving the disposition to try absurd experiments, either physically or mentally, just for amusement, and without any idea of producing any useful or serious results.

PERFECTIVENESS — IDEALITY— ORNATENESS.

"Beautiful! How beautiful is all this visible world! How glorious in its action and itself."—*Byron.*

The creations of nature, and also those of art, differ from each other in their degrees of perfection. Two things may be equal to each other in every respect, so far as their utility is concerned, yet we instinctively prefer one to the other on account of what we regard as its superior beauty. This perfecting propensity is very little cultivated in savage life, but as civilization progresses in any community, and wealth is accumulated in a few superior families, their ambition to outshine each other prompts them to encourage the ornamental arts, and to make comparisons between the various productions of skillful workmen. It is easy to conceive that a great many generations of such rivalry would result in a modification of the upper part of Constructiveness, or rather a superaddition to it, which would constitute a distinct propensity to beautify, ornament, improve, and perfect.

Miss Hosmer, the Sculptress — Fig. 27.

There is no one organ of Poetry. Perfectiveness gives a tendency to ornateness of style; Credenciveness, to romantic and exaggerated ideas; Imitativeness, to personations and dramatic modes of expression; Comparison, to metaphors and appropriate illustra-

Figure 27. In the head of Miss Hosmer we have a fine illustration of the organs requisite to an artist. Constructiveness is indicated by the great width of the forehead; Experimentiveness, by the outline of the left side; Perfectiveness is seen large at the upper part of the right side of the forehead; the heaviness of her brow indicates large Weight; the distance between the eyes, large Form; the breadth of the part of the forehead between the eyes, large Size; and the fullness of the brow, on her left side, large Order.

tions; the organ of Words, to copiousness and readiness of proper language; and (perhaps,) Order and
Number, to rythm. To these may be added a peculiarity of temperament, which produces an almost
unhealthy activity of the brain.

This propensity and Acquisitiveness are naturally
opposed to each other; one delights in mere utility,
and the other in mere beauty; when one is small,
the other is much more active. Artists, poets, and
purely professional persons, generally have Acquisitiveness small; they are delighted with their labor
independently of its profits, otherwise they never
excel. When very large, and the intellect small, this
faculty produces fantastic notions, and tastes inconsistent with common sense. The folly is still greater
if Credenciveness is very large and the temperament
excitable. When small, there is a want of tendency
to the higher kinds of self-education, and to those
artistic improvements that are not of immediate utility.

The history of the discovery of this organ affords
a good illustration of the manner in which the science
of Phrenology has been created. Gall observed that
the upper lateral parts of the forehead were remarkably expanded in the busts of a great many poets, and
proceeding in his usual empirical manner, he called a
certain space the organ of the Poetic Faculty. Spurzheim, by making a great many observations, ascertained that the upper part of the space was very large
on persons who were disposed to believe in the marvelous, and this led him to divide the space into two
organs, both of which are now fully established.

Although at first this organ was attributed to
poets only, it was afterwards observed also to be

equally large on celebrated sculptors, musicians, orators, and all those who were uncommonly devoted to
the fine arts, and manifested a quick perception of the
beautiful. Dr Spurzheim, perceiving the necessity
of changing the name, adopted that of Ideality, which
signifies ideal beauty, or a kind of beauty which is
superior to reality, and which exists only in imagination. Mr. Combe considers Ideality "an elegant and
appropriate name." It is certainly elegant and eupho-
nious, but I cannot admit that it is appropriate; I
have therefore adopted that of Perfectiveness, by
which I mean the propensity to improve and perfect.
So far is it from being related to a kind of beauty
which is superior to nature that I consider it directly
related to the works of nature, particularly those
which are perfect of their kind.

This propensity seems to modify and exalt the aim
of all the powers with which it combines. It disposes
them to rise above mere utility, or rather, it crowns
the productions of utility with ornament. Does Alimentiveness require a repast? this propensity insists
upon its being served up with elegance, and is disgusted with the idea of feeding like a mere animal.
Does Constructiveness inspire the mind with a desire
to build a house? Perfectiveness wishes to have it in
the best style; not merely warm, convenient and comfortable, but splendid and perfect in every respect.
Does Acquisitiveness desire to accumulate property?
it inclines him to do so in the most refined manner;
it soon becomes wearied with the dull monotony of
mere business, however profitable. In this manner it
very much modifies Acquisitiveness, rouses it from
the mean and grovelling pursuits to which it is prone

when this propensity is small, and demands time for improvement. The majority of thieves have this organ deficient, particularly those who commit petit larceny. It frequently deters men from little crimes, not because they are wrong, but because they are mean. I once saw a highway robber with large Perfectiveness, and speaking of himself, he said, "I do not skulk around for my prey like a thieving owl, but I pounce upon it like an eagle." The artist who has it large, is continually searching for the finest forms in nature for his models. The proudest achievements of genius are but imperfect copies of natural beauty. In almost all the complicated productions of nature, certain parts are much more perfect than others; and the artist, by selecting from a great number of specimens the parts which happen to be most perfect, and grouping them artificially together, is able to produce a *combination* superior to any that can be found in reality. The florist can select the most beautiful flowers of the season, and with them form a bouquet more exquisitely beautiful, and better adapted to please the human mind, than any that can be found in nature. The sculptor or painter proceeds upon the same principle when he produces a Venus, an Adonis, or an Apollo. He finds upon one individual a beautiful forehead, upon another a nose, or an arm, and by combining all the individual instances of perfection in one statue, he seems to excel nature, when he has only grouped together a number of imperfect copies of her most perfect productions.

Poetry is the perfection of language. We may combine words in such a manner as merely to be understood; but if this organ is very large, its possessor will choose a noble subject, use the most elegant and refined words, and combine them in the most graceful style; the illustrations also, will be chosen, not for their propriety only, but for their beauty, gorgeousness, and splendor. Every thing low, vulgar, mean, or common, will, as far as possible, be avoided. The images which spontaneously rise in such a mind, and which will be entertained with the greatest delight, will be of the highest order. In looking around upon the face of nature the attention will be particularly directed to such objects as are adapted to this propensity—so that afterward, when writing upon any subject, the images of the objects thus noticed will be involuntarily presented to the imagination, and described in the glowing language of poetry.

> "The poet's eye in a fine frenzy rolling,
> Doth glance from heaven to earth, from earth to heaven,"

to find ideas fitted to illustrate, amplify and adorn his subject; and if his inspired vision cannot light upon any *known* objects "that suit his large desires," he resorts to invention, and his prolific

> "Imagination bodies forth,
> The forms of things unknown."

Like an aspiring æronaut, he cuts himself loose from the dull and prosing circumstances that confine him to the atmosphere of ordinary life; soars above the clouds; takes his station among the stars, and looks down through "the dizziness of distance" upon this lower world, where all common objects are lost in obscurity, and only the grandest and brightest can be distinguished. Such were the aspirations of Shakespeare, when he exclaimed,

> " O for a muse of fire, that would ascend
> The brightest heaven of invention:
> A kingdom for a stage, princes to act,
> And monarchs to behold the swelling scene."

And such also must have been the feelings of Milton, when he invoked the inspiration of Him—

> " Who touched Isaiah's lips with hallowed fire."

This propensity is very dependent upon the highest organs of intellect. Perfectiveness gives the desire to improve, but reflection gives the ability, the talent, the necessary invention. Sometimes a very large organ of Perfectiveness is found combined with a very small intellect. The forehead may be high and wide, but shallow. In such cases the manifestations will frequently be in the highest degree eccentric and ridiculous, especially if combined with very large Approbativeness and Hopefulness. They are continually attempting more than they can perform. They lay out all their undertakings on such a large and splendid scale that they can seldom be realized; their ideas are like monstrous and brilliant bubbles, which burst while they are coming into existence. If we read their compositions, we are entertained with a pompous array of splendid and beautiful nothings; their public discourses are mere

> " Sound and fury signifying nothing."

HOPEFULNESS.

" Hope bears us through nor leaves us when we die."—*Pope.*

This is the propensity to act with reference to the future with confidence of success. Authors and orators have been so much in the habit of giving metaphysical, romantic and poetical explanations of the higher mental faculties, and leaving out of view their utilities and physiological relations, that it seems almost necessary to apologize for treating them in a plain, practical manner. It is difficult to ascertain the primitive and distinctive nature of a faculty if we only study its manifestations amidst a complicated and highly civilized community where the natural and simple is mingled and confounded with the artificial. In primitive and uncultivated communities where the faculties are manifested in their native simplicity we can form more correct ideas of their distinctive peculiarities. If we descend to the most intelligent animals we are inclined by our prejudices to utterly deny them the possession of any of the higher faculties; but the remark of Cuvier that the bodies of animals are experiments ready prepared by nature to illustrate the bodily functions of man holds equally true concerning their minds.

There is no question that all the organs of the Ipseal class are manifested by animals, excepting the improving range, and, perhaps, they exhibit some degree of all these. Tunefulness is possessed by birds, and Experimentiveness in a slight degree by all the higher animals. In regard to Perfectiveness, Mr. Darwin thinks that he has demonstrated that animals in selecting their mates are governed by a sense of the beautiful; and it must be admitted that considerable artistic skill is exhibited by some birds in the construction of their nests. If Hopefulness is primitively a propensity to migrate from a poor region to a better one, it is possessed by several species of animals. Heaven is often described as the happy land to which the Christian at death hopes to emigrate; the Indian hopes to reach the "far off island in the watery waste," or the happy hunting ground where " no fiends torment nor Christians thirst for gold."

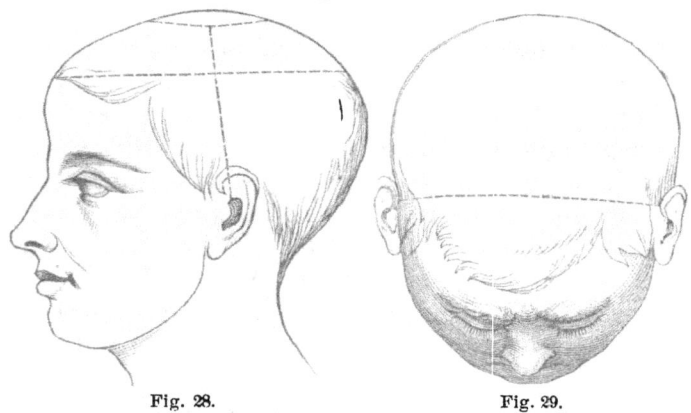

Fig. 28.   Fig. 29.

In all the books and busts that I have seen this organ is placed too high, and to make the blunder still greater, some phrenologists have located what they call " the organ of sublimity " in the very place where Hopefulness has been placed by the Creator. The sense of the sublime depends upon Submissiveness or Reverence acting upon a poetical and cultivated mind. The organ of Submissiveness extends farther laterally than it is commonly represented. To assist beginners in locating Hopefulness, I have prepared the two annexed engavings. A line drawn from the orifice of one ear (*meatus auditorius*) across to the opposite ear, (Fig. 29) will pass through the organ; and another line drawn horizontally around the head, Fig. 28, passing across the upper part of the forehead, will also pass across this propensity; the organ is at the place where these two lines meet.

When large, this propensity causes a person to forget the misfortunes of the past, and undervalue the difficulties of the present, while anticipating the success and pleasures of the future. When Cautiousness is very small and Hopefulness large, there is a tendency to excessive Mirthfulness; with small Acquisitiveness this mirthful tendency is increased, because there is an absence of care concerning pecuniary affairs.

When Hopefulness is small, Cautiousness fills the mind with doubts and sad foreboding, enterprise is checked, and gives way to excessive prudence.

When very deficient, I generally suspect that some of the ancestors have suffered great and long continued misfortunes, or depressing diseases. Disorders of the stomach or liver are frequently accompanied by depression of spirits; diseases of the lungs by abnormal cheerfulness.

This propensity is the highest of the Ipseal Class; like the key stone of an arch it crowns the whole — is intimately related to the whole — and contributes more than any other to human happiness. It produces this effect by combining with the other powers, and inspiring a feeling that they will yet be gratified. In order to fully understand the nature of Hopefulness we must bear in mind its high character, its extensive connections, its relations to the other propensities of its own class, and of the Socials, and especially its relations to the highest Intellectuals. Every propensity is dependent upon the intellect, but the highest propensities are peculiarly dependent upon the highest Intellectuals. The lowest propensities may act effectually and perfectly without the aid of the reflectives; Alimentiveness, Destructiveness and Combativeness, for

instances, can act vigorously and be perfectly gratified
without reflection; the perceptives are to them sufficient guides; not so the highest propensities — their
very definition implies the existence of Causality to
look beyond the present. These remarks apply with
great force to Perfectiveness and Hopefulness; neither
of these propensities can produce the effects which
they were evidently designed to do without the aid of
reflection. I have already shown the effect of a large
Perfectiveness upon a deficient intellect, and its great
dependence upon Causality and Comparison; this is
even more obvious in respect to Hopefulness. I cannot
conceive how this propensity can act at all until Causality has first acted. It is only by means of Causality
that we look forward to the future; we remember the
past and perceive the present by means of the perceptives, but when from these premises we infer the
events to come, we do so only by means of Causality.
Now when we consider that Hopefulness relates to the
doubtful, the contingent, the future — that its very
office is to produce feelings and actions with reference
to subjects concerning which we only know in part,
and believe in part, conjecture in part, and hope the
rest, we must admit that it is especially dependent
upon Causality for the very material upon which it
acts. When anything is present, or within our reach,
we cannot feel any hope in relation to it; but when
the event is one in which we feel a deep interest, and
which by means of Causality we perceive must happen,
though it is doubtful whether the event will be favorable to us or not, then this propensity has its appropriate stimulus, produces agreeable anticipations, dis-

misses all forebodings, and disposes us to act as if success were certain.

The lower animals can possess no more of hope than they do of reason. They know so little of the probabilities of future events, that they can scarcely be said to hope or fear concerning them. But man has intellectual powers sufficiently capacious to store up the events of ages past, and, by the light which they shed upon the future, they enable him to foresee the probable fate of generations yet unborn; without this happifying propensity he would be inconceivably miserable and melancholy. We are not left to conjecture on this point. Hundreds of instances have fallen under my own observation, in which a deficiency of the organ was attended with the most indescribable unhappiness. The more reflective power such persons possess the more melancholy it renders them, by enabling them to see difficulties and troubles afar off, and thus exciting Cautiousness to action while there is not sufficient hope to counteract its chilling effects. The most melancholy people that I have ever seen have large intellects. They have the gift of showing, by the most unanswerable logic, that they are the most unfortunate beings in the world, and they recur to the miseries of the past as data from which to infer the misfortunes of the future.

> " Melancholy is a fearful gift;—
> What is it but the telescope of truth,
> Which strips the distance of its phantasies
> And brings life near in utter nakedness,
> Making the cold reality too real."—*Byron.*

Most of those who commit suicide, have this organ small and Destructiveness large. To them the future holds out nothing sufficiently desirable to make life worth preserving. If Equitableness and Credenciveness are large they are frequently disposed to religious melancholy, and have "a fearful looking for of judgments to come," while the promises of the gospel afford them no consolation.

"On horror's head, horrors accumulate,"

till nature sinks in despair beneath the intolerable load, and they rush into the arms of death in a frenzy of desperation. When the organ is but little below medium, the effect is less severe; then there is a disposition to look at the dark side of every subject, and to foresee evils which exist only in their own imaginations. They are apt to think themselves cursed with *bad luck;* they not only see troubles in the future, but they call up from the recollections of the past only the disagreeable incidents and circumstances, and dwell upon them with mournful interest; they will review their past lives and show that they have been continued scenes of misfortune; they seem to have a great faculty of recollecting disagreeable things, and forgetting those which are agreeable, and they frequently entertain their friends with a doleful account of their misfortunes. One of this kind of persons lately undertook to convince me that he was *naturally* unlucky. "Not long since," said he, "I went a fishing, and every body in the boat caught fish but me. I baited my hook just as they did, put it down into the water in the same way close by the side of theirs, and yet caught no fish, while they hauled them in all around me; and what was most provoking, there was a kind of half fool with us who had better luck than any of the rest." The friends of a young man once requested me to explain, upon phrenological principles, his singular

conduct. He had considerable money left him by his
father, and was surrounded by rich friends who urged
him to engage in business, but he constantly refused
on account of his fears that he should not succeed.
He seemed averse to all kinds of enterprise in which
the results were in any degree doubtful. I found in
him a very amiable organization, but Hopefulness deficient. Although his health was tolerably good, he
undertook to show to me the probability that he should
die with the consumption, as several of his relatives
had fallen victims to that disease, and another, whom
he mentioned, would doubtless have met with the same
fate had he not been killed by lightning.

Hope was Napoleon's "star," and led him on, like
an *ignis fatuus*, first to empire and then to ruin. It
was Hope and courage which dictated the celebrated
remark of Julius Cæsar to the fisherman, when the
storm threatened him with destruction: "Fear not, you
carry Cæsar and his fortunes." Hope is the "good
angel" which hovers around the couch of the pious,
and inspires them with dreams of future glory and
happiness.

> " O Hope! sweet flatterer, whose delusive touch
> Sheds on the afflicted mind the balm of comfort;
> Relieves the load of poverty—sustains
> The captive, bending 'neath the weight of chains."

Those who have this organ large are comparative
strangers to feelings of melancholy; they look forward
to the future with bright anticipations of happiness.
If they have been unfortunate they flatter themselves
that it is all for the best, or that such *bad luck* cannot
last long, but must soon turn in their favor. They
call up hundreds of instances in which, under similar

unfortunate circumstances, the result had proved favorable; and even let the worst happen they still have resources of happiness. When Acquisitiveness is large, they engage with confidence in hazardous speculations, and when small they make the most of poverty — live contented, and free from care and anxiety. So long as they can enjoy the present they " take no thought of the morrow, what they shall eat, nor what they shall drink, nor yet for their clothing what they shall put on." When they are in the greatest straits they feel a hope that by some means, they know not exactly what, they will be able to extricate themselves, and that all will yet be well. Actuated by these feelings they sometimes accomplish apparent impossibilities; they will persevere in undertakings when all but themselves have become discouraged.

" Things out of hope are compass'd oft with venturing."

In the days of childhood we look forward to the happiness which we expect to enjoy after we have come to maturity, and when that time arrives we still have our greatest felicity in anticipation. We still

" Bid the lovely scenes at *distance* hail ! "

The brilliant treasure is always almost within our reach, but continually eludes our grasp. " Time rolls his ceaseless course," and as we are eagerly engaged in the pursuit, our progress is suddenly arrested by the certainty that we are on the brink of death, but even then

" Hope bears us through, nor leaves us when we die."

Dr. Rush remarked that the skulls of insane patients were depressed in the parietal bone, the place where Hopefulness is situated. Those patients were probably melancholics, who suffered from diseases of the stomach and liver.

Marshall Hall writes:

" The temper of the patient is singularly modified by different disorders. The state of despondency in cases of indigestion forms a remarkable contrast with that of hopefulness in phthisis pulmonalis."

Dr. Fothergill, of the West London Hospital, referring to the effects upon the mind of diseases of different parts of the body, remarks:

" The consumptive patient just dropping into the grave will indulge in plans stretching far into the future, ignoring his real condition, and the impossibility of any such survival as he is calculating upon. It is a curious yet familiar state. Hope seems to rise above intelligence, just as in certain abdominal diseases there is a depression which defies its corrections.

" In curious relation to these conditions stand the well known differences of the pulse. In chest diseases the pulse is usually full, sometimes bounding; in abdominal diseases it is small and often thready. The pulse of pneumonia and the pulse of peritonitis are distinctly dissimilar, and contrast with each other.

" The explanation which is shadowed out, for it really does not amount to more, is that abdominal diseases causes a depletion of the emotional centers of which depression is the outward indication, whilst phthisis leads to a plethoric state associated with excited emotional conditions.

" Allied in essence to melancholia is the pamphobia or ' low spirits ' common to women generally. It is the cry of the suffering brain for better nutrition, for a more liberal supply of arterial blood."

THE SOCIAL PROPENSITIES.

These are conveniently divided into three groups, namely: The Domestic, the Governing, and the Conforming.

DOMESTIC GROUP.

RELATED TO SEX, CHILDREN, HOME, AND FRIENDS.

AMATIVENESS.

"Be fruitful; multiply and replenish the earth."--*Genesis*.

The sexual propensity gives an intense love of persons of the other sex. When too large and unbalanced by moral considerations, there is a disposition, for the sake of this love, to neglect business, reputation, and duties of all kinds, for its gratification. When properly governed and directed, it leads to virtuous love and marriage. When very small, there is a manifest indifference toward the other sex. If, however, Adhesiveness is large, there is a steady, though not very ardent attachment to one companion, and indifference to others of the opposite sex. In one

NOTE.—EQUILIBRIUM.—Comparative anatomy, and the experiments of physiologists, combine to indicate that the posterior part of the cerebellum, near the middle line, the vermiform process, is an organ in some way related to locomotion. There is probably no organ in the brain related to motion of any kind *per se*, but it is reasonable to suppose that a propensity is possessed by all vertebrates to maintain their equilibrium, and it is not difficult to understand that it is needed in connection with the function of Amativeness. At present we can only regard Equilibrium as a candidate organ.

(81)

respect this mental organ is analogous to Alimentiveness, and that is that its activity depends upon the
health, the temperament, and other conditions of the
body, which cannot be ascertained by an examination
of the head.

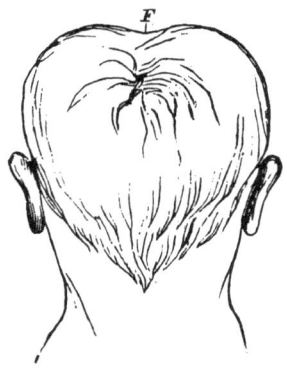

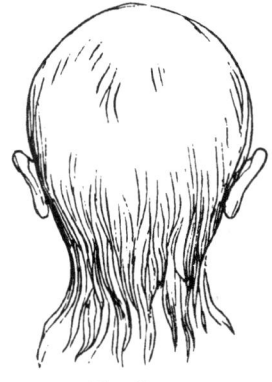

Fig. 30.   Fig. 31.

The cerebellum does not increase much until the
age of puberty, it then begins to expand, and nearly
doubles in size between the ages of ten and twenty;
the character, during this time, undergoes a corresponding change; the opposite sex, which before were
viewed without partiality, become now extremely
interesting, and an indescribable charm seems to be
thrown around them. Their voices are enchanting,
their forms appear exquisitively lovely, and their
favoring smile bewitching beyond all power of expression. Unconscious of the nature of the feeling that
inspires them, they only know that their greatest bliss

The organ, when large, as in Fig. 30, gives width and fullness
to the lowest part of the back of the head, behind the lowest
part of the ears. In Fig. 31 it is small.

is in each other's society; their highest ambition to gain each other's love; and the most dreadful of all apprehensions, that of bestowing their affections without a return. "Love," says the Count De Segur, "creates for us a new world, inhabited by two beings, one of which is to us the whole universe; for that being alone do we value our wealth, our talents, and even our virtue. We prize no worth in ourselves but that which pleases this being. Time seems to linger when it is absent, and fly when it is present; we experience that which Madame de Lambert says: 'we do not find the hours sufficiently long when we have to dedicate them to the beloved one.' But whence comes so sudden a change in the existence of the youth? What has subdued his will, tamed his boldness, overpowered him, and triumphed over his independence? Is it a being more enlightened, more virtuous, or more powerful than himself? No! a very child in purity and power; a young female. She has no other weapon than her looks, no other power than her charms; but she has beauty, and youth imagines that whoever possesses it, is endowed with all perfection. Even wisdom yields blushingly to her empire, and the wise La Bruyere could not refrain from saying, 'A beautiful face is the most enchanting sight, and the sound of the voice of our beloved is the sweetest of melodies.'"

A large development of this organ explains the mysterious fascination which some persons possess, who are not endowed with more than a medium share of other agreeable qualities. It explains why we often see marriages of the most opposite characters. The amiable, virtuous, and talented, united to the morose, unprincipled and ignorant, without any other cause

being alleged than pure love.   If warned by their
friends that they are rushing to their ruin, they cling
desperately to the fatal hope, that by the fabled omnipotence of love, they shall, by some means, they know
not exactly how, escape the threatened danger, and
sail happily down the stream of life.   At all events,
spite of the remonstrances of friends, or even the
pleadings of their own better judgment, they are
determined to run the hazard of the die; and they
only repent of their rashness when poverty, disgrace
and finally perhaps desertion, extinguishes the last
faint embers of their expiring hopes.   But still the
lamp of love burns on, and the deserted one exclaims,

"With all thy faults, I love thee still."

Or, in the language of Byron,

"Though I cannot be beloved, still let me love."

It may be objected, that this ardent attachment is
not produced by Amativeness without being combined with Adhesiveness.   This is true, but neither
can Adhesiveness produce this effect without Amativeness.   It is Adhesiveness that produces friendship, but
it is Amativeness that directs it to the other sex.   So,
also, the admiration of beauty originates in Perfectiveness, and it is Amativeness that directs it toward the
other sex.

The adaptation of Amativeness to the admiration
of personal beauty, seems wisely designed to prevent
the transmission of deformed and imperfect bodily
organizations to posterity.   It is not the effect of mere
youthful fancy, but was implanted in the mind for a
highly useful purpose, and therefore should be by no
means discouraged; on the contrary it seems to be of

the very highest importance that it should be properly directed, and just ideas of what constitutes beauty of constitution, should be early inculcated. This subject teaches us that the knowledge of the principles upon which physical and mental energy and harmony depend, cannot be too highly appreciated as a branch of education. .

I seldom find a person possessing much energy of character who is deficient in this propensity. It seems to give activity to Combativeness, and is generally accompanied with a large development of that organ. Males, among all animals, manifest it in a greater degree than females; and I have seldom found it very large in females, without observing at the same time an uncommon manifestation of the other masculine traits.

FALLING IN LOVE.

At the age ot puberty the organs of the whole constitution, of body and mind, undergo a change. The lungs expand, the circulation of blood increases, the face becomes more full and florid, the eyes brighter, the muscles firmer and more elastic, the brain larger, and the mind more serious and mature; persons of the opposite sex begin to appear more interesting. There is as yet no thought of love, much less of marriage. Young company is sought just for amusement; love and marriage are mentally postponed indefinitely, as something undesirable and inconvenient. If the subject is mentioned to the youth, he acknowledges a general regard and admiration for the sex, but he is in love with no one. He prefers one lady to another very much as he does one gentleman to another. He

sees others fall desperately in love, and wonders at
their folly and infatuation; he fancies that if he ever
marries, it will be pretty much for the same solid
reasons that he would take a mercantile partner.   He
feels sure that he never would marry one who had a
disagreeable mother or sister, or who had red hair or
large hands; indeed, he never will marry at all until
he is rich, or at least has a competence.   The poor
fellow has not the least idea that the love principle is
expanding within him more and more every day, and
that it will soon burst forth and hurry him on to his
destiny with the irresistible force of an insanity.   At
length the time arrives; he is ready to fall in love,
but is utterly unconscious of it; nature has prepared
him for the sacrifice, and he will certainly be in love
with some lady within a short time.   He happens in
company with a person he has long known, and
wonders that he has before been so blind to her
angelic qualities; what a voice; what a smile; and oh,
what eyes.   "Grace is in all her steps, heaven in her
eye, in every gesture dignity and love."   He has no
doubt that the charm that has overpowered him is in
her; but in reality it is in himself.   If he had not
fallen in love with her, he would with some one else.
He fell in love for the same reason that an apple falls
from a tree to the ground, simply because it is ripe
enough to fall there.

PARENTIVENESS OR PHILOPROGENITIVE-
NESS.

" As a hen gathereth her chickens under her wings."—*Luke.*

This is the propensity to protect, nourish and instruct the young and helpless, especially one's own

children. When large it gives tenderness, patience and condescension on the part of parents, nurses, teachers and guardians. When small there is a tendency to treat children with indifference if not with harshness. In females the propensity acquires additional intensity on account of its intimate relations to the maternal functions.

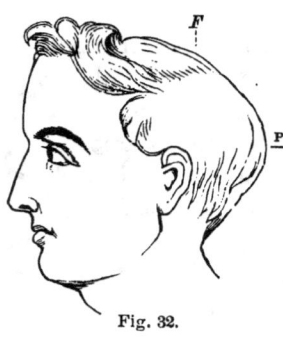

Fig. 32.

It is much the larger in the female sex, they upon whom devolves the care of raising the young, and implanting the first seeds of intelligence and virtue. Who has not felt the influence of a mother's love, and fled from the stern rebuke of an angry father to take shelter behind the bosom of maternal indulgence? Even when compelled by a sense of duty to administer punishment she does so with such evident reluctance as to convince the sufferer that she would gladly refrain, if she could do so consistently with her regard to the future welfare of her child. This awakens a feeling of genuine repentance more certainly than any degree of severity would do if inflicted in a tyrannical manner. When, however, Parentiveness is so much developed as to be ungovernable by the higher powers, the

Fig. 32 is the head of a good natured school master who was repeatedly turned out of his school house by his unruly and vicious boys; but he was so kind and forgiving, and at the same time such an excellent teacher, that he finally won the love of them all and obtained unbounded influence over them. **His Firmness was very small and his Parentiveness and Kindness** both very large.

consequence is a fatal indulgence toward the child, encouraging him in vice, and even in crime, which a salutary correction might have prevented if seasonably applied.

This is certainly one of the most amiable traits in the human character, and when the organ is largely developed in a man it gives a gentleness to his manner which renders him very agreeable to young persons. The president of a college is seldom popular if this is small, but when large he feels a fatherly interest in the welfare of his pupils, which manifests itself in such a manner as generally to win their Adhesiveness in return.   Governors, school teachers, and all persons in

Fig. 33.

situations where authority over juniors is to be exercised in a discretionary manner, need the softening influence of this propensity to prevent them from acting with too much harshness and severity.   When the organ is very large in persons who have no children of their own, substitutes are very frequently adopted.   Orphan children are thus sometimes better provided for than they would have been had they never lost their parents.

Fig. 33 is the head of Junius Brutus, the celebrated Roman patriot and stoic, who condemned his own son to death because he conspired against the state.   In his head the domestic socials are very small compared with the governing group.   Parentiveness (P) is particularly deficient.

Children that have been left by their cruel mothers to perish have frequently found in strangers the most affectionate of parents. The fondness of little misses for dolls, and the affection lavished by older ladies upon pets, such as lap-dogs, kittens, and even plants, is caused by Parentiveness, when it has no more proper object with which it can be gratified; but as soon as the care of an infant devolves upon one of them she immediately neglects all her former pets. To those females who have the organ very large there is a feeling of delight experienced in taking a beautiful infant into their arms, which a man who has the organ small cannot understand. I think Philoprogentiveness too long a name, and have therefore adopted that of Parentiveness.

INHABITIVENESS OR CONCENTRATIVE-NESS.

" It is my own, my native land."—*Scott.*

This is the propensity to fix upon an abiding place, a home, and remain in it. There is an attachment to the village, the house, the lands, the trees, the streams and hills in our vicinity, even though our friends are no longer there. When very small all places are alike indifferent, provided friends and comforts are the same in all. It is generally small and Hopefulness large in sailors and persons who prefer a roving life. This propensity has been denominated *Concentrativeness*, because it has been observed that when large on some persons they seem to be indisposed to change the subject of conversation. They literally *dwell* upon it even when they have nothing new to say in regard to it. I consider this tendency to continuity as an incidental and

secondary effect of Inhabitiveness. Phrenologists have
committed many errors, by not distinguishing between
the primitive uses of faculties and their incidental
modes of manifestation under peculiar circumstances,
and in combination with other faculties.

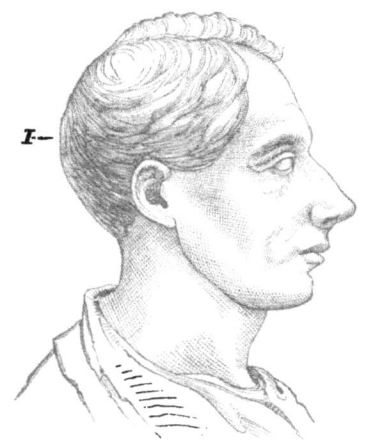

George Combe — Fig. 34.

Mr. George Combe, the distinguished phrenological
author, insisted upon changing the name of this organ
to Concentrativeness, and considered his own head,
Fig. 34, a good illustration of it when largely developed.

One objection that has been made by Dr. Elder and
others to Mr. Combe's views, is that Concentrativeness
is merely continued *attention*, and, therefore, an intellectual function.   But the obvious answer to this
objection is that the intellect attends to those things
that interest the dominant propensities.   I have fully
satisfied myself of the fact that persons full at the
point (I, Fig. 34) are more continuous in all their mental operations than those who are small there, but this

appears to me to be merely one of the modes in which Inhabitiveness manifests itself.

ADHESIVENESS.

"Entreat me not to leave thee."—*Ruth*.

Fig. 35.

This propensity was primitively intended to make children cling to parents, and to those friends who are capable of protecting and defending them. It is larger in the heads of children than in those of adults, and in women than men. Women manifest a preference for men who are brave and strong. "Beauty loves to repose upon the arm of strength." This propensity is one of the principal elements of matrimonial attachment, and partial, enduring friendship and love. When Adhesiveness is very large and Kindness small, there is a disposition to be exclusive, clanish and sectarian, and to exhibit a want of philanthrophy and of courtesy to strangers.

Some phrenologists believe that there is an organ near Adhesiveness related to monogamy or matrimonial attachment to one only. I regard this as an unsettled question.

Figure 35 is the head of Dioclesian, the Roman emperor, who resigned a throne to enjoy the pleasures of domestic life. Observe how long his head is from the ear back to the occiput. Amativeness, Parentiveness Inhabitiveness and Adhesiveness are all large.

THE GOVERNING GROUP.

RELATED TO SELF-WILL, TO SOCIAL EMINENCE, AND TO FIRM AND JUST
GOVERNMENT IN THE FAMILY AND THE STATE.

IMPERATIVENESS OR SELF-ESTEEM.

"When Cæsar says '*do this*' it is performed."—*Shakspeare.*

This is the propensity to command, to take the lead and direct the conduct and affairs of others. It produces independence and individuality of character, and indifference concerning the opinions and wishes of others, especially when Approbativeness is small. The organ is large in the head of Peter the Great — (Figure 36 1).

Fig. 36.

When Imperativeness is large it often takes the form of self-conceit, and tends to unwarranted assumptions of authority. Combined with Kindness it prompts to meddlesome but benevolent attempts to do good by regulating the affairs, the morals and manners of others. Combined with a sense of justice it insists upon establishing just laws and rules of conduct, and forcing others to submit to such laws. When small there is a want of self-assertion, and a tendency to stand back and allow persons of inferior abilities or social position to take the lead. This is more strikingly true when Reverence is large and Imperativeness small. Self-reliance depends upon large Imperativeness, Hopefulness and Combativeness, while the conforming social organs are small.

We often see individuals manifesting this propensity in a most ridiculous manner; putting themselves forward, confidently assuming superiority, and getting themselves into conspicuous situations, while it is obvious to all but themselves that they are miserably deficient in the qualities necessary to fill an important station. It is astonishing to see the success which sometimes attends the ambitious efforts of men of inferior talents, when acting under the influence of Imperativeness. Others, with gigantic intellects, give way before them, astounded at their impudent pretensions and disgusted with their egotism and ignorance. If their favorite hobby is one which is complicated and difficult to be understood, such as theology, medicine or politics, they generally gain the ignorant over to their opinions by the loud, confident and imperious manner in which they assert them, and the supercilious haughtiness with which they bear themselves toward others.

If we examine the busts or portraits of all those master spirits of ages past who have assumed to dictate the operations of others, either in the cabinet, the army, the church, the bar, or the academy, we invariably find a large development of this organ. It is frequently very active in the insane, and is liable to be separately diseased, producing the most singular exhibitions of imperiousness. Gall, Spurzheim and Combe mention several instances in which they have found it largely developed in such patients. I have

also seen similar cases. A few years ago an insane
man escaped from his friends and took his station
upon one of the peaks of the New York highlands.
Assuming that he was the Deity, he began to give
orders to the whole universe; he called in a loud
voice, " Attention, all creation! in battalions to the
right wheel! march!"

APPROBATIVENESS.

"The thought of what men's tongues will say."—*Shakspeare*.

The propensity to gain approval, admiration and
reputation. While Imperativeness aims at authority,
this propensity assists by gaining the good opinion of
those who can confer power and influence. In a weak
mind it assumes the form of vanity and ostentation,
or a silly love of compliments, praise and flattery. It
produces a dread of ridicule, and if unbalanced, it prefers glory and popularity to truth and justice.

When small and Imperativeness large, there is too
much independence of public opinion, a neglect of
reputation, and indifference to praise or blame; such
persons often seem less honest and good than they
really are; they do not flatter or compliment others,
nor expect or desire compliments from them.

The most despotic governments in the world, as
well as the most republican, were originally founded
upon the favor of the people. Cæsar was thrice
offered a " kingly crown, which he did thrice refuse,"
only because he doubted if public opinion was sufficiently ripe for the ultimate purposes of his ambition.
Cromwell could never have driven out the long par-
liament at the point of the bayonet and usurped despotic power, had he not first won the approbation of

his soldiers; nor could Napoleon have mounted the imperial throne had he not been popular with the French army. The extent to which Imperativeness may stretch authority depends in a great measure upon the previous success of Approbativeness; the very same acts of tyranny which Napoleon could perpetrate with impunity, would have cost a Bourbon his sceptre, and perhaps his life. Imperativeness and Approbativeness are twin organs, closely connected in the brain, and in every well balanced mind these propensities mutually assist each other; their combined operation constitutes ambition, which, when properly regulated, is not only useful and laudable, but absolutely necessary to the well-being of society.

Every political election affords illustrations of the influence of these two propensities. The candidate, all other things equal, who has the larger Approbativeness, will get a majority of votes over one who has the larger Imperativeness. The former will be smiling, bowing, deferential and polite; will take great pains to render himself agreeable to the citizens by assurances of his intention to advance their interests; by professions of regard for their welfare, and friendly inquiries concerning their health, their families, their business, etc.; great care is at the same time taken to avoid touching upon any topics calculated to rouse their prejudices, and to say nothing which, if reported, will be calculated to lower him in public estimation. He salutes his acquaintances across the street, and pays the most particular regard to all the little ceremonies that indicate respect and esteem. As soon, however, as he becomes firmly seated in power, so as to be in a degree independent of those who raised

him, his Approbativeness has no longer its appropriate stimulus; Imperativeness is now in the ascen-
dent, and frequently the

> " Proud man,
> Clothed with a little brief authority,
> Most ignorant of what he's most assured,
> Plays such fantastic tricks before high heaven
> As make the angels weep."

" The *proud* man," says Dr. Gall, " is imbued with
a sentiment of his own superior merit, and, from the
summit of his grandeur, treats with contempt or
indifference all other mortals; the *vain* man attaches
the utmost importance to the opinions entertained of
him by others, and seeks with eagerness to gain their
approbation. The *proud* man expects that mankind
will come to him and acknowledge his merit; the
vain man knocks at every door to draw attention
toward him, and supplicates for the smallest portion
of honor. The *proud* man despises those marks of
distinction which on the *vain* man confer the most
perfect delight. The *proud* man is disgusted by indis-
creet eulogiums; the *vain* man inhales with ecstacy
the incense of flattery, although profusely offered and
by no very skillful hand."

Mr. George Combe makes the following remarks
concerning this propensity:

" The feeling which is most commonly experienced
when this organ is large, even when favorably combined with other organs, is anxiety about what the
world will think of us. A youth in whom it is powerful cannot do this thing because everybody will look
at him, or cannot do the other because the people
would wonder. In older persons it produces a fidgety

anxiety about the opinions of the public, or of the circle of acquaintances who compose the public to them. They imagine themselves continually before the public eye, and that the world is occupied with little else than weighing their motives, speculating on their conduct, and adjusting the precise point in the scale of importance and respectability at which they ought to be placed. A great portion of this feeling, however, is the mere inspiration of a very powerful Love of Approbation in their own heads. The public are too much engrossed with themselves and their own affairs to bestow so minute and permanent a degree of attention upon an individual. This anxiety about public opinion, when excessive, is subversive of happiness and independence.

"When the development of Love of Approbation is excessive, while the regulating organs are deficient, it is the cause of great unhappiness. It renders the little girl at school miserable if her dress and the style of living of her parents be not equal to those of the parents of her associates. It overwhelms the artist, author or public speaker with misery if a rival is praised in the journals in higher terms than himself. A lady is tormented at perceiving in the possession of her acquaintance finer dresses or equipages than her own. It excites the individual to talk of himself, his affairs and connections so as to communicate to the auditor vast ideas of his greatness or goodness; in short, vanity is one form of its abuse. 'Sir,' says Dr. Johnson, 'Goldsmith is so much afraid of being unnoticed that he often talks, merely lest you should forget that he is in company.'

"The organ is possessed by the lower animals. The

dog is extremely fond of Approbation, and the horse displays the sentiment not only in his sensibility to marks of affection but in his spirit of emulation in the race. Dr. Gall mentions that in the south of France the peasants attach a 'bouquet' to the mules when they have acquitted themselves well, and that the animals understand it as a mark of approbation and feel afflicted when it is taken away."

Approbativeness is somewhat analogous to Adhesiveness in seeking the support and good will of the powerful and influential, but it embraces a larger number and extends over a wider social field.

FIRMNESS.

"Come one, come all, this rock shall fly
From its firm base as soon as I."—*Walter Scott.*

This is the propensity to resist the influences which tend to produce changes of purpose, such as persuasions, arguments, threats, examples or commands. It tends to bestow stability of character. When very large, and Submissiveness and Kindness small, it produces stubbornness, and an inability to reason fairly against opinions that have once been adopted.

When very small the character is unstable, and the mind is continually liable to change under social influences good or bad. This is especially true when the conforming social organs are large. A great deal of dishonesty is caused by a deficiency of Firmness. The lessons and principles inculcated in early life lose their influence in the presence of immediate temptation when Firmness is small.

This is the propensity to *maintain* authority, to continue in the position, or course, which Imperativeness assumes, to persevere in resolutions which relate to social intercourse. Imperativeness aspires to establish government, Approbativeness to render it popular, and Firmness to give it permanence, fixedness and consistency. It differs from Combativeness in being intended to benefit others, instead of conquering them. It does not attack or oppose, but only holds its own. No man can permanently establish the government o. a nation, a church, or a family, who is deficient in Firmness. It is larger in men than in women, and contributes more than anything else to their universal superiority in government. We frequently see a man with small Imperativeness but powerful Firmness; he may be modest, unassuming, and even cowardly, but still manifest the greatest reluctance to yield his post.

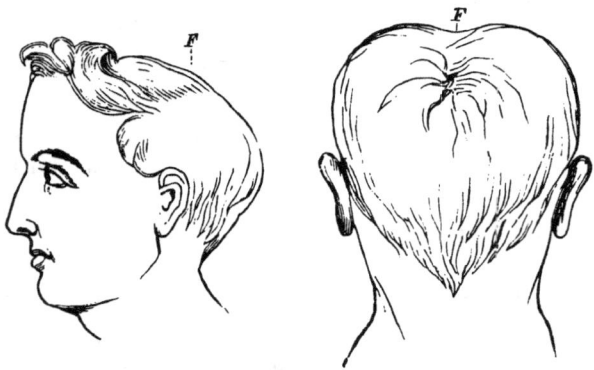

Fig. 37.   Fig. 38.

Fig. 37 represents Firmness and Imperativeness very small and the conforming organs large.

Fig 38 represents the upper back of the head shaped like the end of an orange, depressed in the middle at Firmness and Imperativeness, and very large each side, at Approbativeness and Equity.

Danger, interest or duty may induce him to give way, but he does it with the most evident unwillingness, and returns again as soon as the difficulty is removed. It is common to see a man with very large Firmness and Combativeness governed on ordinary occasions by his wife, and even by his children; the trouble of commanding and directing the affairs of others is to him greater than the pleasure; but his Imperativeness, though small, will sometimes be exited, and when he *does* take his stand he is like St. Helena in the midst of the ocean — nothing can shake his purpose. Firmness is very large in our Indians, combined with Cautiousness and Secretiveness, and accordingly they fight in a cowardly manner, but if taken prisoners they die firmly at the stake, suffering the most cruel tortures without uttering a word of complaint. They have been swept away before the whites, but they have never been reduced to submission, or changed in their manners, habits or opinions. The Negro character is just the reverse, and the forms of their skulls present a striking contrast when compared with those of Indians.

The character of those who have Firmness large, combined with Imperativeness, seems to be stereotyped; they easily resist the influences which others bring to bear upon them; whatever notions they adopt in childhood they are apt to hold through life; and it is therefore of the greatest importance that their first impressions should be correct. If they once acquire vicious habits it is very difficult to reform them; threats, punishment or entreaties, are often ineffectual; nothing but their own wills can change their wills; sometimes they can be *managed* by gently falling in with them, admitting their superiority, and appearing to coincide with them, but at the same time suggesting certain ideas as worthy of their consideration, leaving the final decision entirely to their own pleasure. They should be

"Gently seduced into the paths of truth,"

and the course of conduct which they are led to adopt, must seem to be one of their own choice.

EQUITABLENESS, JUSTICE OR CONSCIEN-TIOUSNESS.

" Be just and fear not."—*Shakspeare.*

The propensity to be impartial and equitable, especially to those who are inferior in power or influence. It does not produce honesty or conscientiousness in the common acceptation of these terms, without the assistance of Submissiveness and other faculties, and a proper moral training and education. This propensity belongs to the governing group, and was designed to produce just and impartial government in the community and the family. Incidentally it tends to fairness in business transactions. When very small, the person is capricious and partial, and decides questions according to prejudice, friendship, resentment or self-interest, and not according to the rules of truth and justice.

The head of Kathleen is a good representation of a numerous class of ladies. She possesses a fine physical form, good health, an emotional temperament, and strong and domestic affections; a full share of the love of dress and display common to her sex; Imperativeness, Firmness and general Kindness small, but Submissiveness rather large, and Equity or Conscientiousness (Fig. 39) very large; a low wide forehead, indicating mechanical skill with uncommon order and neatness in her work. She has all the good qualities and all the weaknesses of her sex; a loving, submissive, devoted wife, whose whole world is within her family; capable of the most passionate love and the most intense suffering from jealousy; constant in love but changeful in her temper and her mood. She takes not the slightest interest in public affairs, and cares

c

Kathleen — Fig. 39.

nothing about women's rights. She is perfectly conscientious, and never intentionally does wrong or omits a duty, but her ideas of right, wrong and duty are derived entirely from education, the teachings of her church and the opinions of her small circle of friends. She is utterly incapable of understanding the characters or doing justice to the motives of people who differ widely from her sect in religious opinions, or who violate what she regards as the sacred rules of conventional propriety. She has faith, hope and a good conscience, but no charity, or toleration for sinners of her own sex.

Conscientiousness is greatly dependent upon the higher organs of intellect. It is by means of reflection that we are enabled to understand our relations to others, and Conscientiousness is affected according to the views which the intellect takes of a subject. If a person is so deficient in the intellectual organs that he is incapable of understanding his duty, Conscientiousness alone will not guide him right. It only gives the *disposition* to do justice, and not the *ability* to ascertain what constitutes it. It is only by means of the intellect that we *know* anything. After the intellect has acquired a knowledge of all the facts in a case which affect the right of God or man, Conscientiousness inspires the mind with a desire to act according to justice, and respect those rights. Sometimes we see persons who, like Lord Bacon, know very well what is required of them, but are little disposed to perform it; and again we see others who have a strong desire to do their duty, but are deplorably ignorant of it, and " need that some one should teach " them.

It has frequently been urged as an objection to phrenology, that if men commit crimes on account of a deficiency of Conscientiousness it is unjust to punish them, and therefore they should be set at liberty. But whatever may be the cause that prompts men to violate the rights of others, society is certainly justified in protecting itself from their outrages, whether they are idiots, criminals, or insane; and any criminal code that has for its object the safety of society and the

improvement of the offender, will be in accordance
with phrenological principles. I must insist, however, that nothing can be found in phrenology to jus-
tify unnecessary punishment. The safety of society
renders it necessary that criminals should be deprived
of the liberty which they have abused, and so guarded
that they can do no more mischief to their fellow men,
but any farther proceedings against them should be
intended for their reformation and improvement.
Society has no right to punish any one for revenge, or
merely for an example to others. I am aware that
throughout the world the most severe inflictions are
excused on the ground that they frighten others; and
in some countries the most horrid cruelties are per-
petrated under the sanction of this principle. But,
in the name of humanity, does not the history of man
furnish already a sufficient number of examples of the
consequences of iniquity? Is it necessary to keep
continually before the community the example of several thousand individuals in misery for the purpose of
warning others ? Does the history of the past prove
that severity is the best preventive of crime? Has
society any right to protect itself by such barbarous
and unmerciful means as those now in use, when
milder means may be made equally effective? I confidently believe that when the sublime principles of
phrenology are universally understood, the present
criminal laws and criminal discipline will undergo an
important change; and the convict, instead of being
treated like a beast of prey, will be managed like a
moral patient. Instead of being considered a fit object
for the exercise of unnecessary severity, he will be
pitied as the most unhappy of mankind, and a remedy

applied adapted to the nature of the disease. While
he will be secured, and every means taken to prevent
him from repeating his crimes, every means will also
be taken to render his situation as happy as circumstances will permit, and to restore him again to society
better qualified and disposed to respect the rights of
others.

THE CONFORMING GROUP.

I ELATED TO SOCIETY IN GENERAL, AND PRODUCING CONFORMITY TO ITS
REQUIREMENTS IN OPPOSITION TO SELFISHNE·S, CLANNISHNESS, AND
SELF-WILL.

SUBMISSIVENESS, OR REVERENCE.

"Thy will, not mine, be done."—*Jesus.*

The propensity to obey commands, to submit to
authority, and to admit others to be superior. It
recognizes excellence or superior power, with pleasure,
whether it is found in nature or in society. The
immensity of space, the vastness of the celestial system, the velocity of the planets, the destructive force
of earthquakes, the power of genius, the greatness of
moral heroes, and above all, the omnipotence of God—
these are subjects calculated to excite this propensity.
It produces respect for parents, teachers, magistrates,
and superior persons of all classes. It is probably the
principal element in the sense of the sublime, the
grand and the awful. When small, there is an uncere-
monious bluntness, a want of respectfulness in the
manners, and a tendency to treat superior persons
with undue familiarity. This kind of irreverence is
still more manifest when Imperativeness and Combat-

iveness are large, and Approbativeness, Secretiveness, and Equitableness are small.

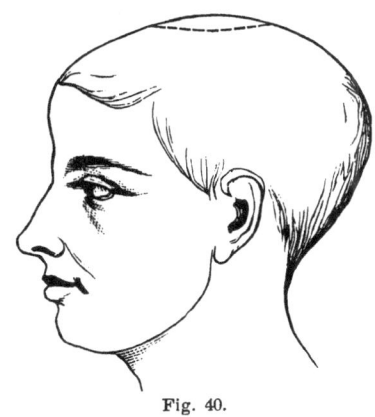

Fig. 40.

Imperativeness, or Self-Esteem, is the propensity to compare ourselves with others, and if possible to establish a claim of superiority. Submissiveness, or Reverence, on the contrary, is the propensity to compare ourselves with others and admit our inferiority. It recognizes authority and humbly sits at the foot of its throne, listening and learning. It unites itself with the other conforming propensities, and if there is no personal superior present, it resorts to books, traditions, relics, and monuments as substitutes. It seeks for something to admire, worship, imitate and believe. Even if the intellect is very

Fig. 40 is so drawn as to give an idea of the appearance of the top of the head when this organ is large, and also when small. There are, in early infancy, two open places, caused by the bones of the skull not having completed their full development, so as to come together and cover the brain. One of these is located at Imperativeness and the other at Submissiveness. The bones at these two points oftentimes join imperfectly, so as to mislead novices into the belief that there is an uncommon development or deficiency of the organs. But the prominences made by mere bones are angular and sharp, and easily distinguished from those made by brain. A bony projection behind the ear is often mistaken for an organ, and so, also, is a bony prominence at the occiput.

large, it becomes filled with the ideas thus acquired from others, and is destitute of originality; the opinions are all borrowed, and are sustained by authorities instead of facts derived from experience. There is in such a head more of learning than of practical wisdom, or of the executive ability which springs from self-reliance.

Sir Walter Scott—Fig. 41.

Fig. 41. Sir Walter Scott's head is extremely high in the Conforming region. All four of the organs of this group are large in his head. It was said of him that he was prouder of being invited to dine with the king than he was of all his works. His reverence for royalty and rank, and ancient families is manifested in all his writings. His heroes, unlike those of Dickens, were invariably chosen from among princes and nobles.

KINDNESS OR BENEVOLENCE.

"Charity suffereth long and is kind."

This is the propensity to treat all persons with suavity and benevolence, especially if they are strangers, and have no claims upon us. Its motto is, "Come, send abroad a love for all that live." It is the basis of philanthropy, and the love of humanity in general. It is opposed to sectarianism, clannish-

Dr. B. Franklin — Fig. 42.

Fig. 42. Benjamin Franklin. There is no trait in the character of Franklin more remarkable than his benevolence. In him it never degenerated into a weakness. His charities and kind deeds were always accompanied with prudence, and administered with shrewdness and wisdom. He was industrious and economical that he might have the means of being charitable. It is doubtful whether the American continent has produced a character with fewer faults, and a greater number of virtues. Kindness is indicated by the height of his forehead in the middle line.

ness, and exclusiveness in society. It gives a tendency to acquire general knowledge concerning human affairs, instead of limiting inquiries to the immediate circle in which we live. This is especially true when the front part of the organ is large, and is combined with a large intellect. When small, there is a manifest indifference to the general interests of mankind, and a tendency to concentrate the feelings and thoughts upon self and home friends, upon the church, the village, and the community, or society in our near vicinity.

Sometimes there is an apparent contradiction exhibited by persons in whom Kindness is large, combined with large Acquisitiveness; they will not give away property, but they will give their personal services, attend the sick, show kindness in their manners, words, etc. A similar inconsistency appears in those who have Kindness with the Governing Group large; they will be kind to those who obey them, and conform to their notions; but they will be tyrannical, oppressive, and intolerant to those who treat their authority with contempt; or who are opposed to their views of politics, religion, or morality. Again, we may see a person with large Destructiveness and Kindness, and Acquisitiveness small; he will be profuse with his property, and therefore take great credit to himself for his benevolence; but perhaps he will at the same time commit deeds of wanton cruelty. All these facts are explained on the principle that the large organs predominate over the smaller.

IMITATIVENESS OR SYMPATHY.

"Catch the manners living as they rise."—*Pope.*

The propensity to adopt the manners, language and habits of associates, and especially of those whom we admire and regard as examples worthy of imitation.

Socrates — Fig. 43.

It disposes a person to give up his old manners and practices, and conform to those of his associates. It tends to make all the members of a community act and dress and speak alike. It is the natural auxiliary of Kindness, and is opposed to all manifestations of stubbornness and self-will. It is the principal element of sympathy, since it not only prompts us to

Figure 43 is the head of Socrates, the moral giant of antiquity. What a magnificent head! All the capabilities of human nature appear to have been exhausted in producing his brain. His forehead is broad, high and deep. This immense cerebral mass was not developed at the expense of his bodily vigor. He was a brave and hardy soldier, but his most noted deed in this capacity was the saving of the life of a comrade on the battle-field, at the imminent risk of his own. He was a sculptor, having learned the art from his father, and his broad forehead indicates a mechanical propensity. He was an original, shrewd and unequalled logician and reasoner, and this agrees with his capacious intellectual lobe. His intuitive knowledge of human nature was probably never surpassed even by Shakspeare, and do as others do, but it makes us endeavor to conceive of their feelings, wishes and thoughts. It therefore tends to make us study human nature. In 1838, in my "New System of Phrenology," I pointed out the fact that persons with the front part of Kindness and Imitativeness large, are more prone than others to study human nature. Upon this hint several phrenologists announced the discovery of a new organ, which they called Human Nature, between Causality and Reverence. They mistook a peculiar manifestation of a known faculty for a distinct faculty. The truth is that Kindness and Imitativeness, combined with the reflectives, produce a tendency to study the characters of all sorts of people. Those in whom these organs are deficient may study the characters of their particular acquaintances, but they fail to understand people who differ from themselves, or from their limited circle. Shakspeare is a wonderful instance of a writer who could describe with accuracy a great variety of characters. Walter Scott also excelled in this respect; and they are both remarkably large in the region between the reflectives and Submissiveness.

this is indicated by the vast expansion of the upper part of his forehead. Without being a fanatic or a sectarian, he was a truly pious reformer, and fell a martyr to the cause of moral and religious truth. Among his other peculiarities he possessed a talent for imitation and drollery, and a faculty of illustrating his ideas in an exceedingly amusing and facinating manner. One of the charges brought against him on his trial was that by his undignified and humorous manner of expression he captivated and corrupted the youth. Instead of teaching in the formal and grave manner of the schools he condescended to amuse and entertain the young in order to gain their attention and instruct them more successfully. The organ of Imitativeness is large in his head. It is located at the dotted line (Fig. 43.)

This faculty is an important one to an actor or an orator, as well as to a dramatic author, as it enables one to temporarily forget himself and "enter in" to the feelings of an imaginary character.

A person having Imitativeness very large, with Kindness small, will be able to conceive how another feels; will, as it were, imitate or repeat imperfectly in his own mind the feelings of others, but will have no very strong desire to gratify or relieve them; yet this is one kind of sympathy, though not such as proceeds from a well balanced mind. Lavater remarks, in substance, that by imitating the expression of another we may partially experience his feelings, and I doubt not that this is true, especially of those who have Imitativeness very large.

The importance of making a distinction between propensities, feelings and actions, upon which I have so much insisted in this work, must now be obvious. Spurzheim, Combe, and all other phrenologians, agree in denominating this propensity a *feeling* of Imitation; but imitation is an *action* produced by the *propensity* of Imitativeness. It would be absurd to say "I *feel* imitation," but it is perfectly proper to say "I *act* in imitation," and it is also proper to say "I feel sympathy." I therefore name this the propensity of Imitativeness — the feeling which it produces I call sympathy — and the actions which it produces I denominate imitations. If the term *sympathy* does not convey the precise idea of the feeling produced by Imitativeness, then I know of none in our language that does. I have, in writing this work, often felt a necessity for new terms to express more precisely the different feelings, and I doubt not that as the science continues to progress, improvements will be introduced in this important part of the nomenclature of mental philosophy.

Those who have this organ large, are capable of conforming to the manners and habits of those with whom they associate much more readily than those who have it moderately developed; they seem to have the power of approaching in a proper and successful manner those who occupy eminent stations. They are more easy and graceful in their manners, and can readily adapt themselves to the feelings, actions and situations of others. It is large in those who are capable of representing the feelings and actions of others in writing or speech; and no man can easily excel as an actor, orator, artist, dramatic author, ventriloquist, dancer or musician, unless this is fairly developed. In proof of this, we find it large in the portraits or heads of all who are eminent in either of these professions. It gives the dramatic author the power of calling up in his own mind the same train of ideas and feelings that he supposes the characters to possess whom he describes; and having thus, as it were, imbued himself with their spirit and made their case his own, he proceeds to pour out their feelings in language such as that of Shakspeare, Voltaire, Walter Scott, N. P. Willis, and Longfellow.

Those authors who are incapable of reasoning profoundly, but who can write racily and pictorially, and readily adapt their style to the subject, will invariably be found to have moderate reflectives and large perceptives and Imitativeness. They

" Catch the manners living as they rise."

They describe things as they see and feel and hear

them, but do not attempt to account for them.   Most
of the writings of novelists are of this character.

CREDENCIVENESS— MARVELOUSNESS— WONDER — SPIRITUALITY— SUPER- NATURALITY.

"Lord, I believe; help thou mine unbelief."—*Matthew.*

The various names that this organ has received
prove that it has not been well understood.   Gall
included Credenciveness and Perfectiveness, or Ideality, under one name, (the poetic faculty,) and regarded
them as one organ.   Spurzheim separated them, and
demonstrated that the upper portion is related to
Faith, and the lower to Beauty; one is more especially
devoted to religion, and the other to the fine arts.

I regard this as the propensity to believe the assertions of others; to assume what they say to be true.
It is very active in the young.   By its promptings
they acquire knowledge concerning what has been
said or written.   It is therefore an essential element
in the love of literature, biography, and history.   It
fills the mind with the materials required for conversation, and for writing in a general and varied manner.   The organ of Language gives memory and
facility in the use of unusual words, but it does not
bestow the *disposition* to use language; this springs
from the conforming Socials, and chiefly from Credenciveness.   When the intellect is small, or the
knowledge deficient, this organ tends to produce
superstition in its thousand forms.

It is unfortunate for business men to have this
organ large.   They trust their customers and endorse

for their friends too readily. They allow themselves to be drawn into novel and doubtful schemes, from which a little more natural skepticism would have saved them. Women who have this organ large, and Secretiveness small, are too confiding. A scientific head is generally skeptical, but a literary and poetical head is credencive. This faculty does not prompt to deception, but it tends to unconscious exaggeration. It is an important element in a poetic and romantic imagination. The manifestations of this faculty are often confounded with those of Perfectiveness, (Ideality,) but there is a vast difference between the exaggerated and the beautiful.

Paine—Fig. 44.   Gibbon—Fig. 45.

Every proposition, the truth of which we cannot test by the evidences of our own senses, if it is probable, or even possible, is calculated to excite and gratify Credenciveness. But its most natural stimulus is the *testimony* of intelligent beings. I consider it as specially designed to make us act upon the testimony of

others, and particularly of our superiors, in cases
where we cannot have the evidence of our senses.
Impressions enter through the senses to the perceptives, and are analyzed, classed and connected by the
reflectives. Causality performs the last and highest
process of intellect; and if the proposition is not perfectly self-evident, it becomes a matter of belief or of
skepticism; that is, it becomes an appropriate stimulus for Credenciveness. This propensity is of course
modified in its action according to the nature of the
subject, the amount of evidence, the proportion of
Credenciveness to intellect, and the effect which it is
to have upon our interests, or our hopes. Whether
an individual will be skeptical or credulous, depends
upon the *proportion* which his intellect bears to Credenciveness and Submissiveness. Those who have
very high but shallow foreheads, are apt to be foolishly
credulous; and those who have low and prominent
foreheads, are inclined to skepticism. They wish to
investigate much and believe but little. There is a
third class who have foreheads wide, high and prominent; they love to believe when they can, but they
cannot without proper investigation. They examine
thoroughly, and believe sincerely, many controverted
doctrines; they seem to take pleasure in revolving in
their minds doubtful subjects, even if they cannot
quite believe them. If it is something which chal-
lenges belief—if it has probability or even possibility
in its favor, it is a proper subject to stimulate and
delight this propensity, and produce the feeling of
of marvelousness. This enables us to understand
the characters of novelists, romancers, and dramatic
authors, such as Scott, Voltaire, Shakespeare, and

Tasso, who all had very high foreheads, particularly in the region of this organ and Imitativeness. Those who have been remarkable for faith upon religious subjects, have the same development, combined with Submissiveness; such are Bunyan, Baxter, Swedenborg, Irving, Wesley, and hundreds with whom I am acquainted.

I consider this as one of the most important elements of a love of knowledge. The ability, or the talent of *knowing*, depends upon the intellect; but the desire, the love, the proneness to learn, depends upon the propensities. Each propensity produces a desire to know that which will be gratifying to itself. The highest gratification of Credenciveness consists in knowing what people have said or written. It is easy, therefore, to understand why those who have it large should be very fond of reading or hearing the extraordinary assertions of others, and of inquiring into their truth. If the intellect is large, they will be commonly successful in their inquiries, but if it is small they may be induced to give credence to the most absurd statements. It is this propensity that makes us love to hear or read extraordinary things, even if we do not believe them. It seems as if some love to stretch their faith to its utmost, just to give it exercise; the more marvelous the story, the better it suits them; and if Submissiveness is large, and the statement is made upon high authority, it becomes perfectly charming. This organ is larger in youth than adults, and in women than men. It accounts for the love of the marvelous manifested by children; for the pernicious novel reading habits of girls; and for the ease with which impostors of all descriptions succeed with the

generality of women.   I have noticed that those
persons who in youth read the most novels, and the
least science, in maturer years are the most prone to
superstition and fanaticism; they are much greater
sticklers for matters of mere faith and form than for
moral and christian practice.

The exposition which I have made of this propensity shows that it is one of very great importance in
society.   It is the grand lever by means of which the
few can govern the many more despotically than by
any other.   It is for this reason that the union of
church and state is a desirable object with all despots,
and adds immensely to their power.

Hume — Fig. 46.   Tasso — Fig. 47.

This is plainly, then, a *conforming* Social propensity, since it is the means by which children and all
ignorant persons are guided.   Nothing renders a man
more ungovernable, or unamiable, than a disposition
to doubt every thing he hears, and to rely entirely

upon his own judgment and observation, instead of giving due weight to the testimony of others.

In regard to the lower animals, it is more difficult to show that they possess Credenciveness than any of the other Socials. It is certain that they have it in a less degree than any of the others, which alone is sufficient to prove its exalted nature.

Fig. 47 is the head of Tasso, who divides with Milton and Shakespeare the highest honors of exaggerated poetry. Shakespeare differs from his rivals in the fact that "in the very tempest and torrent" of his mythical creations he never entirely loses sight of the actualities of human nature, but Milton, Tasso, and Dante constructed high pyramids of wonderful and beautiful improbabilities and crowned them with things impossible. If we analyze poetic genius, we find it compounded of various elements: 1. There is the ability to use good language with facility; 2. The talent for rythm and rhyme; 3. The sense of the beautiful; 4. The inventive or experimentive imagination; 5. The propensity of Credenciveness, which, when large, bestows the tendency to imbibe the marvelous and exaggerated, and so to mingle it with the beautiful and the true in their expressions that it is difficult to separate and distinguish them. Contrast the head of Tasso, Shakespeare, Milton and Scott, with those of Paine, Hume and Gibbon, and then compare their productions, and you will find them equally in contrast. One class delights in contemplating and relating beautiful wonders that no sane man is expected to believe, while the other smiles with contempt upon historical statements which the whole Christian world regards as absolute truth.

There is no faculty of the mind that is manifested in such a great variety of modes, or that influences so many important human affairs as this credencive propensity does. A person who has this organ very large is certain to manifest it in some way or other. Many men are skeptical upon subjects with which they are thoroughly conversant, or in relation to which they have a prejudice, yet they are foolishly credulous concerning other things in regard to which they are comparatively ignorant. We frequently see a Spiritualist who does not believe in Christ, but he believes in A. J. Davis; he does not believe in the Virgin Mary, but he believes in Kate Fox; he does not believe in the Apostles, but he believes in the Davenport boys; he does not believe that the Omnipotent God could assume the human form, to make communications to man, but he believes that Katie King, John King, and any number of dead savages can become incarnate and exhibit themselves to believers ! !

If an organ is *very* small it is not manifested in any combination or in any manner, and if it is large it may not be exhibited by any two persons alike. This remark is especially true of the higher faculties; their functions are more relative and complex than those of the lower, and it therefore requires a more searching and discriminating analysis to detect and illustrate their manifestations. One often sees a merchant who is skeptical and shrewd enough when dealing with mercantile sharpers, but who, in regard to spiritual manifestations, or love affairs, is credulous beyond measure.

MEMORY.

The only plausible theory of the physiology of Memory, is that every conscious impression made upon a brain fibre produces such a change in the structure of some part of the fibre that when it is vibrated again, from any cause, it will repeat the same peculiar vibration and state of consciousness as at first. When a person is young the impressions upon the brain are easily and permanently made, but in old age, or after the brain has been diseased, the impressions are less effective, and consequently the memory is poor.

The association of ideas probably depends upon associations among the phrene organs and fibres. The intellectual organs are so related that the excitement of one generally calls them nearly all into action to a greater or less degree. Thus the name of a thing recalls its form and color and its connections with other things; so also the form of a thing recalls its name and the events that transpired when we saw it before. If the thing thus called to mind is in some way connected with a pleasant or a disagreeable event in our lives, the feelings formerly experienced are again in some degree excited on account of the natural tendency to association in the action of organs.

THE TEMPERAMENTS.

The word temperament originally signified *mixture*. It is applied to those proportions and conditions of the body, and appearances of the face that denote peculiarities of character, independently of phrenology and physiognomy. The probability is that the different temperaments, originated long before the commencement of the historic period, when men lived in widely separated localities, under various climates, where they fed upon very different kinds of food, and were subjected to greatly contrasted influences and conditions. The low, moist climate of Holland appears to produce men who are broad in the pelvic region; the elevated plains of the Peruvian Andes, where the pressure of the atmosphere is less than elsewhere, produce extraordinary expansion of the chest; the cold, clear air of the Scandinavian and British highlands produces fair skins and flaxen or red hair; the sandy and dry deserts of Arabia produce slender, agile forms and swarthy features, greatly in contrast with those of people of the same race who inhabit more northern climates. Even in a single lifetime, the constitution and complexion of an Englishman undergoes a remarkable change in the warm miasmatic climate of India.

In order to treat the subject systematically, and place the doctrine of Temperaments upon a scientific basis, we may consider the whole constitution as consisting of seven distinct classes of organs, and assume that the predominance or deficiency of one of these produces a simple or elementary temperament, while a combination of two or more classes produces a compound temperament. By adopting this method we can represent the temperament of any individual by numbers, just as we do his phrenological developments.

The ancients, who knew very little of physiology, believed that there were three different colored fluids in the body — the sanguine or red, the bilious or black, and the lymphatic or white. According to their ideas the dominance of one of these fluids produced a particular temperament. Experience has demonstrated the accuracy of their observations. Dr. Thomas, of Paris, was the first to suggest that the three great cavities of the body, namely, the cranium, the thorax and the abdomen or pelvis, may be made the basis of three temperaments. I believe that I was the first to propose the addition of the muscular system as the basis of a seventh simple temperament. The following description of the temperaments will now be understood. I will first describe the three that depend upon the fluids; next the three that depend upon the great cavities; then those that depend upon the muscular system, and, lastly, several that are produced by combinations of the simple temperaments:

1. THE SANGUINE TEMPERAMENT is indicated by a florid face, blue eyes and brown, flaxen, auburn or red hair. It abounds in the highlands of Northern and Western Europe. Probably exposure to the cold air originally *produced* this florid sanguine condition, by forcing the blood to the face to sustain it and keep it from freezing. Accordingly, it is generally found upon people who are fond of exercise in the open air, and who have an aversion to sedentary employments. Even if they have good intellects, and are fond of reading, the confinement required to study is irksome, and often injurious to the health; they manifest vivacity, and a love of various kinds of pleasure and sportive exercises of body and mind. Many authors commit the mistake of saying that the sanguine temper-

ament is indicated by large chests; but the fact is that florid complexions and light hair may be seen upon people of large or of small chests.

2. THE BILIOUS TEMPERAMENT was formerly supposed to depend upon the predominance of a black fluid in the body; it was therefore denominated the Melancholic temperament, from *Melan*, black, and *cholia*, a fluid or bile. It is probable that the sallow complexion and dark hair and eyes, when seen in the white race, is caused by the predominance of the dark, venous blood over the arterial. Possibly extreme cases of this temperament have resulted from diseases of the liver in tropical and miasmatic countries. The word melancholy, when used to signify a sad condition of the mind, was undoubtedly derived from the observation that this mental condition was frequently observed upon persons of this complexion. The word sanguine, on the contrary, is used as synonymous with hope and confidence, because people of the sanguine temperament were notoriously cheerful, and inclined to look upon the bright side of the future. That there is no necessary connection between a dark complexion and melancholy, is proved by the well known fact that negroes are the most cheerful of human beings.

Habitual sadness is unquestionably a manifestation of vital depression, which in most cases has resulted from the diseases of ancestors.

3. THE LYMPHATIC TEMPERAMENT is indicated by softness of the flesh and indolence of expression and action. It probably originates in a disease of the blood, and is most frequently seen in persons of scrofulous constitutions. Excessive fatness is often

confounded with this temperament, but there is no necessary connection between the two conditions. Persons of all temperaments may become fat after middle age, and lymphatic people are occasionally seen who are quite lean. It is not the quantity but the condition of the flesh that is to be considered. Persons of this temperament are generally, but not always, light complexioned.

Let us now describe the temperaments that depend upon the predominance of one of the three great cavities.

4. THE CRANIAL OR CEREBRAL TEMPERAMENT results from a large brain and a slender body, particularly small in the thorax. Of course such a person might excel in study, and in mere intellectual operations, that require but little expenditure of animal vigor, but in everything else he would be deficient.

5. THE THORACIC OR RESPIRATORY TEMPERAMENT results from a large chest and a small head and pelvis. This bestows bodily energy and vigor without long continuance, and without a disposition to study.

6. THE PELVIC OR ABDOMINAL TEMPERAMENT is produced by a broad pelvis and capacious abdomen, with a relatively small head and chest. Such persons are slow, unenterprising and uninteresting, but they have remarkable power of continuance.

7. THE MUSCULAR TEMPERAMENT is indicated by a large frame and large, firm muscles, bestowing uncommon strength without much activity.

The seven temperaments that I have described may be regarded as elementary, and as such they are seldom found. All other temperaments are compounded of these seven elements united in different proportions.

COMPOUND TEMPERAMENTS.

8. THE MERCURIAL TEMPERAMENT, erroneously denominated the *Nervous Temperament*, results from
small muscles and well developed chest, and a head of
at least average size. This may be combined with any
complexion. It is the combination that bestows the
greatest degree of activity, but without unusual
strength. The leanness and delicacy of muscles that
results from disease is often mistaken for this temperament, but the genuine mercurial temperament is often
seen in whole families, and even in tribes, in whom
the health is unimpaired. The ancient Greeks represented the God mercury, the wing-footed messenger of
Jove, as possessing this combination.

9. THE CEREBRO-MERCURIAL TEMPERAMENT. — The
combination of the cerebral with the mercurial gives
the highest degree of mental activity and power. This
is the temperament most favorable for the manifestations of imaginative genius.

10. THE EMOTIONAL TEMPERAMENT results from the
combination of the cerebral with the sanguine and
thoracic. A large brain acting upon a sanguine and
vigorous constitution is favorable to powerful emotional expressions. This is frequently seen in Irish
people.

11. THE PLETHORIC TEMPERAMENT is generally indicated by a large chest and pelvis and a short neck, with
generally a florid complexion. There can be no doubt
that this form of constitution is inherited from ancestors who have indulged to excess in the pleasure of the
table.

12. THE ANÆMIC TEMPERAMENT is the reverse of the
plethoric. I do not know of any other appropriate

word in our language that conveys the idea of a deficiency of the vital organs. The word anæmia and anæmic is used by medical practitioners to describe indications of vital weakness; and it is certain that we see many persons who have well formed heads, of at least average size, who are so deficient in vital power that, without suffering from any positive disease, and without being decidedly lymphatic, they are constitutionally inefficient, and practically incapable of accomplishing any important results.

13. THE HERCULEAN OR PONDEROUS TEMPERAMENT is the reverse of the mercurial, and results from a large frame, large muscles, and large chest and pelvis. Such persons are not active, but they are powerful; and if the brain is large they exercise great personal influence. Such a man was Washington.

14. THE SANGUINE AND BILIOUS TEMPERAMENTS combined are indicated by dark hair and eyes and a florid complexion. Napoleon the First had dark brown hair, sallow skin and blue eyes; this indicates a union of vigor with endurance.

15. THE MERCURIAL AND BILIOUS TEMPERAMENTS indicates activity and excitability with endurance.

16. THE MERCURIAL WITH THE LYMPHATIC TEMPERAMENT indicates activity without endurance.

The different species of animals afford good general illustrations of temperament. The lion represents the thoracic; the beaver the pelvic; the greyhound and the hawk the mercurial; and the ox, buffalo and elephant the ponderous.

LARGE BRAINS AND SMALL.

It is a fundamental axiom that size is a measure of power, all else equal. Practical phrenology is rendered possible on this principle. The question is, therefore, of considerable importance: What differences are we to expect between the manifestations of two persons who, as far as we are able to discover, differ only in one having a much larger brain than the other? Let us suppose them at the same time to be situated and educated, and in every essential particular circumstanced alike. In a word let us eliminate every condition of the problem excepting the difference in the magnitudes of the brains. The characters of the two would be the same so far as the dominant traits were concerned. The faculties that predominated in one would also predominate in the other. Now the question is, in what manner would the larger brain display its superiority? It is evident that the differences must be *quantitative* and not qualitative: in other words, there must be something that both brains do precisely alike in manner, aim and intent; but one must do *more* than the other of the same things — must do it longer or stronger, or both. After some reflection, I am forced to conclude that the larger brain will continue in operation longer without weariness or a disposition to change or rest, provided the subject under consideration is important and worthy of occupying the attention. A large brain does not bestow great physical or motor power. Those whose brains are large perform less with their limbs than those with small brains. They think more and do less. They speak and act much less promptly or excitedly, but **more wisely. Mr. Darwin** has remarked that animals that can give the most attention can be taught the most easily. A large brain can attend longer than a small one. All animals, as well as men, can attend longer to those things that interest their largest organs. A cat will attend to a place in which she suspects a mouse to be hidden, and watch and wait a long time for her victim to appear; a dog will attend his master's footsteps, or wait for his return during many hours without his attention flagging for a moment. A man with some organs of the propensities very large and others small, will generally manifest continued attention to those matters that interest his larger organs only. But if the whole brain, and all its parts are large and well proportioned, he will attend equally well to any or all subjects that interest him. I must protest against comparing a large, ill-proportioned brain with a small one of very different proportions, or with one that is joined to a very different bodily temperament. Children and persons with very mercurial temperaments manifest less continued attention than mature persons or those who possess less active temperaments. Persons with very large conforming and small governing organs have their attention easily diverted. Persons with large intellects and moderate temperaments are capable of longer attention to *study* than those whose intellects, particularly the reflectives, are small, or whose temperaments are mercurial. Persons with large Inhabitiveness are less disposed to change the subjects of conversation or of contemplation than those who have it large. But when we compare a large brain with a small one we must distinguish between differences produced by general

size and those produced by singularities of proportion.
If two persons have bodies nearly alike, but one has
much the larger brain, the influences of the emotions
that proceed from the larger brain will be more continuous, and will, therefore, cause a greater drain upon
the blood making system. We see this fact illustrated
by those large headed, small bodied children, whose
minds bloom so prematurely, and whose bodies suc-
cumb so early. It is often said in such cases that the
head is too large for the body, but no one has informed
us heretofore in what manner the larger head operates
to injure the body. Surely the mere exercise of the
intellectual faculties does not injure the health if the
emotions are unexcited.

It has been estimated that the average quantity of
blood received by the brain is one-sixth of that furnished to the whole human system. No physiologist
will doubt that an organ which receives so much blood
must perform some labor of great importance. With
this fact in view we can readily understand why severe
and long continued mental labor frequently produces
direful effects upon the health. When we perform
bodily labor it is well known that the quantity of blood
required and expended is in a definite ratio to the exertions; when we perform mental labor the same rule
holds good. In these estimates we must distinguish
between the intellectual and emotional faculties. Mere
intellectual study uses up but little blood, and probably never *per se* injures the health or exhausts the body,
provided the emotions are not involved. But love,
anger, emulation, ambition, anxiety or religious en-
thusiasm cannot be long sustained without drawing
heavily upon the stomach, lungs and heart.

PRACTICAL PHRENOLOGY.

1. In order to learn to make examinations, procure a plaster bust and a book and impress upon your memory the definitions, locations, sizes and forms of all the organs, together with the class, range or group to which each belongs.

2. Distinguish the organs concerning which all phrenologists agree, from those that may be considered as doubtful or candidate organs, and suspend your opinions in regard to the latter.

3. Acquire clear ideas concerning the traits that result from an uncommon development or deficiency of each organ.

4. Learn the effects of various combinations of large and small organs. This is the most difficult task, and requires time, patience and good judgment.

5. Learn the modifying effects of particular temperaments and bodily conditions, both from the book and from observation.

6. Learn to distinguish the effects of the original temperament from the effects of diseases or unhealthy habits.

7. While you are learning to examine, confine yourself as much as practicable to persons whose characters you know before hand, and see if the heads indicate the known traits. You can afterwards apply the knowledge thus acquired to strangers.

8. When you begin to examine strangers do not *guess* at anything; confine your remarks to the organs and combinations that are so decidedly developed or deficient that if phrenology is true you cannot be mistaken.

9. If the persons examined or their friends dissent from your opinion, do not dispute with them, but make a careful re-examination, and if you have doubts of your own accuracy, do not be ashamed to say so. It may be humiliating, but it is your duty. If you have made no mistake in regard to the size of the organs, adhere firmly but politely to your statement. You and the dissenting friends may both be right. An organ may be small, and yet for some unknown cause it may be very active, or it may be large and inactive; perhaps a local disease or some ante-natal cause may affect an organ for several years. A young man in Philadelphia manifested a remarkable want of Firmness, which his head did not indicate externally, and the celebrated Dr. McClellan (father of the General) cut off a large tumor which had long pressed upon that organ. In this case the cause of the discrepancy was revealed.

10. Do not attempt, as some do, to tell whether the person examined belongs to a long-lived family or not; you cannot tell this by phrenology. It is true that persons with apparently well formed bodies will probably live longer than others, but the family physician is much more capable of giving an opinion upon this subject, or any other relating to the health, than you are. The truth is that the causes of longevity are not yet known to any one. Who can tell why a robin dies of old age in eight years, and a crow in eighty; a horse in twenty, an ass in sixty, a dog in twelve, and a lion in seventy?

11. Do not pretend, as some do, to tell by the developments of the head what organs have been exercised

most. When this pretence is subjected to a severe scientific test it fails.

12. Do not pretend to tell what kind of a husband or wife the person examined should choose. The only rules known to physiology are, 1, that both should be well formed and in good health, and belong to families that are healthy in body and mind; 2, that there should be slight but not extreme differences of complexion, form, size, features and mental traits.

13. In examining children you should recollect that the brain continues to grow until thirty, and undergoes a rapid and important change near the age of puberty. The direction that the changes will take depends upon causes that existed several generations back, and are, in a great measure, beyond our control. But they are not altogether so. I have no faith whatever in the doctrine that after a person is twenty-one any particular employment or exercise of the organs will vary the form of the head. But I have very great faith in the effects of early training — especially in the effects of such patient, persevering, loving and forgiving influence as a judicious mother often exerts over the moral character of her children. I have seen some wonderful instances of shockingly bad children converted to good men and women by the sleepless vigilance and exhaustless love of Christian parents and teachers. No one but an insane fiend can resist such influences.

14. Children and youth are much oftener temporarily insane than is supposed — probably much oftener than grown people. Their conduct is frequently such as can be explained upon no other hypothesis. Instead of being punished or treated severely, they should be

pitied and restrained, as other lunatics are, kindly but firmly. We must not allow ourselves to be blinded or misled by the fact that such young persons show intelligence and shrewdness on ordinary subjects; all lunatics do this. We should consider that the brain is growing and changing; new propensities are coming into power, and revolutions are taking place in the character. This is especially true during several years after the commencement of puberty. I have observed in many of these cases that the body has grown much more rapidly than the brain, and the higher organs of the brain are, to a certain degree, arrested in their development.

15. In making an examination the intellectual organs should be compared only with each other and not with the propensities. So also the propensities should be compared with each other, and not with the intellectuals. We may with propriety compare the whole intellect with the whole of the propensities in order to determine their relative magnitudes. But it is clearly improper to estimate the strength of a single intellectual by comparing it with the magnitude of the whole brain. Causality, for example, should only be compared with Comparison, and with the perceptives in order to determine its influence in the intellect.

The principal object of an examination is to ascertain the relative influences of the different antagonistic organs in the formation of the character. But the Intellectuals and propensities never antagonize one another; the whole Intellect, and each of its parts, is the servant and guide of the dominant propensities, but never their antagonist. The Intellectuals only antagonize each other, the largest being the most influential; for this reason they should be compared only with each other, in order to ascertain the peculiar intellectual character of the person examined. The propensities that prompt to aggressive and energetic conduct should be compared with those that restrain or moderate the conduct; thus Combativeness and Hopefulness should be contrasted with Cautiousness; Imperativeness and Firmness with Reverence and Kindness; Acquisitiveness with Kindness, with Hopefulness and with Perfectiveness. When Hopefulness is small and Cautiousness and Acquisitiveness large, there is a tendency to engage in small and sure transactions, and even to be penurious. If Hopefulness is dominant it tends to hazardous speculations.

16. If phrenology has had incapable expounders and imprudent friends, it has also had some not over scrupulous opponents. The assailants of a new science, whatever may be their motives, often render it a service by pointing out its defects and weak points. None of the objections that have been urged have produced as much effect upon simple minds as those concerning several of the small perceptive organs near where the nose joins the forehead. It has been objected that there is a cavern in the skull at this part called the *frontal sinus*, which renders a correct estimate of the sizes of the organs impossible. Let me confess that in regard to these organs this is a real difficulty; but let me also remark that the sinus does not exist, or is very small, in youth, and only becomes an obstacle at maturity. When the time comes, as it undoubtedly soon will, that every person will be examined in early life, and a record made of the examina-

tion in the books of a permanent institution, this
difficulty will entirely disappear.

17. Another objection is that the perceptive organs
are so very small that they cannot make differences
enough in the skull to be practically distinguished.
It must be admitted that this also is a real difficulty.
Within a space, the radius of which is not more than
an inch, phrenologists have located, or rather have discovered, as they suppose, five organs, namely: Individuality, Form, Size, Weight and Locality; and,
unfortunately, four of these occupy the very place
where the sinus interposes itself between them and
the outer part of the skull. There is no doubt that
several of the lowest organs of the intellect are located
in this central place; a decided depression here indicates a serious defect in the intellectual character. Dr.
Gall denominated this part the organ of the Spirit of
Observation. His definition was judicious. Spurzheim changed the name and called the most central
part (immediately above the nose) the organ of Individuality. It is defined as the faculty of noticing
things without reference to their qualities. I cannot admit that there is such a faculty in the mind.
When we have noticed the form, size, color, weight
and locality of a thing, we certainly have noticed the
thing. A faculty of Individuality is, therefore, unnecessary. By examining extreme cases, we may be
able to prove that organs of Form, Size, Weight and
Locality exist where they are located; but in ordinary
cases the examiner is forced to content himself with
observing the general fullness and width of the part
of the forehead where these organs are situated, and
assuming that if one is large the others are also.

18. It has been objected to practical phrenology that only a part of each organ (each convolution) is immediately under the skull. There is some force in this objection, but not much. Show any artist or comparative anatomist one finger of a man and he will approximate very nearly to the size of the whole hand. Give a mathematician a small section of a circle and he will tell you precisely the diameter of the circle.

Phrenology was discovered and established by observation, and not by argumentation. It is founded upon facts derived from millions of examinations, and can only be overturned or improved by more correct observations. I never yet knew an opponent of phrenology who became one in consequence of examinations. I have met a great many who thought that they knew without any investigation that it *must* be untrue. They remind us of the opponents of Gallileo, who condemned him without condescending to look through his telescope to see whether his new planets existed or not; they were sure that such planets *could not* exist, and that was enough.

19. It is furthermore objected that phrenology is imperfect, and therefore ought not to be practiced. What science is not imperfect? Is medical science perfect? The ablest physicians frankly confess that it is so imperfect as scarcely to deserve the name of a science. The homœopaths, allopaths and eclectics treat each other with quite as little respect as they do the phrenologists. But they all continue to practice their profession in spite of its imperfections and their mutual contempt for each other. With what consistency, then, can they complain of the phrenologist

who imitates their example, by practicing his profession honestly, according to the best of his knowledge and ability? This treatise contains abundant evidence that I am fully aware of the defects of phrenological science, and that I have exerted the limited talents I possess to remedy them.

A reproach has been thrown upon phrenology on account of the practice of itinerants and others examining heads for a fee. Those who raise this objection, however, are the very ones who deny that there is any truth in phrenology. The moment we admit that it is a science, and an art capable of being made immensely useful, the objection to itinerants vanishes. If the only objection is that the itinerants are ignorant of this important science, and incapable of doing it justice, no one laments it more than I do; but I would remark that there is quite as much reason for lamenting the ignorance and incompetence of doctors and clergymen. No doubt it would be more dignified to make examinations merely to improve the science, but there are few if any who would devote years to such a thankless task. I regard it as a fortunate circumstance that phrenology has become a practical profession, and that some men can support themselves by making examinations. It prevents phrenology from becoming obsolete, and tends to test the accuracy of the observations of the founders of the science. If phrenology is at fault, who is so likely to know it and correct it as the men who have devoted ten or twenty years to making examinations? It is these men who have unanimously agreed that Time and Tune are unreliable organs; that Language and Number, notwithstanding they are very small and theoretically objectionable, are perfectly established, and that nearly all the other organs are correctly located. The only persons who are competent to give an opinion concerning the merits of phrenology, are those very ones whose daily business it is to apply it practically; they know that it is true, and therefore smile with contempt at the objections raised by those who admit that they never made any examinations.

20. Phrenology, as a scientific system of mental physiology, is much more advanced than as a practical art. It must in candor be acknowledged that several organs that have been discovered by comparing extreme cases of development with remarkable manifestations of traits, cannot, in ordinary cases, be measured and their relative strength determined with sufficient accuracy for practical purposes. This is a valid argument against the perfection of phrenology as a practical art, but not as a scientific system. There are no advantages possessed by other mental philosophers that the phrenologists do not possess in common with them, and the latter certainly have an important source of information of which the more metaphysicians are deprived.

PHYSIOGNOMY.

"There is no art to find the mind's construction in the face."—
Shakspeare.

There is an impression on the minds of people who know scarcely anything of phrenology, that physiognomy affords a surer guide to a knowledge of character than phrenology does. I have studied both of these subjects with great care for many years, and find, as a result, that very little can be known by the face alone. In function the face is related to the organs at the base of the brain, and to those only. The higher organs of the brain have no direct or functional relation to the face, and they may, therefore, be large or small, without the face affording any indication of the fact. The form of the face indicates only a few of the lower — the animal — traits of the mind, and even these but vaguely and imperfectly. I have often seen a man who had a brutal-looking face, and who possessed the traits that his face indicated, but he also had the higher cerebral organs large enough to counterbalance the lower, so that in reality he was a noble character — such a man was Socrates; such also was Luther. Again, I have seen a man with a similar face who was deficient in the higher organs, and his face really did indicate his character truly. I frequently see persons whose faces denote innocence and gentleness, but the higher organs being deficient, their characters are low and contemptible. This idea may be well illustrated by the head and face of Franklin. Let the face remain and surmount it with a low head, and in an instant the character of Franklin is gone.

Those who have faces like bull-dogs generally have Destructiveness or Combativeness larger than people whose faces resemble those of peaceful animals. Persons with retreating chins and with teeth like beavers and squirrels, resemble those animals in their artistic and sometimes in their economical habits. Large nostrils denote energy, because they generally accompany good respiratory organs.

The movements of the muscles of the face constitute a kind of natural language, by which the present passing emotions of the mind are often expressed with

great accuracy. Keen, experienced observers are sometimes enabled, by watching the faces of people, to
infer their thoughts and feelings with remarkable precision. But a hypocrite, a confidence man, or a good
actor can assume any of these expressions and deceive
the shrewdest of men. The face can be made to lie
quite as effectually as the tongue can, but the head
always speaks the truth. The expressions of the face
sometimes become chronic and fixed, so as to indicate
habitual mildness, cheerfulness, melancholy, morose-
ness, gravity, levity, and many other traits. These
expressions may be hereditary, just as other peculiarities are. The children of refined and social people
have different expressions from those of persons who
have for several generations been deprived of the ben-
efits of cultivated society. We frequently infer, the
moment we glance at a face, that it belongs to an
Irishman, an Englishman, or a German, but we seldom detect these expressions in their American grand-
children.

The face undergoes important changes as a consequence of development from infancy to old age. In
childhood the jaws and nose are small, while the forehead is prominent, especially at its upper part. Probably the reason of this is that the child, being cared
for by its mother, and fed mostly upon fluids, does
not need the same amount of strength in its jaws that
it does when older.

We sometimes see a face upon a full grown person
that reminds us of the features of a child, and in fact
it is what is called an "arrest of development." The
nose will be small, short and flat, or the chin retreating, or the frontal sinus will be wanting, while the

upper part of the forehead is prominent. This is frequently seen in idiots, in whom the brains as well as
the faces have been imperfectly developed.

INSTINCTIVE FACULTIES.

The bee, the spider and the beaver, without instruction or experience, perform tasks which man can only
accomplish after having had the advantages of both;
yet men are in the habit of speaking of their own
slow and toilsome method as if it were immensely
superior to what they contemptuously term *mere
instinct*. When a poet, a musician, an orator, or an
artist, exhibits faculties that approximate to those of
animals in precocity and spontaniety, we hail him as
a child of extraordinary *genius*. The genius of blind
Tom for music is evidently of the same nature as animal instinct. The fellow is in some respects idiotic,
and nature seems to have developed one faculty at the
expense of all the others. The musical faculty which
he exhibits is not different in *kind* from that of other
men; it is only different in degree. I have no doubt
that this is true of all animal instinct; they do not
differ in kind from the faculties possessed by man,
but they differ in intensity, and in the fact that they
require no cultivation or instruction. The quail, as
soon as it is hatched, has the perfect use of its external
senses and its voluntary muscles; it can run, and
choose its food, and hide itself from approaching enemies. A child only learns to do this after tedious
years of experience, during which it commits a thousand blunders. The human being can boast that he
has the capacity to learn to do those things which the

animal does at first without learning. It is folly to speak of the superiority of human beings in this respect; the truth is that they are very much inferior. Now the question is, why should man be made inferior to other animals in respect to the lower mental and voluntary faculties? The answer is, because the young of human beings are cared for by their parents during several years, and *do not need* the full use of their mental and voluntary faculties. They learn slowly because there is no necessity for their learning rapidly. As soon as the child is born it is capable of seizing the breast and drawing forth its nourishment; it needs this instinct and it has it in perfection; it needs nothing else but the protection of its parents, and it has the faculty of crying aloud for that. These two faculties of sucking and crying need no more education than do the faculties manifested by the newborn quail. I believe that the law is universal that the less care the parents bestow, the more perfect the faculties of the young are.

The capacity which man has for improvement has been regarded as his crowning glory; but this very capacity springs from his imperfection at birth. It requires several years of improvement to bring man up to an equality with many animals that are not more than six months old. It is often said that animals have instinct *instead* of reason; it would be nearer the truth to say that they reason instinctively wherever reason is necessary to them. Their reason, like their other faculties, is limited to certain subjects and adapted to certain wants, but so far as it extends, it is perfect. Insane people, and patients who are laboring under temporary delirium, often astonish their friends by manifestations of mental or bodily force far beyond their normal capacities. Mesmerized and entranced subjects, and spirit mediums do the same. The manifestations of great special genius, of partial insanity, and of animal instinct, may all be referred to one cause, and that is a highly exalted condition of some portions of the mental organism.

PLAY OF THE FACULTIES.

When there are no occasions for the faculties to act in earnest, and in accordance with their primitive purpose, they often become spontaneously and playfully active without any real occasion. For example, the parental propensity, which was originally designed to impel to the care of helpless children, manifests itself playfully in young girls, and prompts them to treat little images as if they were actual infants. So also boys, who are naturally pugnacious, and yet have no real cause for quarreling, will wrestle and box, and strive for victory. In playing with a ball, they will divide into nearly equal parties, and contend long and earnestly, under the influence of the same propensities which prompt them afterwards to risk their lives upon the battle field.

Young people are fond of manual and pedal exercises; and in the absence of occasions for useful action, their faculties will manifest themselves in dancing, foot-racing, skating, and other similar exercises. Young girls will assemble together, and play that they are giving parties, and they will imitate the fashionable parties of their parents. All kinds of plays **are representations** of realities, and the same faculties are active in both the representative and the real. It has been considered difficult to give a satisfactory definition of *wit*, but we find the key to it here; it is the playful action of the intellect and of Experimentiveness expressed in words. The primitive action of the same faculties is serious and earnest, and relates to utility or necessity, while wit relates only to amusement. Theatrical representations are properly denominated *plays;* they give pleasure because they are a playful mode of exercising many of the mental faculties at times when there is no occasion for their serious action. Historical novels belong to the same class of performances, and so indeed do all works of fiction.

The mental emotions are of two kinds, the exalting and the depressing. The depressing, (fear and awe,) require the solemn, terrible, and tragic drama and play for their gratification. These faculties require playful exercise quite as much as do the more numerous class of exalting propensities. There are many people who experience a "melancholy pleasure" in shedding tears and in sympathizing with the misfortunes of heroes and heroines in distress. They enjoy the thrill of horror which they experience when the beautiful and innocent Desdemona dies, or the conscience-stricken Macbeth shudders at the sight of his blood-stained hands. Tragedies gratify not only the depressing propensities of Cautiousness and Reverence, but also the more savage faculty of Destructiveness, which delights in the terror and misery exhibited in the drama. The spectators admire and sympathize with the hero, hate the tyrant, despise the villain and pity the victim at the same time, and thus gratify a variety of faculties. The depressing propensities are gratified by solemn, funereal religious exercises, independent of any sense of duty or obligation to God. Persons with these faculties dominant take pleasure in contemplating the tragedy of the crucifixion; the terrors of death; the awful magnificence of the judgment day; and the dreadful doom of the wicked. The pleasure is of course very much enhanced if they are fully satisfied that they themselves are among those who are elected to enter heaven in triumph. Ceremonial religion is often a mere play of the serious faculties, without any necessary connection with sincere and intelligent piety; the solemnity of the performances contrasts so strangely with the vivacity and hilarity produced by the play of the more vigorous propensities, that we have been prevented from regarding them both as playful modes of action of faculties that were primitively created for very different purposes.

This subject is intimately related to moral and religious education. By managing the sports of children in such a manner as to excite the moral faculties that need cultivation, we can do more to modify the character, initiate good habits and instill good principles than by any other means. In this manner they can

"Be taught as though you taught them not."

Those teachers who have the art, possessed in such a high degree by Socrates and by Franklin, of preserving their dignity while they convey instruction in an amusing manner, are always eminently successful. For the same reason vicious and immoral men, who have an uncommon faculty of amusing, are dangerous companions for youth.

MYTHS.

When we see a play or read a work of fiction, we gratify our propensities by playfully imagining the characters and scenes to be real. In these cases we are not in the least deceived; for we never for a moment think of treating the subjects of contemplation as actualities, or of regulating our serious conduct by them. But there are some things, equally unreal, the existence of which many people have not the slightest doubt; they not only believe in their reality, but they allow them to influence their most important concerns; these imaginary existences are called *myths*. The Greeks believed in the existence of a multitude of gods; the Irish and English in fairies; the Scotch in warlocks, and all nations in something similar. There is scarcely any department of human affairs in which myths do not abound; they intrude even into the domain of popular science; its early history is crowded with them; astrology, alchemy, animal magnetism, modern spiritism, are suggestive of little else. There are few religious systems that are not more or less adulterated by myths, and, indeed, some are entirely composed of them. Many of them were originally adopted playfully, but they gratified several powerful propensities to such a degree that they at length came to be believed in. Our propensities oftentimes become fathers to our opinions. Many religious ceremonies and creeds that have taken a strong hold upon the minds of people, owe a large part of their influence to this cause. They are myths founded upon slight and fallacious evidence, but they are entertained and fostered because they give occa-

sion for the playful exercise of many powerful pro
pensities. The religious creeds of a people are generally adapted to their characters. The higher and
nobler phases of the Christian religion can only be
popular among a cultivated people, while its mere
outward forms and pagan excrescences are suited to
inferior and superstitious minds. Intellectual persons often wonder that men of good sense can believe
in such absurd things, and upon such slight grounds
as they do. The key to this mystery is found in the
fact that the intellect is the slave of the dominant
propensities. When the propensities desire a particular conclusion, they blind the intellect to the truth
that opposes it. We see this fact exemplified every
day by political and theological partisans, and indeed
by zealots of all kinds. The conduct of sincere spiritists affords a good illustration. The following may
be taken as an example: A man lost a dear and only
son; while his feelings were greatly affected, he was
informed that the spirit of the deceased had taken
possession of a certain medium; he knew very little
of spiritism, and thought it probably false; but he
wondered if it might not possibly be true. In this
frame of mind he went to a circle of spiritists, and
from a writing medium received what purported to
be a communication from his son. He did not believe
that it came from him, but he fervently wished that
he really could be thus favored. He tried it again
and again until his wishes conquered his intellect and
his prudence, and he became a convert. If his *feelings* could have been unbiased, the evidence would
not have made the slightest impression upon his judgment. It is useless to argue with such a man. If

you succeed in demonstrating to him that he has been imposed upon, instead of being grateful he feels as if you have robbed him of a treasure. When Jacob and his wives deserted from their father Laban, and carried his idols with them, the only complaint of the unhappy idolator was, "Ye have taken away my gods, and what have I more?"

It is the function of the senses and the intellect to receive and *understand* evidence; it is the function of Credenciveness *to believe* that kind of evidence which consists of human testimony. If the testimony is gratifying to several powerful propensities besides Credenciveness, and not disagreeable to any, we become *prejudiced* in its favor, and are almost certain to adopt it as truth and *act* accordingly. If the evidence is contradictory, the propensity of Equity inclines us *to weigh* the arguments for and against fairly; but it is exceedingly difficult to do this if Acquisitiveness, Parentiveness, Approbativeness, or any other powerful propensity is enlisted on one side. Skillful lawyers, politicians and pulpit orators avail themselves of these principles in their public appeals.

It has been said that there are more false facts than false theories. It may be added that there are very few false theories that are not founded upon false facts — upon myths. Logic consists in reasoning correctly from certain premises; but logic does not ascertain the soundness of the premises; that is the function of positive science. Metaphysical reasoning has been brought into disrepute, not because the reasoning was illogical, but because the premises were so frequently mythical. If the conclusions of reasoning are false, the resulting conduct must be erroneous, and it is oftentimes disastrous beyond measure.

THE BRAIN

STRUCTURE DOES NOT REVEAL FUNCTION.

Dr. Gall, the discoverer of Phrenology, never stood as high in the opinion of the medical profession as he does to-day. Those among them who do not believe in, or rather know nothing about Phrenology, admit his extraordinary merits. Dr. Flint, in his work just published, pays a just tribute of respect to the character and genius of Gall, and intimates that nothing but his Phrenological *theories* have prevented him from receiving due credit for his great services to science. Dr. Flint ought to make himself better acquainted with the facts concerning Gall's teachings. Gall never proposed any theory whatever; this was one of his faults; he mererly proclaimed the *facts* which he had observed. He did not attempt even to systematize his observations, much less to give any theoretical explanation of them. As for Phrenology obscuring his merit, the contrary is notoriously true. Had it not been for Phrenology, his name would never have been heard of beyond his native province. It was that which led him to examine the brains of men and animals, and to dissect them with such care and accuracy. He was desirous to know whether the internal structure confirmed the external indications. The results surpassed his most sanguine expectations. Mr. Solly, in his treatise on the brain — a standard work in our medical colleges — says, "Phrenology alone can account for monomania," and he proceeds to give his reasons for regarding it as true. He adds: "The first philosopher who attempted to prove that the brain does not minister to the intellect as a single organ, but as a combination of organs, was Gall, and I think he is entitled to the gratitude of mankind."

When a few days ago, I requested Professor Jewell, of the Northwestern University, to refer me to the best work on the relations of the mind and body, he recommended the treatise of an English author, the learned and able Dr. Tuke,* I find that he has not over-estimated this excellent work. On page 158, speaking of Dr. Gall, he says: "Whatever may be the fate of the details of his organology, (Phrenology,) he was an original observer, a true philosopher, and infinitely superior to his critics." This is the language of one of the first medical philosophers of England in 1872, concerning a man whose name, during his life-time, was never spoken in any college of Great Britain excepting with contempt.

The scientific opponents of Phrenology, or those who profess to be such, often endeavor to produce an impression upon young students that their opposition arises from their profound knowledge of the anatomy and physiology of the brain; while the truth is, that all the useful knowledge that they possess upon the subject, has been derived from the founders and advocates of Phrenology. 1. Gall was the first who taught Phrenologists that the passions and emotions are

* Dr. Tuke, in a note at p. 25 of his work, does me the justice to refer to the testimony of one of my pupils, Dr. Darling, during his visit to Europe, that I first performed the experiments which were afterwards repeated by Mr. Braid and others. Although my first work on the subject was published in 1845, the experiments were performed by me in Buffalo, N. Y., as early as 1838, but at that time I had no physiological explanation to offer.

located in the brain; the highest medical authorities in Europe, including Bichat and Brousais, denied this fact, but it is now admitted by all physiologists. 2. The convolutions or folds of the brain were supposed to be permanent structures until Gall succeeded in actually unfolding them and forcing his opponents to change their views. 3. The fibrous structure of the brain was not understood, and when Gall and Spurzheim demonstrated that the fibres proceed to and from the convolutions and the oblongata, passing through the striatum and thalamus, and receiving reinforcements in them, they were shamefully misrepresented and slandered. The Edinburg *Review* contained an article by Dr. Gordon, Professor of Anatomy in the college, denying the fibrous structure. Dr. Spurzheim visited Edinburg, and there, says an eye witness, "with the *Review* in one hand and a brain in the other, he opposed fact to assertion, and that day won over five hundred witnesses to the fibrous structure of the brain." No one now denies it; on the contrary every medical college in the world teaches it. 4. There are several parts of the brain the uses of which are now admitted to be to connect the different regions of the brain together so as to allow of intercommunication. They have received such fanciful and foolish names as the fornix, the tenia semicircularis, the ourlet, and the callosum. Gall, Spurzheim, and Solly, the three greatest Phrenological anatomists, were the first to point out their real structure and probable uses. I defy any anatomist to mention a single fact in regard to the anatomical structure of the brain, that throws any light upon its functions, which has not been borrowed from the founders and advocates of Phrenology. It is the custom of the professor of anatomy in nearly every medical college, during the term, to dissect a brain in the presence of the students, and show them the different objects brought to their view, describe their shapes and positions, and endeavor to impress these things upon their memories, together with the ridiculous names indicative of ancient and profound ignorance, by which the parts are known. But unless they admit Phrenology to be true, they are unable to even conjecture the special function of any part of the brain.

The reader will naturally ask how it happened that the Phrenological investigators were more successful in their researches concerning the structure and functions of the brain than their learned opponents? The reason is that they pursued a different method. Instead of dissecting brains to learn their functions, or tormenting living animals for that purpose, they compared the external developments of well-known persons of greatly contrasted characters, and learned by Phrenology and mental philosophy the functions of the different parts; and *then* dissected brains, and of course discovered that the structure harmonized with the functions which they had already ascertained. Structure seldom or never reveals function. The structure of the heart, the arteries, and the lungs were known to Harvey and his cotemporaries, but this knowledge did not teach them the great fact of circulation. The structure of the brain did not teach Cuvier, Bichat and Brousais that the passions reside in it. It was the undignified method of examining and comparing heads, that removed the passions and emotions from the body and enthroned them in the brain. 5. Knowing as they did that volition proceeds from the oblongata, they inferred that there must be a fibrous connection between it and the parts immediately beneath the skull, they therefore dissected brains and demonstrated the existence of the fibres that converge toward the oblongata. 6. Finding that the cerebral fibres pass through and form the principal portion of the striatum, and also of the thalamus, they inferred that those two apparently distinct bodies are but the trunks of the higher cerebral masses that seem to grow out of them. 7. After Gall and Spurzheim were dead, and Combe had published his last work, I was so fortunate as to discover that all the organs of the brain are developed in three classes—the Intellectual, the Ipseal and the Social—which correspond with the three classes of bodily functions, namely, the volitional, the nutritive, and the reproductive. This being ascertained by observation and analysis, I was at once met by the confirmatory fact that the brain has always been regarded as having three lobes, the anterior, the middle, and the posterior, and that each of the classes was located in one of these lobes. The structure of the brain and its division into three lobes did not reveal the fact that each lobe performed a distinct class of functions.

8. Again: In attempting to account phrenologically for various mental phenomena, my attention was arrested by the fact, that notwithstanding the great number of nerves and phrene organs that communicate with the mind, the mind itself is a unit, in which one organ may predominate at one time and another organ at another. This being the case, these phrene organs and nerves should have some common central

point where they could meet and contend for the mastery and control of volition. In looking into the structure of the brain, I found such a central point in the oblongata. In 1845, when I first announced this idea, no one had suggested that Conciousness was located in the oblongata. 9. The structure of the sympathetic nerve has been known for a long time. Gall was the first to suggest that it is the channel through which the emotions affect the vital organs; his opinion has been generally adopted, though few seem to be aware that this truth was one of the first fruits of phrenology. This idea of Gall has been abundantly confirmed by the important discoveries of Brown-Sequard, and others. 10. It never occurred to any anatomist that the mental emotions are *functionally* related to the heart and other vital organs until the writer was led to that conclusion by studying the phenomena of trance.

I have in the following pages gone more into detail in explaining and illustrating the anatomy of the nerves and brain than is usual in works of this character, and I have done so not because I found it necessary in order to *prove* any of my positions, but to show that, so far as anatomy has any bearing one way or the other, it is all in favor of the principles which I have advanced in this treatise.

TECHNICAL TERMS,

AND THE NAMES OF VARIOUS PARTS OF THE BRAIN.

The unprofessional reader who looks at the engraved representations of the brain, and reads below them the strange names that have been given to the different parts, will naturally suppose that his inability to understand the matter arises from his ignorance or stupidity, and his mind will probably be filled with something like envy of those distinguished professors who are supposed to be skilled in such mysteries. Reader, let me hasten to relieve your mind. The most learned professors know no more about it than you do. The absurd names by which the different parts of the brain are now known, were bestowed upon them a long time ago by men who had no idea of the functions of the parts. Like the names of places in a new country, they were determined by accident, by caprice, or by fancy. It may assist and at the same time amuse the reader if I give the literal definition of a few of the terms used by anatomists in describing the brain:

1. *Medulla Oblongata*—Something of an oblong form.

2. *Corpora Restiformia*—A rope-shaped body.

3. *Corpora Pyramidalia*—A body resembling a pyramid in form.

4. *Corpora Olivaria*—An olive-shaped body.

5. *Pons Varolii*—The bridge of Varolius that passes over the oblongata and connects the right and left sides of the cerebellum.

6. *Cerebellum*—Little brain or little cerebrum.

7. *Ganglion*—A knot or mass of grey nerve-matter.

8. *Cineritious Matter*—Grey, pulpy, nervous matter, that is of the color of ashes.

9. *Corpus Striatum*—A striated or striped or fibrous-looking body.

Thalamus—A bed. The original name was the *Thalami Nervorum Opticorum*—The bed of the optic nerves. It is now known that it is not the bed of those nerves; but the name — thalamus — is continued for convenience.

Fornix — A vault — fibres that assume something of an arched or vaulted form.

Fissure of Sylvius — A depression that separates the anterior lobe of the cerebrum from the middle lobe.

Vermiform process — The worm-shaped part of the cerebellum, situated in the middle line, and is supposed to be related to the motions or the equilibrium of animals and men.

The Rhomboideum — A ganglion in the interior of the cerebellum that is of a rhomboidal form.

Corporo Mammalaria, or Mammary bodies — Two small bodies that look like breasts.

Tenia semi-circularis — A white skein of fibres that runs between the thalamus and striatum.

Crura Cerebri — Legs of the cerebrum.

Corpus Callosum — Hard body — a bridge of white fibres that connects the two halves of the upper part of the brain.

Pes Hippo-Campus — A part that looks like the print of a horse's foot.

Locus Niger — A dark place — a mass of grey, pulpy matter in the crura cerebri.

Ourlet — Fibres that connect the anterior and posterior parts of the cerebrum. They are seen in Figure 58, running above the Callosum in the median line.

STRUCTURE OF THE BRAIN.

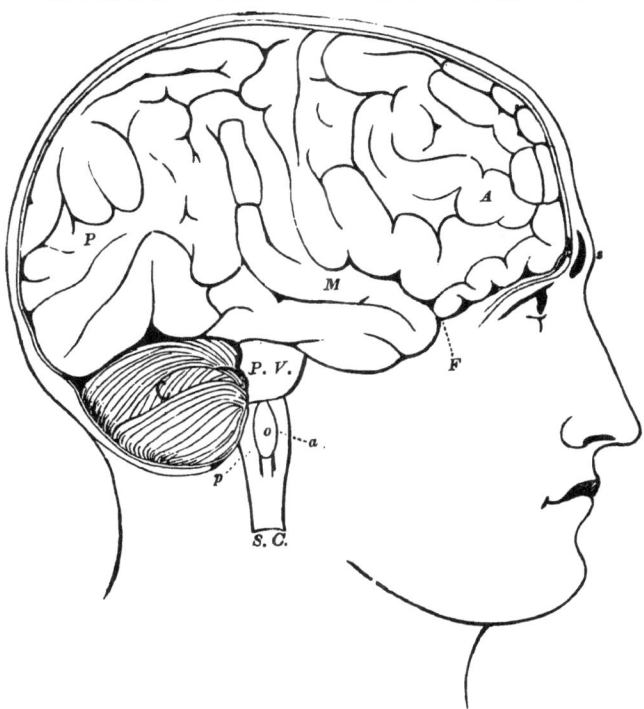

Fig. 48.

Figure 48. Side view of the brain, in its true position, showing the convolutions or folds of its surface. *A*, Anterior lobe.
M, Middle lobe. *P*, Posterior lobe. *C*, Cerebellum — separated
from the cerebrum by a fold of the dura mater called the ten-
torium. *P. V*. Pons Varolii. *o*, Olivary body in the oblongata.
a, Anterior column of fibres. *p*, Posterior column of fibres. *S.
C.* Upper part of spinal cord. *s*, Frontal sinus — a hollow
between the outer and inner tables of the skull, which, in some
cases, renders craniological indications uncertain. *F*, Fissure
of Sylvius, which separates the base of the anterior from the
middle lobe.

The disposition and directions of the convolutions, or folds of the brain, indicate that the brain was first compressed laterally, to make longitudinal convolutions, such as we see in lower animals, and afterwards compressed antero-posteriorly or from front to back, so as to shorten the brain; this is evident in all the convolutions, but particularly in those over the eyebrow, over the letter *M*, and over the cerebellum.

The Cerebrum is enclosed in the skull, and corresponds with it in general form. It is sometimes said that we cannot judge by the external form and appearance of the head what is the shape of the cerebrum, or the size of its parts. The varying thickness of the integuments and the skull are supposed to render it difficult, if not impossible, to determine, with the requisite accuracy, the development of the phrene-organs. I can testify that it is a real difficulty, in some cases, where the head is nearly balanced, and it is desirable to apply phrenology practically in an individual case. But so far as establishing the truth of Phrenology is concerned, the difficulty is entirely imaginary; for when we are at liberty to resort to extreme cases, we can easily prove to the satisfaction of any candid person the reality of a large majority of the organs which I have set down as established. Those persons who still talk about phrenology not being true, are, of course, to be treated with reasonable charity and courtesy; but it is difficult to resist the disposition to intimate to them that such opinions belong to an age that has passed away, and are no longer deserving of respectful attention.

There has been considerable dispute among anatomists as to the best mode of dissecting a brain, to learn its true structure — the old school preferring to commence by slicing off sections, until the callosum and the parts beneath come into view. The new, or phrenological school, on the other hand, contend that the brain should be dissected from the oblongata upwards, to the convolutions. The truth seems to be, that human brains may be examined in both ways, with ever so much skill, without their actual structure or functions being ascertained, unless the simpler brains of other animals are made to perform the parts of alphabetical interpreters of the more complicated language of the human brain. Take a human brain out of the skull, and place it with the base downwards, and we see nothing but the cerebrum, with a part of the cerebellum, enclosed in a tough membrane, called the *dura mater*. Removing this, we come to a very delicate membrane, which dips down between all the folds of the brain, and seems to sustain the blood-vessels. This is called the *pia mater*. Between the dura mater and pia mater, if we are very observing, we can see a delicate web-like membrane, which has been called the *arachnoid*, or spider's web. The surface of the brain is folded like a piece of thick cloth that has been crowded into a small box. Cut into the brain, and we find that it is composed of two substances, the outside being grey-neurine, or cortical substance, extending to the depth of half an inch, and below this is the white substance, composed of fibrous neurine.

Looking at the brain from above, we notice that it is in two equal halves, with a deep fissure between; and when we attempt to separate the two halves, by pulling them apart, we observe about an inch below the surface of the top of the head that there is a white bridge of fibres passing across from one side to the other, as if intended to unite them into one apparatus.

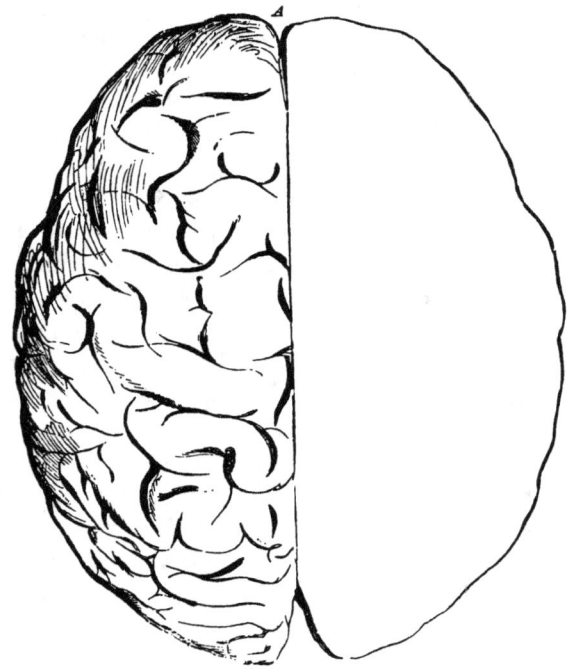

Fig. 49 — Top view of the left side of the brain.

Figure 49. *A*, Anterior. *P*, Posterior extremity. On the left side, the convolutions are represented, showing that most of them are transverse; whereas, in the side view, most of them are longitudinal. This is accounted for by the upper part of the human brain being more exposed to antero-posterior pressure, and not being as well protected by the skull-bones.

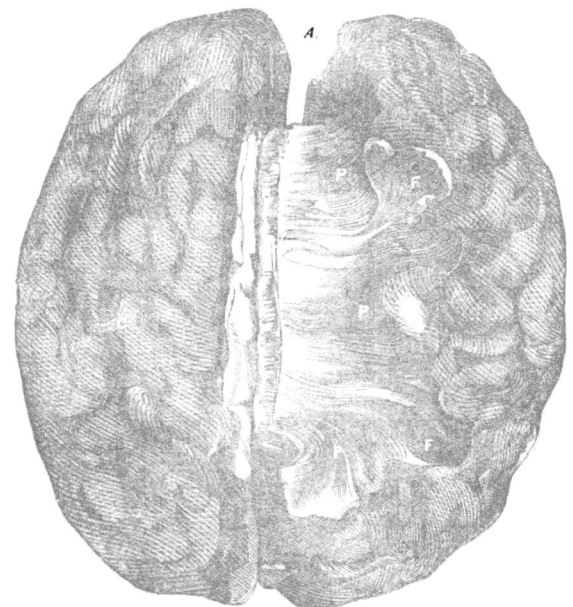

Fig. 50.

Figure 50. Top view of the brain (from Solly), with the right half dissected away, down to the callosum, to show the fibres of this great commissure, extending across from one side to the other, and terminating in the convolutions. The left half of the brain, *C*, remains undisturbed. *P P P*, Fibres of the corpus callosum radiating into the right hemisphere. *F F*, Fibres, terminating in the convolutions. *A*, Anterior lobe. *B*, Posterior.

This bridge is called the corpus callosum. Its precise connections with the other parts are yet unsettled. *Foville* declares that it is not connected with the convolutions, but that it proceeds from the crura of one side across the median line to the crura of the opposite side; thus making a kind of arch, which is analogous to the pons varolii, that connects the two halves of the cerebellum. *Solly*, on the contrary, contends that the callosum does not connect directly with the crura, but that it connects the convolutions of one side with those of the other. Most anatomists agree with *Solly;* but *Dr. F. S. Grimes*, (who had made a great many dissections of the brains, in order to settle points concerning which the authorities differ) assures me that in several instances he found that the callosum was composed of two horizontal layers of fibres; the superior layer could be distinctly traced to the convolutions of the lateral parts of the brain, as described by *Solly;* but the inferior layer was disposed in the manner described by *Foville.*

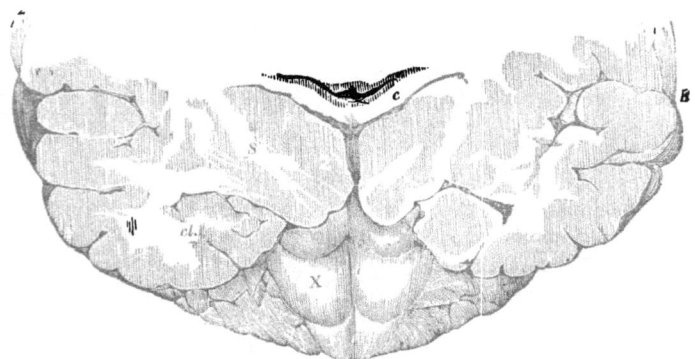

Fig. 51.

Figure 51. A transverse section of the middle lobes of the cerebrum, from Solly. The parts above the callosum, *c,* being sliced away by a horizontal incision; the posterior parts of the brain, *X,* are seen beneath in perspective. *S,* Section of the striatum, from which the anterior lobe is developed. *c l,* Section of the claustrum from which the middle lobe is developed. *c,* Section of the callosum. *B,* Fissure of Sylvius.

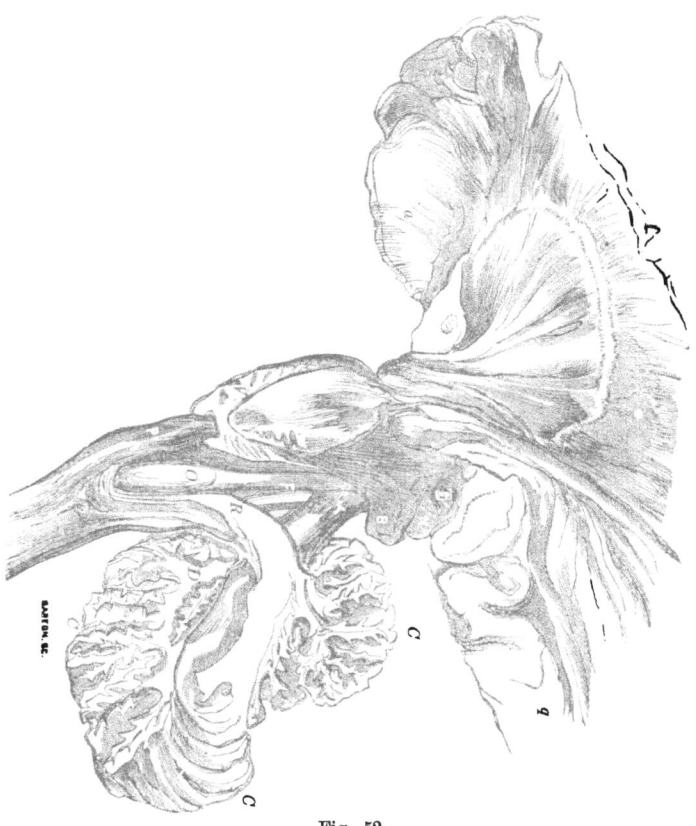

Fig. 52.

Figure 52. Diagram showing the fibrous structure of the brain, and the direction of the principal fibres, as they appear when carefully dissected. *O*, Olivary body. *D*, Rhomboideum, or central ganglion of the cerebellum. *C*, Cerebellum, showing the arbor vitæ, or tree-like structure, produced by alternations of white and gray neurine. *T*, The fibres that connect the cerebellum with the crura cerebri; they have been called, by Solly, the inter-cerebral commissure. *F*, Olivary column, or optic nerve, connecting the optic ganglion with the olivary body. *N*, *B*, Optic ganglia. *G*, Two geniculate bodies, which seem to belong to the optic ganglia. They are about as large as coffee-beans. P, Anterior pyramids, or columns of fibres, that connect the oblongata with the anterior part of the brain. V, Pons Varolii. a, Anterior lobe. q, Posterior lobe. R, Restiform, or rope-form fibres that connect the spinal cord and oblongata with the cerebellum.

This figure, drawn by Mayo, represents in a very perfect manner the improved — the phrenological — method of dissecting the brain introduced by Gall and Spurzheim. Instead of commencing at the top, as other anatomists do, and cutting away horizontal slices, the brain, after having been kept in alcohol about a week, is dissected from below upward — not by cutting, except when absolutely necessary, but by gently scraping and tearing and following the fibres from the spinal cord into the convolutions.

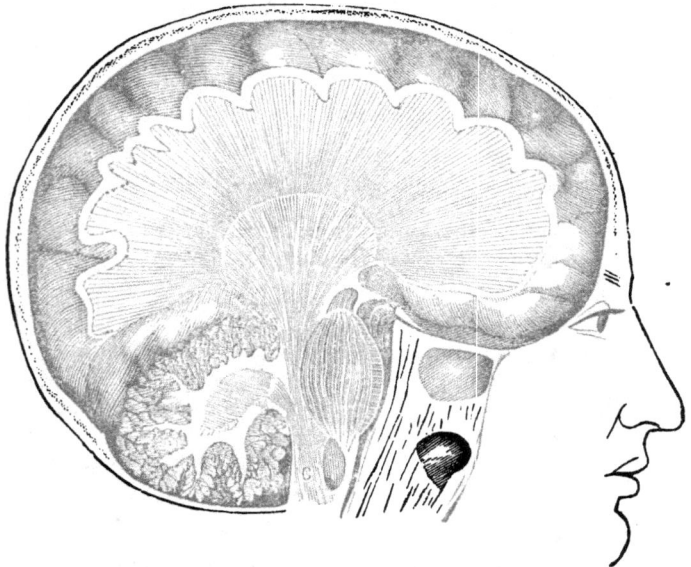

Fig. 53—(c), Conscious Centre in the Oblongata.

This figure is copied from Spurzheim. It represents the cerebrum as consisting mostly of white fibres, similar to those that constitute the nerves of volition. These fibres proceed from the outer parts of the brain and converge toward the oblongata (c). If we may compare the brain to a rose, the oblongata represents the stem of the rose; and just as the leaves of a rose converge toward its stem, so do the cerebral fibres converge toward the oblongata. The cerebellum, or little brain, like a smaller rose, also sends its concentrated fibres to connect and merge into the same oblong stem.

Gall and Spurzheim had no theory to support, as I have, in demonstrating this convergence of the cerebral and cerebellar fibres to a central point — the same point that receives all the nerves of sensation from the head and body, and the same that sends forth all the nerves of volition. The illustrious founder of the greatest of the sciences, expressed no opinion concerning a conscious centre distinct from the phrene organs. I believe that I was the first to advance the idea that consciousness is located in the oblongata, in a work that I published in Boston in 1845. The engraving, Fig. 53, is the same that I then used for an illustration, and it was again used in another work which I published in 1850, entitled *Phreno-Geology.* I am induced to make this statement by the circumstance that several eminent English authors have lately adopted my views of this subject. In a very learned and able work, published in 1872, by Daniel Hack Tuke, M. D., on the influence of the mind upon the body, I find the following quotation from a work by Professor Lacock:

" There are phenomena, however, in favor of the

doctrine that the medulla oblongata is the common sensory of all conscious states — whether they refer to corporal processes or the purely encephalic changes associated with ideas."

Dr. Tuke remarks: " It is striking to observe how many cerebral physiologists have arrived at the conclusion that the emotions are connected in some special way with the medulla oblongata, or the adjoining encephalic ganglia."

Dr. Tuke also quotes from Brown-Sequard, who, in 1860, said: " I am ready to admit that the pons varolii, particularly by its part connected with the roots of the auditive nerve, is a portion of the centre of emotional movements, but not the seat of the whole of this centre. The medulla oblongata is also a part of this centre."

Referring to Mr. Herbert Spencer, Dr. Tuke remarks, that as respects the medulla oblongata, Mr. Spencer regards it "as the seat of emotional feeling, considered as a mental state apart from the movements to which it gives rise. Not, of course, that it by *itself* can generate emotion, but that it is that out of which emotion is evolved by the co-ordinating actions of the great centres above it."

In my Phreno-Geology (*Boston and Cambridge, James Monroe & Co.; London, Edward J. Whitfield*, 1851,) I use the following language (p. 64): " It should be understood that according to my peculiar system of phreno-philosophy, the brain is not considered as the organ of mind; mind, or consciousness, is exclusively confined to the medulla oblongata. The doctrine taught by all phrenological authors, before I published my phreno-philosophy in 1845, *was*, that thought and feeling were performed by the brain itself, and that instead of there being one central organ of mind for a sensorium, each organ of the brain had in itself the power of feeling, thought or consciousness. It seems to me that the truth as well as the

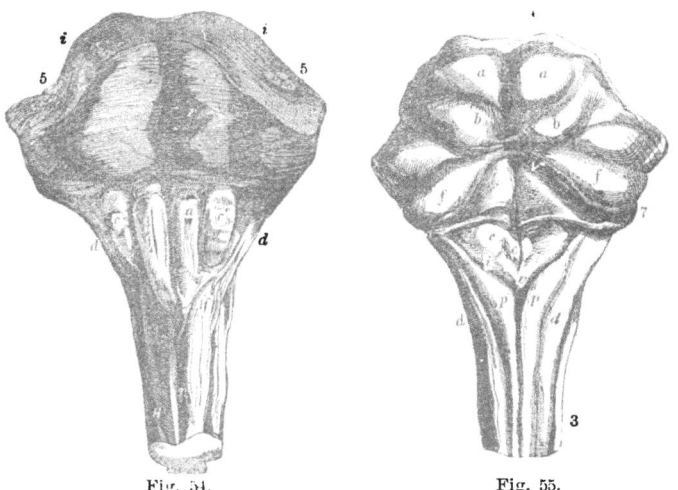

Fig. 54.   Fig. 55.

Figure 54. An anterior view of the medulla oblongata. *a*, Anterior pyramids. *c c*, The olivary bodies. *d d*, Restiform bodies. *f*, Fibres shown by Solly to pass from the anterior column of the cord to the cerebellum. *P*, Pons Varolii. *i*, Its upper fibres. 5 5, Roots of the trigeminus.

Figure 55. Posterior view of medulla oblongata, and back of the pons Varolii. The peduncles of the cerebellum are cut short. *d d*, Restiform bodies, (fasciculi cuneati;) passing up to become inferior peduncles of cerebellum. *p p*, Posterior pyramids. *v v*, Posterior fissure, or calamus scriptorius, extending along the floor of the fourth ventricle. *a b*, Optic ganglia. *f f*, Superior peduncles of cerebellum. *c*, Eminence connected with hypo-glossal nerve. *e*, With glosso-pharyngeal nerve. *i*, With vagus nerve. *v*, With spinal accessory nerve. 7 7, Roots of auditory nerves.—*Quain and Sharpey*.

beauty of my phreno central theory will be so apparent as to render it acceptable, not only to phrenological students, but even to those metaphysical philosophers who have hitherto regarded phrenology as crude and imperfect, for want of that very unity of plan which this system establishes."

The oblongata is a part of great importance, for the following reasons:

1. It is undoubtedly the phreno centre, or seat of the mind.

2. All the principal fibres of the brain converge toward it or diverge from it.

3. All the nerves of sensation from the face, and from all parts of the body, in man and in all animals, can be traced into it.

4. All the nerves of voluntary motion proceed from it.

5. All the nerves that convey the influence of the emotions of the mind to the heart and other vital organs, proceed from it.

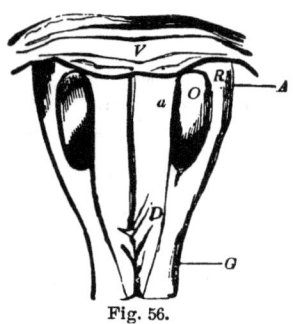

Fig. 56.

Figure 56. Front view of the oblongata. *a*, Anterior pyramid. *O*, Olivary body. *D*, Decussation or crossing of the fibres of the two halves. *R*, Restiform fibres. *V*, Pons Varolii.

The most intelligent invertebrated animals, such as the spider and bee, that have no proper brains, have this part in which their nerves of sensation and volition centre, and in which their mind seems to reside.

THE STRIATUM AND THALAMUS.

Each half of the brain contains a cavity or ventrical. At the bottom of this ventrical are two bodies called the striatum and thalamus. The anterior and middle lobes of the brain are developed from the striatum, (S,) and the posterior from the thalamus, (T.) If we slice away the top of a brain by horizontal slices until we come to the bottom of the ventricles, we have presented to us the view represented in Fig. 57. I doubt whether the real nature and character of the sub-cerebral parts will ever be fully understood until the doctrine of evolution is brought to bear upon them. I suspect that there are many parts of the brain, as well as of the body, that have been developed in different stages, in different geological ages; and that their forms can only be accounted for by the light of their past — their geological history.

Spurzheim says, "the posterior cerebral lobes proceed from the thalami." Solly says there is scarcely any rudiment of the thalami in fishes; their proportional size increases in reptiles, birds, and in the lower mammalia. Again he remarks, the spinal columns appear to terminate superiorly in two large tubercles; the striata and thalami, from the sides and under parts of which the cerebral hemispheres spring out, being afterwards reflected so as to completely envelope the bulbous extremities—the thalami and striata.

1. Phrenology demonstrates that the anterior lobe of the cerebrum, (the forehead,) is the seat of the intel-

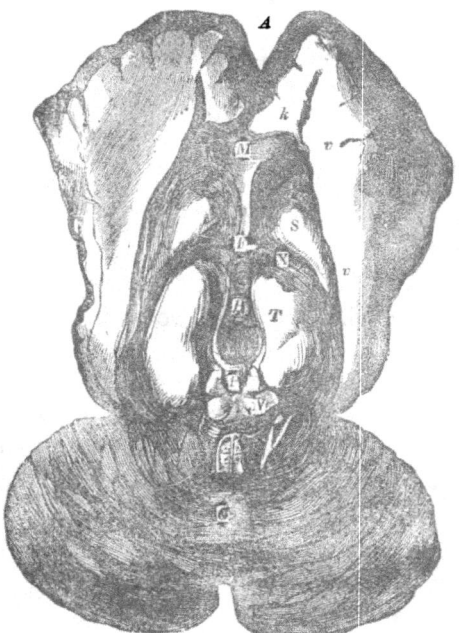

Fig. 57.

Figure 57. Top view of subcerebral organs; the cerebrum above being cut away. *A*, Anterior. D, Posterior part. *S*, Striatum. *T*, Thalamus. *C*, Cerebellum. *v v*, Parts of the cerebrum around the great lateral ventricles. *k*, Anterior cornua, or continuations of the ventricles. *X*, Tenia semicircularis. *F*, Anterior pillar of the fornix, where it turns down to form the mammillaria. *B*, Middle commissure. *A*, *N*, Optic ganglia. *P*, Pineal gland, with its peduncles, or connecting fibres. *M*, Place where the fornix unites with the callosum in front.

This figure gives a good idea of the relative positions of the cerebellum, thalamus, striatum, and the cerebrum; and it enables the student to understand how the ventricles can be formed by the cerebrum developing over the subcerebral organs.

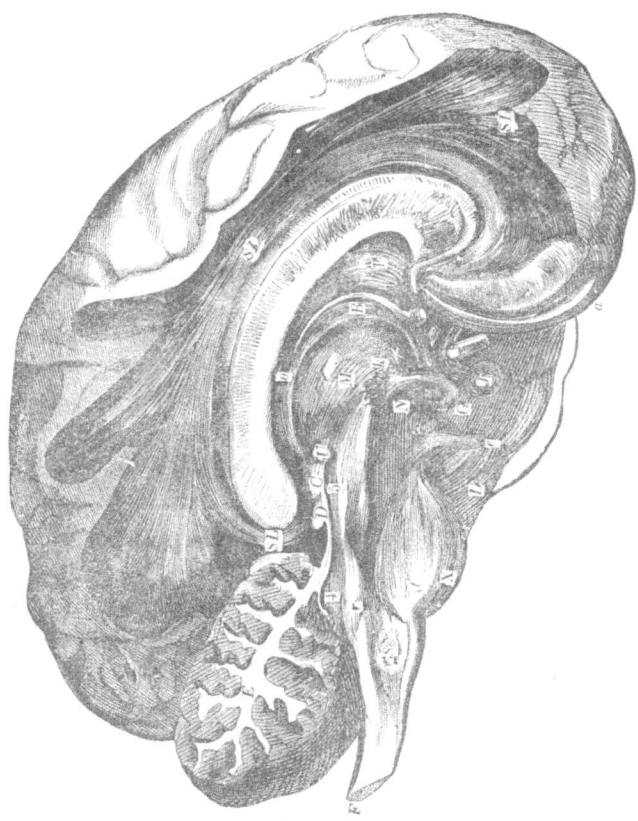

Fig. 58.

Figure 58. *F*, Spinal cord. *B* is between the semicircularis
and the peduncle. *G*, Mammillaria. *L*, Fibres of the fornix.
t, Fibres of the anterior pyramid. *r*, Fibres of the olivary, or
optic, tract. *S L, Ourlet. P*, Striatum. *K*, Thalamus. *M*, Section of the middle commissure. *O* is called the peduncle of the
pineal gland; parallel with it is tenia semi-circularis, a white,
semi-circular skein of *D C*, Optic ganglia. *U*, Section of the
fibres, running in a furrow between the thalamus and striatum.
posterior commissure. *J*, Pituitary gland; just above which is

lectual class of faculties. Anatomy demonstrates that this lobe grows out of the small bulbous mass below, called the striatum.

2. Phrenology demonstrates that the middle lobe of the brain, (the side of the head,) is the seat of the Ipseal or Self-relative functions, and anatomy shows that this lobe is developed from the posterior and lateral part of the striatum.

3. Phrenology demonstrates that the posterior lobe of the cerebrum is the seat of the social propensities, and anatomy demonstrates that this lobe is developed from the thalamus.

From these facts it is natural to conclude that the striatum is a lower degree of development of the Intellectual and Ipseal organs that constitute the anterior and middle lobes, while the thalamus is a lower degree of development of the social organs that occupy the posterior lobe, precisely as a bud is a lower degree of development of the rose. Embryology and comparative anatomy sustains this conclusion.

The next three figures are well calculated to give a good idea of the fibres, (commissures) that connect the different parts of the brain with each other. Fig. 48 is a section of the brain, directly in the middle line, so made as to separate the right from the left half, the inner side being scraped and prepared with great skill

the divided optic nerve. *a*, Olfactory ganglion. *N*, Crus cerebri, or leg of the cerebrum. Between *N* and *J* is the mammillaria, *G*, a loop formed by a twist of the fornix, proceeding from the thalamus. 4, Fourth ventricle. 5, Iter a tertio ad quartum ventriculum, or passage from the third ventricle to the fourth. These ventricles are of no account. *S*, Section of olivaria. *X*, Section of pons. *E*, Section of cerebellum.

to show the directions of the fibres, that instead of constituting phrene organs, (as those do that we represented in Fig. 52 and 53, are designed to connect the different regions of the brain with each other to produce harmony and co-operation. It will be observed that these connecting fibres or commissures are of two kinds, the longitudinal or antero-posterior, the principal of which are the Fornix and the Ourlet, and the transverse, that connect the right and left halves

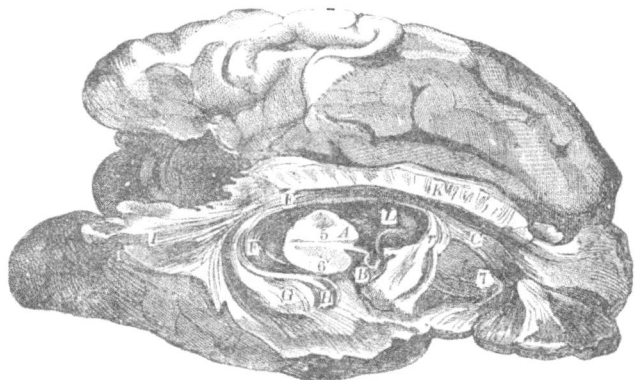

Fig. 59

Figure 59. This is a section of the cerebrum in the mesial line, as far down as the callosum, but below that it passes to the left of the mesial line, so as to show distinctly the direction of the fibres of the fornix below the callosum, *K*. *L*, Thalamus. 5, Section of the crus cerebri. 6, Niger. 7, Striatum. *A*, Fibres proceeding from niger to *B*, mammillaria, where the fibres turn down and up again, and proceed to *r*, called the anterior pillar of the fornix. *C* is the septum lucidum, which is an extremely thin sheet of fibres proceeding from the anterior lobe. *E*, Trunk of the fornix. *F*, Fibres of fornix descending to *G*, hippo campus major, and *H*, hippo campus foot in the middle cerebral lobe. *I*, Fibres of the fornix in the posterior lobe, passing over the hippo campus minor.

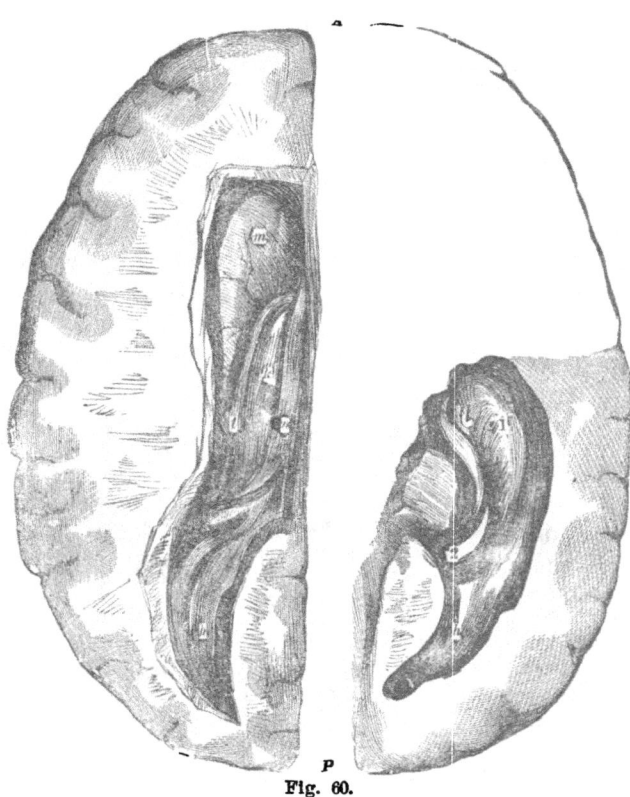

Fig. 60.

Figure 60, modified from Solly, represents the fornix in a very perfect manner. *A,* Anterior lobes of the brain. *P,* Posterior The figure gives a good view of the interior of the brain, it having been sliced away from above, so as to expose the great lateral ventricle. *m,* Striatum *k,* Thalamus. *t,* Tenia semi-circularis. *r,* Body of the fornix. *h,* Hippo-campus minor, a part covered over by the fibres of the fornix, which extend to the posterior lobes. 1, An internal eminence, which somewhat resembles a horse's foot, and has, therefore, received the name of pes hippo-campus, or horse's foot. 2, Fibres of the fornix,

of the brain; of the latter, the principal are the callosum (c,) above the ventricles anterior and the middle
and posterior commissures below them.

In order to convey an idea of the order in which the
different parts of the brain are developed and superadded to each other in vertebrated animals — the only
animals that have proper brains — I have made a series
of diagrams, the first of which (Fig. F) represents the
lowest known vertebrate, the amphioxus, a species of
small fishes that have nervous systems like other vertebrates, but no brain. They have an oblongata in
which all the nerves of sensation terminate, and from
which volition proceeds, and that is all. The crosses
represent the aconscious spinal centres; (1) represents
the terminus of the nerve from the stomach (the
vagus) and the end of the Ipseal class of propensities;
(2) is the the terminus of the nerves of the external
senses and the root of the intellectual class; (3) is the
terminus of the posterior column of the spinal cord,
and the root of the social propensities.

Fig. G represents the lowest vertebrates that have
even rudimentary brains; (4) is a striatum or bud of

which, after proceeding backward, and winding over and
around the thalamus, proceed forward to connect with the internal part of the base of the middle lobe.

NOTE.—The objection has been made to practical Phrenology
that there is a large space between the hemispheres in the middle line which cannot be examined during life. But it will be
seen by inspecting Fig. 58, (S. L.) that this space is not occupied
by phrene organs, but by longitudinal connecting fibres. This
objection, therefore, goes where many others have gone—to the
place where it belongs.

the anterior or intellectual lobe of the cerebrum; (3) is a small cerebellum. The striatum and the verm, a central portion of the cerebellum, were created in the Silurian period, before any other parts of the brain existed.

Fig. H contains all the parts that the preceding diagrams do, with the addition of a latteral development (5) which is seen in the highest fishes — the shark and skate. It is probably the bud of the middle lobe, and is related in function to (1) the vagus or stomach nerves.

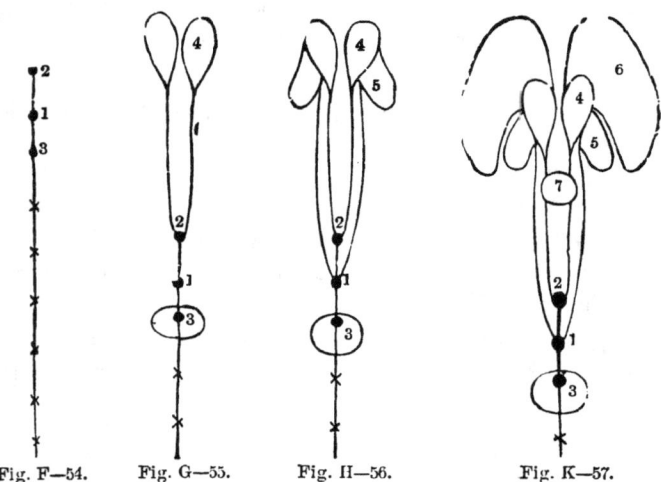

Fig. F—54.   Fig. G—55.   Fig. H—56.   Fig. K—57.

Fig. K is like the preceding, except that it has an addition of (6) an anterior lobe growing out of (4) the striatum, and it also has (7) a small thalamus, or root of a posterior lobe, situated behind the striatum. This is the degree of development of the brain in the reptiles.

Fig. L is like K, with the addition of a middle lobe (8) which has grown out of (5) the latteral part of the striatum. This represents the degree of development of brains in birds. The cerebellum has also a lateral addition.

Fig. M is like L, with the addition of (9) posterior lobes which have grown out of (7) the thalamus. The cerebellum is left out of this diagram. This is the degree of development found in mammels and man.

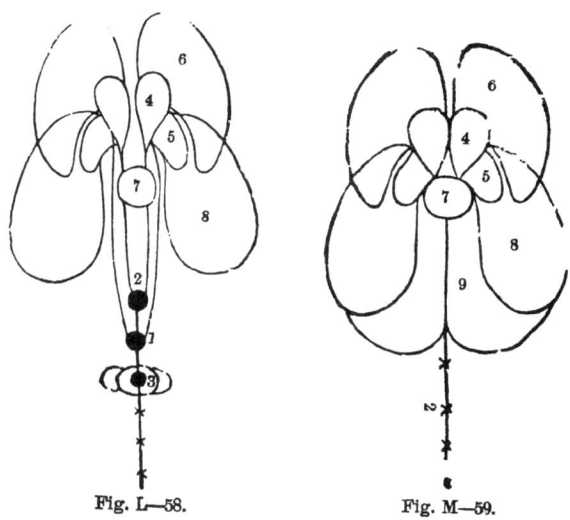

Fig. L—58.   Fig. M—59.

A comparison of the human brain six months before birth, with the brains of animals, shows that at that time it only equals the degree of development which is permanent in reptiles.

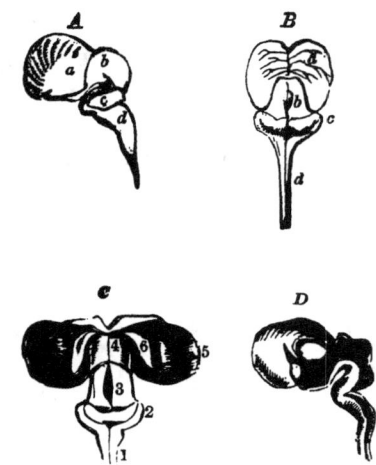

Fig. 60.

FIGURE 60. Four views of a human brain, six months before the time of birth. *A*, Side view. *a*, Cerebrum. *b*, Optic ganglion. *c*, Cerebellum. *d*, Oblongata. *B*, Top view — references same as *A*.

C, Top view, with the hemispheres reflected, or pushed back, to show the sub-cerebral organs. 1, Oblongata. 2, Cerebellum. 3, Optic ganglion. 4, Thalamus. 5, Cerebrum. 6, Striatum, imbedded in the cerebrum, as it is in birds.

D, A longitudinal section in the median line, showing that the spinal cord and oblongata are hollow, as in fishes. It will be observed that the cord has the appearance of being bent up in a serpentine manner, as if to shorten and accommodate itself to the small space into which it is crowded. We can easily understand from this, that the parts in the back and front of the human brain are crowded out of their natural places, to make them occupy a shorter skull.

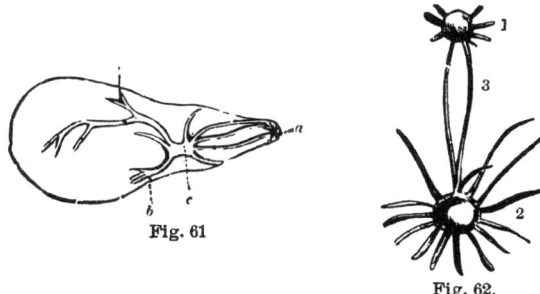

Fig. 61

Fig. 62.

FIGURE 61.   Ascidia mammillata, an animal quite as low in the scale of progression as the oyster, and is essentially a mere stomach, into which food enters at the mouth, *a*, and if not used, passes out at *b ; c*, is the analogue of the oblongata of higher animals.   Below the oblongata, *is d*, a stomach-nerve, or vagus. Above is a mouth-nerve of taste and motion.

FIGURE 62.   Crab-fish.   1, is the cephalic or ganglion of the senses, which is situated above the throat.   2, Is a ganglion in which all the nerves relating to locomotion centre.   This is situated in the body, and connected with the ganglion, 1, in the head, by two slender nerves, 3, which, with the ganglia, constitute an oblong nervous ring.   The ganglion, 2, is, in effect, a whole spinal cord concentrated into one aconscious ganglion, which surpasses in size the conscious centre, or oblongata, 1, in the head.

The spider has a similar nervous system ; but animals which are lower in the scale of organization, such as the caterpiller, earthworm, and centipede, have a great number of spinal centres, and limbs, which produce the same results in a much less powerful, concentrated and economical manner.

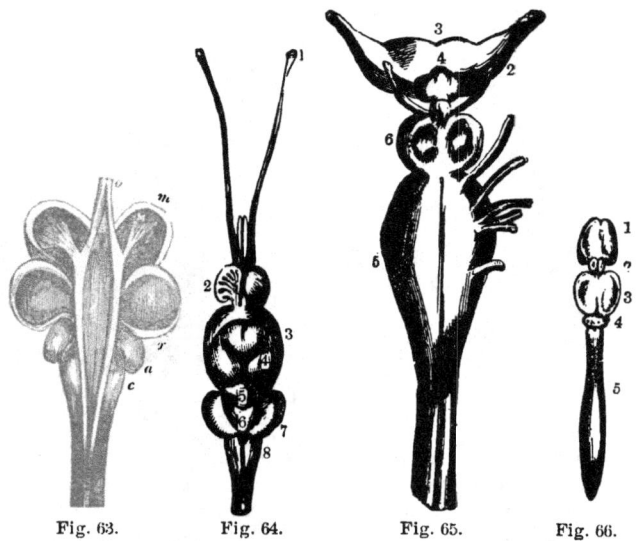

Fig. 63. Fig. 64. Fig. 65. Fig. 66.

FIGURE 63. Brain of a codfish, dissected to show the continuation of the spinal cord up into the oblongata, and then still further up, to unite with the olfactory nerve. *o*, Olfactory nerve. *m*, Striatum. *x*, Optic ganglion. *a*, Cerebellum. *c*, Oblongata. *s*, Spinal cord.

FIG. 64. Brain of the carp, seen from above. 1, Potentive ganglion on olfactory nerve. 2, Striatum. 3, Optic ganglion. 4, Ganglion, function unknown. 5, Cerebellum. 6. Auditory ganglion. 7, The ganglion of the vagus. This fish is remarkable for the distinctness of its potentive ganglia on its nerves of special sense, and yet its striatum and cerebellum are very small. 8, Oblongata. *s*, Spinal cord.

FIG. 65. Brain of the skate, seen on its under surface. 1, Olfactory nerve, terminating in, 2, the claustrum, or lateral part of the striatum. 3, The striatum proper. Below 4, is the pituitary gland, which is very large in fishes. 5 Is the oblongata, which is very large, compared with the rest of the brain. 6, Optic ganglion.

FIG. 66. Brain of a tadpole, or young frog, from Grant. 1, Striatum. 2, A small thalamus. 3, Optic ganglion. 4, The cerebellum, which is very small. 5, Spinal cord.

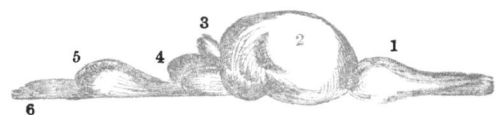

Fig. 67.

FIG. 67. Side view of the brain of the turtle. 1, Olfactory nerve, with a large potentive ganglion on it. 2, Cerebrum, in which is inclosed a striatum and thalamus. 3, Pituitary gland. 4, Optic ganglion. 5, Cerebellum. 6, A part of the oblongata.

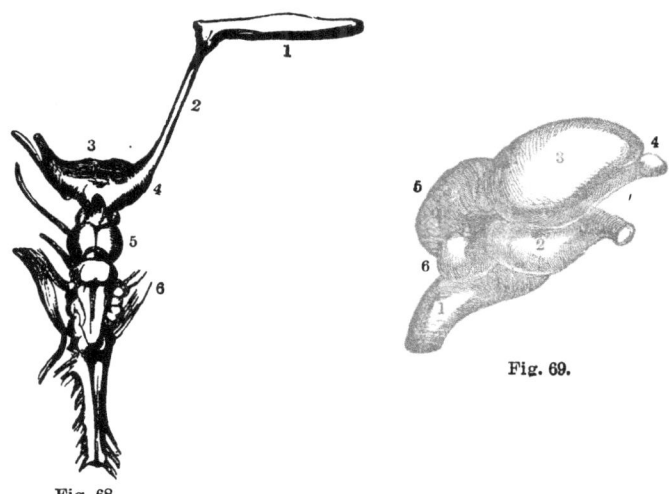

Fig. 69.

Fig. 68.

FIGURE 68 The brain of a skate, removed from the skull, and seen from above. 1, Potentive ganglion of the olfactory nerve. 2, Olfactory nerve. 3, Striatum, or brain. 4, Claustrum, or lateral part of the brain. 5, Optic potentive ganglion. 6. Potentive ganglion of the vagus, or stomach nerve.

FIGURE 69. Side view of the brain of a bird. 1, Oblongata. 2, Optic ganglion. 3, Cerebrum, which conceals a striatum and thalamus. 4, Olfactory potentive ganglion. 5, Verm of the cerebellum.

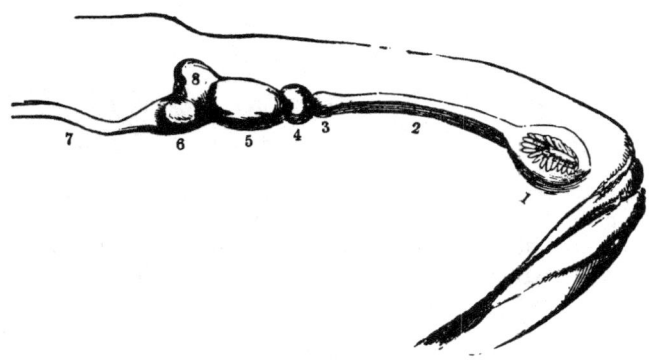

Fig. 70.

FIGURE 70. Brain of a perch, side view. 1, The impressorium of the olfactory nerve. 2, The olfactory nerve. 3, The potentive ganglion of the olfactory nerve. 4, The striatum, or brain. 5, The potentive ganglion of the optic nerve. 6, The oblongata. 7, The spinal cord. 8, The cerebellum.

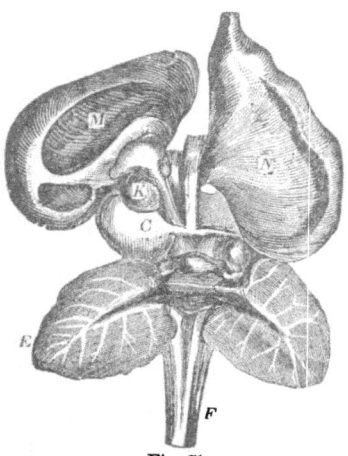

Fig. 71.

FIGURE 71. Dissection of the brain of a goose, which does not differ essentially from that of any other bird. On the right side

N, is seen a fan-like radiation of fibres, which are supposed to be rudiments of the fornix. On the left side, *M*, are the striatum and the claustrum, so enormously large as to constitute most of the cerebrum. *K*, Is the small thalamus, which does not appear to be connected with the cerebrum; yet, in man, more than half of the cerebrum seems to be developed from the thalamus. *C*, Optic ganglion. *E*, Cerebellum. *F*, Oblongata.

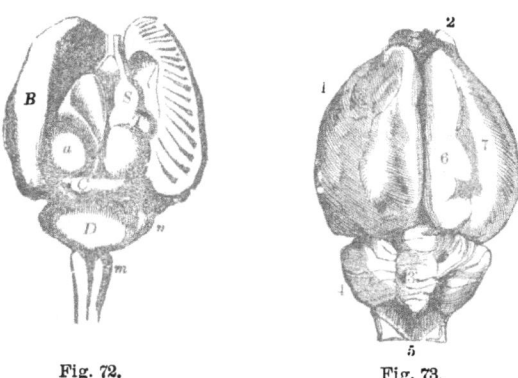

Fig. 72.   Fig. 73.

FIGURE 72. Top view of the brain of a squirrel, the upper portion of the cerebrum being cut away, to show the parts below. *S*, Striatum. *T*, Thalamus. *a*, Anterior optic ganglion. *C*, Posterior. *D*, Verm of the cerebellum. *n*, Lobulus of the cerebellum. *m*, Oblongata. Here it will be observed, that the striatum is small, and the thalamus is comparatively large.

FIGURE 73. Top view of the brain of a beaver. 1, Region of Constructiveness, where the beaver is full and the rabbit is narrow. 2, Olfactory ganglion. 3, Verm of the cerebellum. 4, Lobulus of the cerebellum. 5, Oblongata. 6, 7, Between these figures is a small rudimentary convolution, indicating lateral pressure.

It is an interesting fact, in regard to both animals and men, that, when they change from a pastoral to a mechanical mode of life, or from the condition of wanderers to that of citizens and builders, they become wider in the temporal region. Ethnologists have lately made the observation, that the first inhabitants of England were not mechanics nor warriors; and their skulls were narrow. The next were warriors, and their skulls are wide at the base behind; those of the present industrial ruling race are wide above in front. Phrenology will give a solution of all these various problems, and I commend it to the consideration of those learned ethnologists to whom we are indebted for these curious observations.

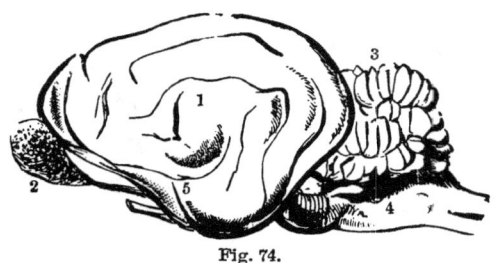

Fig. 74.

FIGURE 74. Side view of the brain of a common cat. 1, Cerebrum, showing simple convolutions, or folds in the brain, such as would be naturally produced by pressure from side to side, and afterwards from front to back. 2, Olfactory ganglion. 3, Verm of the cerebellum. 4, Oblongata. 5, Fissure of Sylvius.

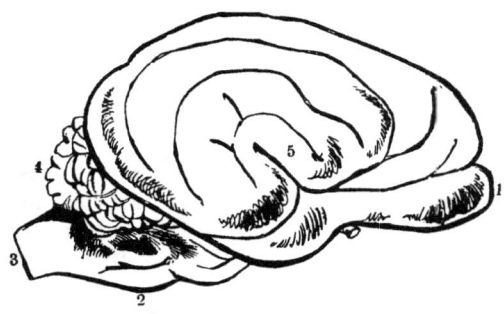

Fig. 75.

FIGURE 75. Side view of the brain of a fox. 1, Olfactory ganglion. 2, Oblongata. 3, Spinal cord. 4, Cerebellum. 5, Cerebrum. The brain of the fox is very much like that of the cat, but larger, and a little more complicated in its convolutions.

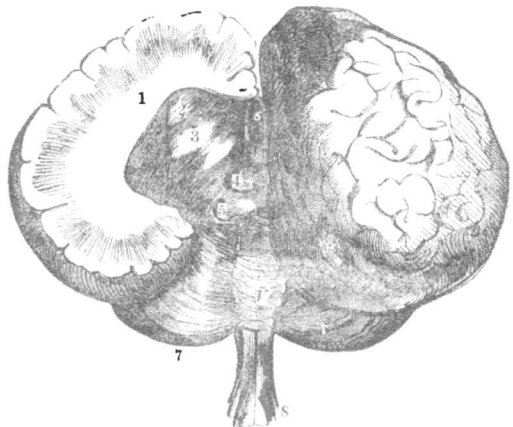

Fig. 76.

FIGURE 76.   Top view of the brain of the porpoise.   1, On the left side, the upper part of the cerebrum is cut away, to expose the sub-cerebral parts beneath.   2, The striatum, which is comparatively small.   3, The thalamus, which is very large.   4 5, The optic ganglia — the posterior, 5, being the larger.   The verm of the cerebellum, V, is exceedingly small, while the lobulus, 7, is very large.   8, Spinal cord.   This animal, and indeed, all the cetacea, are remarkable for the great size of the thalamus and cerebellum, and the deficiency of the posterior lobes.

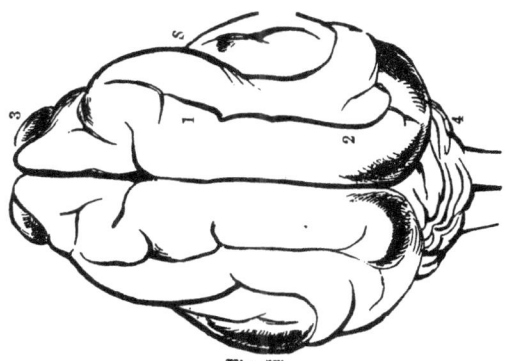

Fig. 77.

FIGURE 77. Top view of the fox's brain. *S*, Fissure of Sylvius. 1, 2, Longitudinal convolutions — the transverse convolutions being merely rudimentary. 3, Olfactory ganglion. 4, Cerebellum.

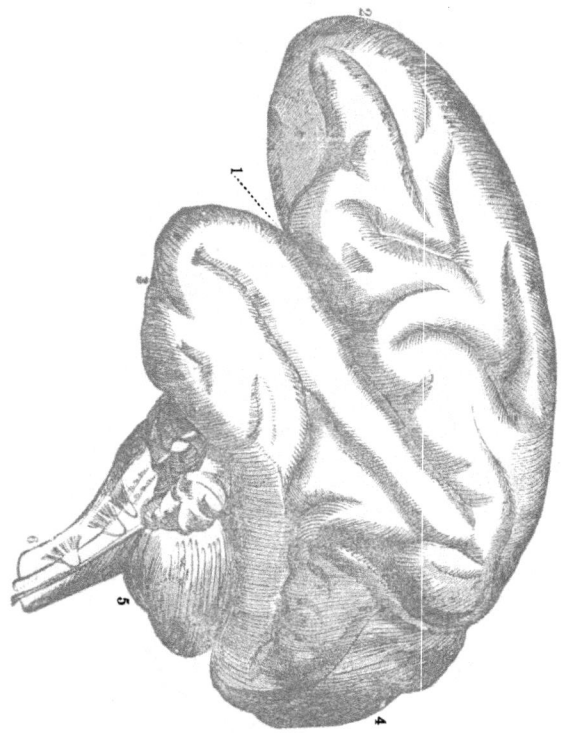

Fig. 78.

FIGURE 78. Side view of the brain of a baboon. 1, Fissure of Sylvius. 2, Anterior lobe. 3, Middle lobe, enormously developed. 4, Posterior lobe, developed beyond the cerebellum. 5, Cerebellum. 6, Oblongata.

EVOLUTION OF THE MIND AND ITS ORGANS.

Naturalists are at the present time divided into two parties upon questions relating to the origin of species, and especially the human species. One party, of which Mr. Charles Darwin is the most distinguished representative, point to a vast number of facts which tend to the conclusion that all animals now existing are the natural descendants of a lower species that previously existed. The other party consists, mostly, of those who are influenced by theological considerations. They do not deny the essential facts brought forward by the Darwinians, but they demur to their conclusions. They say, " It is very true that upon comparing all the vertebrate animals, the higher seem to be mere modifications of the lower, but upon a thorough examination of the subject, no evidence can be found that, in a single instance, one undoubted species of plants or animals is the offspring of any other species. The facts that seem to indicate such descent or evolution of species, can be best explained by assuming that several plans or types existed in the Divine Mind, upon which it was preordained that all animals should be formed. One of these was the vertebrate plan. Each distinct species of vertebrates that now exists, or ever did exist, was separately and miraculously evolved from the mind of the Creator in a manner which the human intellect cannot comprehend. The evolutionists admit that there is no direct proof of the production of one species by another during the short period of human history, but they insist that during the vast eons of geology the slight variations that are known to occur in species would so accumulate as to produce all the differences that now exist among vertebrates. The first scientist who distinctly taught this doctrine was Lamark, a distinguished French naturalist, and a cotemporary of Gall and Cuvier. In 1848 an anonymous author published " *The Vestiges of the Natural History of Creation*," in which, with unimportant modifications, he advocated, with great ability, the doctrine of Lamark. This work produced a remarkable sensation both in Britain and America, but it was denounced in severe terms by the leading naturalists, and especially by Professor Agassiz, who declared that no one would advocate such a doctrine unless he were ignorant of the very elements of natural history. In 1850, I published " Phreno-Geology," in which I advocated the same doctrine as that since promulgated by Mr. Darwin, excepting that I assumed that Divine Providence superintended the *natural* evolution of organized beings. Although the work was stereotyped, only five hundred copies were issued. Dr. Jarvis, the histriographer of the Episcopal church, in a letter to my friend and pastor, the Rev. Orange Clark, declared that a man who advocated the gradual and progressive creation of the brain from one geological age to another, was only fit for a mad-house. My publisher, Mr. James Munroe, of Boston, who lived in Cambridge, consulted with Professor Agassiz, and he denounced the idea in still stronger language. He asserted, what was then undoubtedly true, that no respectable naturalist in Europe or America held the views of Lamark, or any modification of them; and my personal friends objected to the work, as impolitic, for the reason that

the religious portion of the community would become
prejudiced against me, and regard me as an infidel.
The result was that I boxed up the stereotype plates
and have them still in my possession. A quarter of
a century has passed since then, and brought with it
remarkable changes. Dr. Gill, of Washington, in a
speech made at the meeting of the American Association for the Advancement of Science, in 1874,
stated that three-fourths of the naturalists now living
are advocates of natural evolution. I propose, in a
short time, to issue a second edition of Phreno-Geol-
cgy, and submit it once more to the judgment of the
world.

I do not propose in this treatise to discuss this
question, and will merely remark that the order of
arrangement and super-addition of the organs of man,
both bodily and mental, is in perfect accordance with
the great law of evolution — the existence of which
both parties admit — and concerning which they
only differ as to the manner in which it has been
executed. There is no positive proof that man has
descended from a lower species of creatures, but it is
nevertheless true that the whole constitution of man
is built up by several series of super-additions or
specializations, that are powerfully suggestive of the
idea of a natural evolution and progressive development.

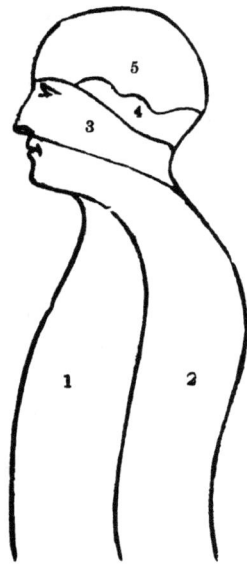

Fig. 79.

The diagram, Figure 79, illustrates this hypothesis in a very general manner. The lowest space (1) contains the organs of those functions which man performs in common with all other organized beings, both plants and animals. They may be denominated the vegetative organs. In the second space (2) are the superadded organs which man possesses in common with the very lowest animals. In the third space (3) are the additions possessed by the highest of those animals that are destitute of proper brains, but have otherwise well developed nervous systems. In the fourth space (4) are the rudimentary brains of fishes, the first created vertebrates. In the fifth space (5) are the cerebral organs of the higher animals, including man. If we wish to carry this analysis further, we must resort to phrenology.

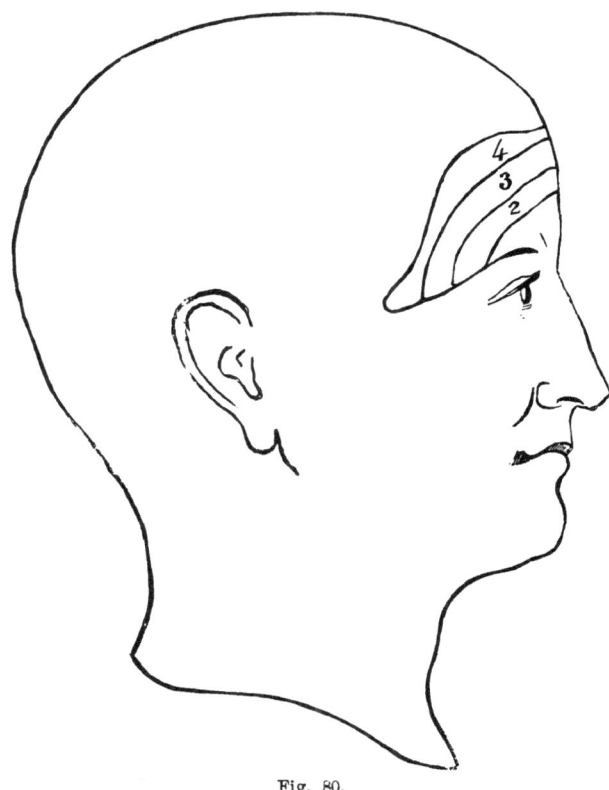

Fig. 80.

Figure 80 is made to convey an idea of the manner in which the Intellectual organs were developed by superadditions. We may assume that the lowest division (1) was possessed by fishes and reptiles, and that the next two (2 and 3) were superadded in higher animals. The highest (4) is peculiar to man. Those who are most developed in the fourth division excel in profound mathematical and philosophical reasoning.

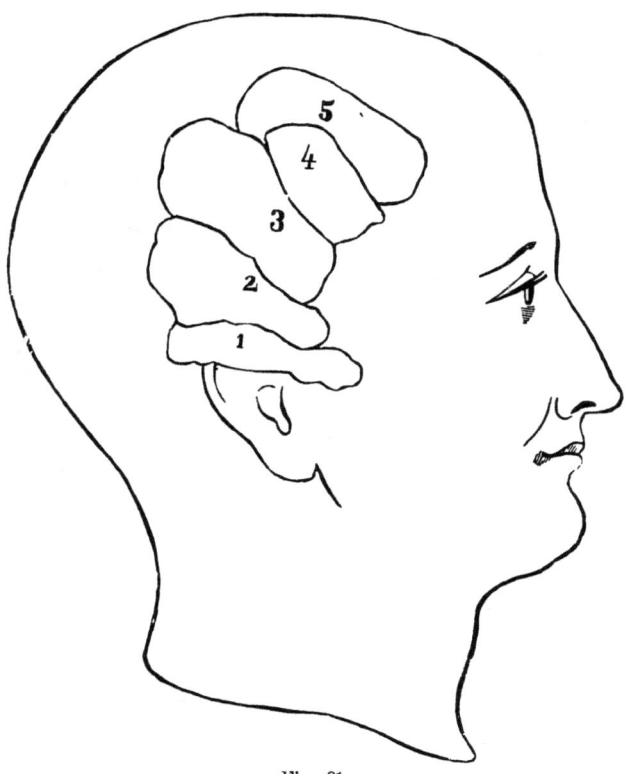

Fig. 81.

Figure 81 represents the Ipseal class of organs and is intended to illustrate the idea that the ranges or strata of organs were superadded in the order of the numbers; 1 is the corporeal range; 2, the belligerent; 3, the prudential; 4, the industrial, and 5, the improving or human range.

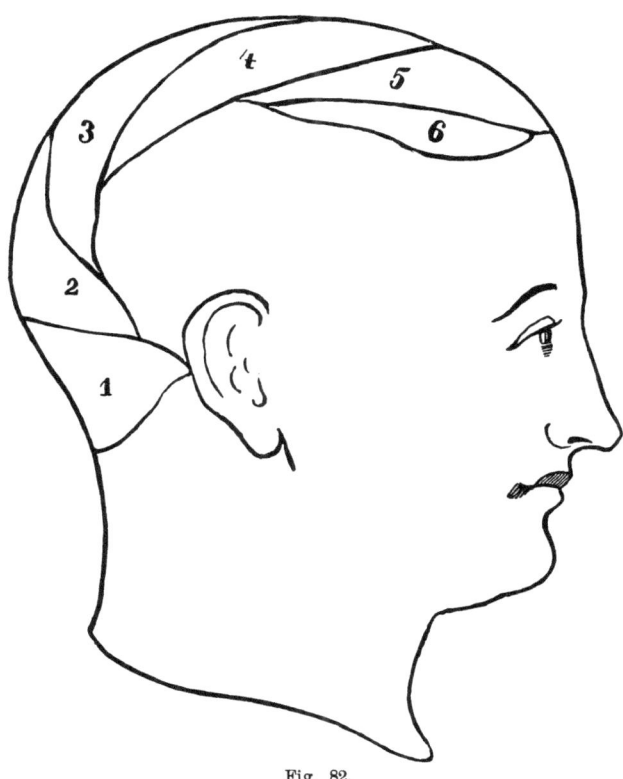

Fig. 82.

Figure 82 is designed to give an idea of the manner in which the Social propensities received additions during the successive geologic periods; (1) is the cerebellum, or little brain. In fishes and reptiles, the first created vertebrates, the cerebellum and the striatum, or anterior lobe of the cerebrum, are two separate masses — one situated in the anterior and the other in the posterior part of the skull. As the brain continued to grow, its additions were made to the

anterior portion in such a manner as to make it expand
laterally and backward until it covered the cerebellum, without uniting with it. This is probably the
reason why the cerebellum is now separate from the
cerebrum. In birds the anterior and middle lobes
are one mass, or only partially divided, and the thalamus is another distinct and separate mass, which
afterwards, in higher animals, coalesced with the other
lobes and gave birth to the posterior lobe (2).

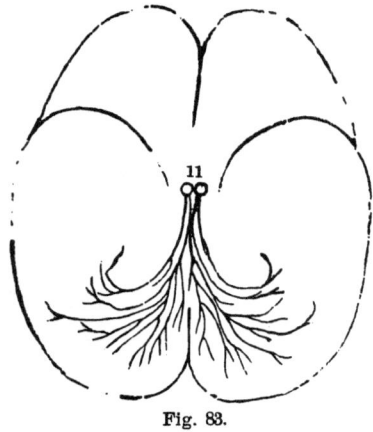

Fig. 83.

Figure 83 is a diagram made to represent the manner in which
the fibres from the right and left thalami — two distinct masses
—develop backward to form the posterior lobe.

Anatomists and phrenologists have often been puz-
zled to account for the fact that the cerebellum is a
distinct little brain by itself. If these views are correct,
comparative anatomy furnishes the probable explanation. The brain as it developed from before, backward
(Fig. 82), reached the occiput (2, Fig. 82) and then
turned upward as it continued to develop until 3, 4, 5

were added, and I have no doubt some degree of all these are possessed by the higher animals; but the last development (6 Fig. 82) is certainly possessed by man and manifested in a manner which elevates him vastly above any other creature. This is the part of the brain that is so deficient in the lowest savages. It is an interesting fact that the highest Intellectuals, Ipseals and Socials come together at the upper lateral part of the forehead.

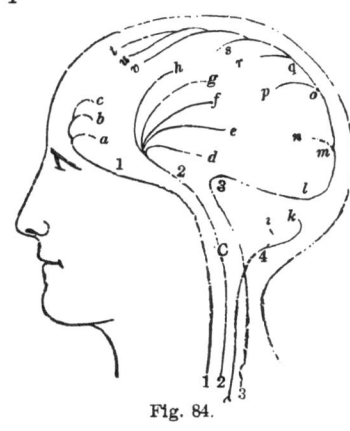

Fig. 84.

Figure 84 is a diagram made to express, in a general manner, my conception of the manner and order in which the different parts of the brain were developed.

This theory of the creation of man by superadditions is of great practical value in enabling us to understand that in some idiots and in a great many semi-idiots and natural born criminals the development of the higher organs has been arrested, in

1, In the oblongata, proceeds to 1 in the brain, to form the striatum, and then to *a b c* in the forehead, to constitute the intellectual class of phrene-organs.

2, In the oblongata, proceeds to 2 in the brain, to form the claustrum, or middle lobe, and then to *d e f g h*, the five ranges, or strata of Ipseal organs. 3 in the oblongata, proceeds to 3, the thalamus, and then to *l m n o p q r s t u v*, the social phrene-organs of the cerebrum.

4, in the oblongata, proceeds to 4 in the cerebellum, to form the rhomboideum, and then to *i* and *k*, the lowest social organs.

consequence of ante-natal causes, and that special and extraordinary pains should be taken in their education and moral training. We can also understand that the higher organs are in some cases developed late in life, and in the mean time the individual acts like a mere wild animal in some respects, and like a stupid animal in others, and stands in continual need of a guardian and teacher until near the age of thirty.

THE POSTERIOR LOBES.

An Objection Answered.

A very plausible objection has been made by Dr. Wm. Carpenter, of London, to Phrenology, drawn from the comparison of the brains of different classes of animals with each other and with that of man. Some animals possess only the anterior, and others only the anterior and middle lobes of the cerebrum, and are destitute of the posterior lobes, in which phrenologists locate parental love; yet these animals, thus lacking in the organ, are not wanting in manifestations of the affection. Birds, porpoises, and

C, Conscious centre, or place where the sensory nerves and the mental organs all converge, to communicate with the mind.

This figure illustrates the idea that the phrene-organs of the cerebrum are developed in three classes, and that each class is progressive, rising and branching like a tree, each higher branch being of a more general character, and adapting its possessor to a more extensive and complicated state of society. The figure is also a perfect illustration of the idea that the direction of the development of the Intellectuals and Ipseals is first forward, then upward, and then backward; but the Socials develop, first forward, then backward, then upward, and forward again, following the same course as the cerebral band, or fornix and ourlet, and that the whole head is thus made of a convenient form.

rabbits, are careful of their young, but have no parental lobe in their brains. Dr. Carpenter remarks, " this seems fatal to Phrenology." To one but slightly acquainted with comparative anatomy, it will very naturally seem so; but I am surprised that Dr. Carpenter does not understand that it is really no proper objection at all. The following remarks will, I hope, make the matter clear and fairly remove the objection.

1. The very lowest animal known to naturalists is that of the amoeba, a mere minute mass of jelly. It cannot be said to have any particular permanent form, but it has the ability to assume almost any imaginable shape, according to circumstances. It can protrude a portion of itself forward in the form of a limb; it can thus produce a dozen limbs; it can spread itself out into a thin sheet, and envelope and absorb what it wants, and then change its form again. This creature occasionally manifests a degree of mechanical skill that is not surpassed by the beaver, and not even equalled by uncivilized man. We learn an important lesson here, and that is, that nature is capable of manifesting superior mental qualities without any *special* organs whatever that can be perceived. Next observe the spider; he has nerves but no cerebrum nor cerebellum, no thalamus nor striatum. He has something that appears to be analagous to the human oblongata, and that is the nearest approach to any thing like a brain, yet he surpasses the beaver in mechanical skill, the fox in cunning, the monkey in dexterity, and the tiger in malicious cruelty. He surpasses all animals that have brains, excepting man. What is the explanation? The answer is obvious; the spider has the organs of his mental faculties, call

them by what name you will, located somewhere in
his body, in his nerves, or in his ganglionic masses.
He has no brains; no animal has them except fishes,
reptiles, birds and mammals. Fishes have what is
called a brain, but it is a mere bud of the anterior
lobe of a brain, and that only. They have what appears to be the homologue or equivalent of what in
man is called the striatum, and from which the anterior lobe is developed. There is not in all nature a
more interesting lesson than that which is conveyed
by a comparison of the animals that have no proper
brains with the fishes, the lowest of those that have
them; and then a comparison of these with the next
class above them, the reptiles; and these again with
the birds that are one step higher still; and then the
birds with some of the lowest animals of the next
higher class, the mammals, such as porpoises and rabbits; then higher mammals—cats, foxes, dogs, horses,
elephants, apes, men.

The lesson that we learn is this, that the Creator
commenced by producing animals with mental faculties diffused throughout the body, and without any
special organs; next he introduced animals with nervous systems of the body, some of which are almost
as complicated and perfect as that of man, but to
these no brains are added. Whether these brainless
creatures have their mental organs diffused throughout the body or concentrated in their nerves and ganglia, we do not know; but there is no doubt that the
mass of nervous matter nearest the head is analagous
to the oblongata of man, and is their conscious centre.
When we examine the brain of a fish, we find that it
is only the rudiment or bud of one class of mental

organs, the Directives or Intellectuals. The propensities of the fish are not represented in its brain, but
are still retained in the body. Now, if we look at the
brain of the reptile, we see that it is like that of the
fish, but no longer a mere bud, for an anterior lobe
has developed out of the front part of it, and has, (for
want of room in front,) turned over backward, like the
collar or cape of a coat. Now look at the brain of a
bird, and we find that the lobe or cape has not only
developed further backward, but it has a latteral
offshoot, which in man is the middle lobe, and contains the Ipseal or self-relative class of propensities;
still there is no posterior lobe to represent the social
propensities; these are still retained in the body. Let
us examine not only the brain of the bird, but of the
lowest species of the class next above them, and
we find in these no posterior lobe, but we find a small
body called the thalamus, situated behind the striatum, just as the body of a bird is behind its spread
wings. This thalamus is very large in all those animals that have anterior or middle lobes largely developed, but are destitute of posterior lobes. In birds,
in whales, and in porpoises, it is *very* large, and probably performs, in some degree, the office of a posterior
lobe; for when we come to the animals that have the
posterior lobe well developed, we find it growing out
of this very thalamus, just as the branches of a tree
grow out of its trunk. Let us continue this investigation further. The posterior lobe is developed back-
wards in some monkeys more (relatively) than in man.
And now we learn a lesson from Phrenology that we
could not learn from any other source, and that is
that the posterior lobe is devoted to the lowest social

functions, and that in the highest animals, and especially in man, these social organs, that commenced
their development in the back of the head, continue
upward along the middle line, and then forward, producing the higher governing and conforming groups.
Strongly confirmatiory of this explanation is the fact
that the human brain, about six months before birth,
has only the anterior or intellectual lobe developed.
(See Fig. 60.) It continues to develope more and more
backward until, at birth, the posterior is the largest
part of the brain. Still the brain is low, especially
in front; the highest organs are not fully developed,
and will not be until after puberty.

PART SECOND.

THE HEART.

PHYSIOLOGY OF THE EMOTIONS.

AND THEIR PROPER AND USEFUL INFLUENCES UPON THE HEART AND OTHER VITAL ORGANS.

It has long been known that the emotions produce powerful effects upon the heart, but hitherto these effects have been regarded by physiologists as altogether abnormal and injurious. I propose to demonstrate that this idea is erroneous, and that the effects of the emotions upon those organs are functional, normal, and highly important. That the undue excitement of the emotions sometimes produces injurious effects is certain, but the same may be said with equal truth of every species of functional excess. Physiologists seem to have assumed that the emotions should normally confine their operations to the brain and the voluntary muscles. If they occasionally intruded their forces within the sphere allotted to the involuntary and vital organs, such intrusion was regarded as mischievous and deranging. They do not appear to have had any idea of the important fact that *the emotions influence the vital organs to compel them to conform to the exigences of the mind.*

(203)

There are two classes of emotions — the exalting and the depressing; one class tends to impel the body to act with energy, and the other to restrain or moderate its action. When an exalting emotion — anger for example — is excited, it not only impels the voluntary organs to act with uncommon vigor, but it influences the heart to increase the supply of blood to sustain the exertion. On the contrary, when a depressing emotion is excited, such as fear, it not only restrains the *voluntary* organs, but it influences the heart and other vital organs in such a manner as to diminish the vital action, and the circulation of the blood.

PRELIMINATION.

It cannot be fairly objected to this statement, that the increased vital action is caused by the uncommon voluntary exertion which is made when the emotions are excited, for in all cases the change in the vital action *precedes* the exertion. For example, when anger is excited, the blood rushes to the limbs and face instantly, and before the *mind* is made up whether to exert the limbs or the tongue in a contest or not. The influence of the emotions upon the vital organs is always of a preliminary and preparatory character. I know of no word in our language that expresses the idea I wish to convey with precision, I shall therefore take the liberty to vary the word preliminary, to make *prelimination* and *preliminating*, and use them to characterize the preparatory influences of the emotions upon the vital organs. The word *vasso moter* has been applied to the nerves that increase the circulation in the capillaries when certain emotions are excited, but that term cannot properly be applied to the restraining or inhibitory effects produced upon the blood vessels by the depressing emotions; and, besides, it does not convey the idea that prelimination does, which is, that the emotional influence is in all cases such as to prepare the body, and put it into proper condition to perform the voluntary actions that may follow.

Before we do anything intentionally, we think of doing it; this is an *intellectual* process; in the next instant the action of the vital organs is changed in such a manner as to prepare the body for what is to follow, this is an *emotional* process; then we do what we intended to do, and this last is a *volitional* process. Of these three processes, the two first are preliminary to the last.

RELATIONS OF THE BODY AND MIND.

There appears to be, at the present time, a strong disposition manifested by physiologists to acquire more correct ideas concerning the relations of the mind and body to each other. Until very lately the opinion has prevailed that mind, especially the higher faculties, were so entirely independent of the material organs that they could exist and perform their functions when separated from those organs. The body was regarded as the temporary prison of the mind, from which it was only released by death. Shakspeare expresses this idea:

> " Look how the floor of heaven
> Is thick inlaid with patines of bright gold;
> There's not the smallest orb which thou beholdest
> But in his motion like an angel sings,
> Still quiring to the young-eyed cherubims:
> Such harmony is in immortal souls;
> But *whilst this muddy vesture of decay*
> *Doth grossly close us in, we cannot hear it.'*

In common language, when a man dies his soul is described as "taking its flight." Byron inquires:

> " When coldness wraps this suffering clay,
> Ah, whither strays the immortal mind ? "

What will be the condition of the mind after death, can only be learned by Divine Revelation; the eye of science cannot see beyond the material world. The scientist knows nothing of mind except by experience and observation, and that is all limited to this life and this world. Let those who doubt the absolute dependence of the body and mind upon each other during life, consider the following facts:

1. All the organs at the base of the brain are so directly related to the bodily functions, that they evidently must have been expressly designed by the Creator to serve the body.

2. It is safe to assert that mankind, as a whole, spend nineteen-twentieths of the time of their lives in exertions of body and mind to support and gratify the body.

3. The most powerful and constant impressions made upon the mind, are those that proceed from the body and relate to its wants.

4. All the good as well as evil deeds of mankind are done by means of the body.

5. The mind and all its faculties is governed by physiological laws.

6. The brain is more dependent upon the blood than is any part of the constitution. This is made evident by the fact that the brain of man is only one-fortieth of the whole constitution, by weight, and yet it receives one-sixth of all the blood, instead of merely one-fortieth.

7. If from any cause — bad air, bad food, poison, bad digestion, intemperance, or inherited scrofula — the blood is poor in quality or deficient in quantity, the mind suffers in consequence *much more* than the body does.

8. If, in youth, while the body is growing, the brain is very large and much excited, it robs the body of its needed share of blood and thus ruins the health.

9. If the brain is very small, or is malformed, the mind is imperfectly manifested.

THE NERVES.

Before proceeding farther with this inquiry, I will give a brief description of the Nervous System. I do not propose to weary my readers with a long and tedious account of the anatomy of the nerves, for it cannot be expected that any but professional students will take the trouble to master the details and technicalities of the subject. But a general idea will be useful to all classes of readers, and especially to those who desire to acquire a clear understanding of the physiology of mesmerism and trance.

Under the general term "Nervous System," is included all the nerves, and also the brain; but as I have described the brain in another place, in this section I shall confine the term to the nerves proper.

The nerves are, in some respects, like errand-boys, who are of no special importance themselves, and derive all their dignity from the masters whom they serve. All nerves perform one and the same function; they are the mediums through which dispatches are sent to and from important organs; this being the case, if we wish to learn the function of any particular nerve, we must inquire concerning the functions of the organs which employ it, and to and from which its messages are transmitted.

NERVE SUBSTANCES.

The word *nerve* literally signifies a string or cord. The nerves received this name from their appearance before their uses were known.

The substances of which the nerves are composed are found in three forms:

1. *Tubular Fibres.* These are small, white tubes, which inclose a dusky gray substance; the material of which the tubes are composed is called " the white substance of Schwan," it having first been described by an anatomist of that name; the internal gray substance is called the *axis*, to distinguish it from the tube. Around the tube is a delicate membrane. Careful observations, by the aid of the microscope, tend to the conclusion that the axis is the essential part of the nerve, and the conductor of the nervous influence. The membrane and the Schwan substance appear to be useful as mechanical protectors and insulators of the axis.

2. *Fine Gray Fibres*, without tubes, are found associated with white tubular fibres, and the present prevailing opinion is, that the gray fibres differ from the white only in being destitute of tubes or sheaths of Schwan substance. This opinion is confirmed by the fact, that, in some instances, the tubular fibres are without tubes at their extremities, where they are connected with delicate tissues. It is also found that the fine gray fibres, mostly, if not all, belong to the sympathetic system of nerves.

3. *Gray* vesicular neurine is nerve substance which is commonly found in masses, called ganglia, or knots, instead of being arranged in fibres. It is composed of granules, or small grains, in which are embedded a variable number of small cells, vesicles, or corpuscles; each corpuscle has a central nucleus, and each nucleus has a central nucleolus; in other words, there is a cell within a cell, and another within that.

The ganglionic-neurine is of a purple gray color, and it has, for that reason, been named the cineritious, or ashes-colored substance. It covers the brain to the depth of half or three-fourths of an inch, and for that reason it was anciently called the cortical, or bark-like substance. From its soft consistence it is sometimes denominated the gray pulp. It is now generally considered as the generator of the nervous force; and the fact that it contains a large number of minute blood-vessels, and also the fact that it is most abundant at the extremities of the sensory nerves, sustains the idea.

There is no evidence that nervous and electric influences are identical; but the nerves appear to transmit their forces in a manner analogous to that in which the telegraph wires operate; so also does the gray neurine appear to generate force from the blood, in a manner that must necessarily remind us of the galvanic battery. We are, therefore, justified in concluding that the nervous apparatus is similar to the galvanic, whether the two forces are identical or not.

Fig. 85.

Figure 85 represents a large nerve, consisting of many smaller nerves, wrapped up in a common cellular sheath. 1, The nerve. 2, A single cord, or fibre, drawn out from the rest.

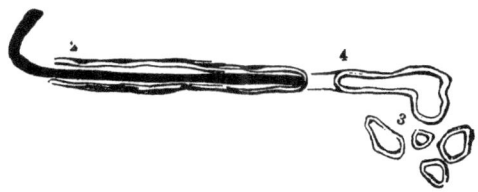

Fig. 86.

Figure 86 is intended to give an idea of the appearances occasionally seen in tubular fibres. 1, The axis, or conducting substance, projecting beyond the tube, and bent upward. 2, Membrane, and white sheath. 3, Parts of the contents of the tube escaped. 4, A part where the membranous tube is seen empty.

The size of the nerve fibres varies, and the same fibres do not preserve the same diameter through their whole length, being largest in their course within the trunks and branches of the nerves, in which the majority measure from one-two-thousandth to one-three-thousandth of an inch in diameter. As they approach the brain, or spinal cord, and generally, also, in the tissues in which they are distributed, they gradually become smaller. In the gray, or vesicular substance of the brain and spinal cord, they generally do not measure more than from one-ten-thousandth to one-fourteen-thousandth of an inch.

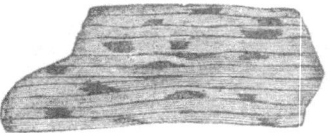

Fig. 87.

Figure 87, fine gray fibres, magnified three hundred and forty times, according to Professor Hanover.

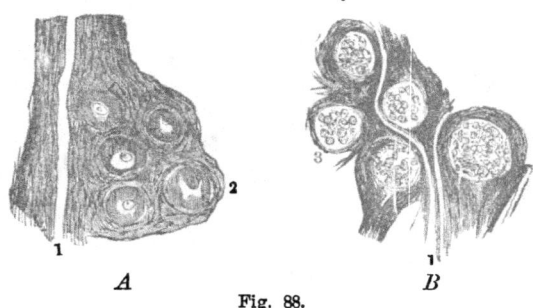

Fig. 88.

Figure 88, *A* and *B*. Magnified representations of ganglion corpuscles, imbedded in fine gray fibres, with several tubular fibres 1, 1, Tubular fibres passing through. *A* shows some of the corpuscles. *A*, 2, With nuclei containing nucleoli within them. *B* shows large corpuscles covered by capsules of granular cell nuclei.

A NERVOUS APPARATUS.

A nervous apparatus is sometimes called a nervous circle, and is composed of several parts, each of which performs a distinct function.

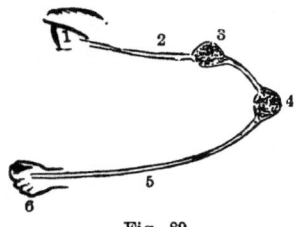

Fig. 89.

1. The impressorium is the place where an impression is made (1 Fig. 89.)

2. An afferent sensory or centripetal nerve, which transmits the impression to a central terminus or ganglion (4.)

3. A potentive or power-giving ganglion, which is found on nearly all nerves of sensation, and which *probably* have the power to act on the capillary bloodvessels, and increase the circulation in a nerve of sensation when it is exercised for a long time and needs sustaining.

5. A motor nerve.   6, A muscular terminus.

A commissure is a set of fibres that pass from one nervous apparatus on one side of the body or brain to a corresponding apparatus on the opposite side, in order to make the two sides act in concert.

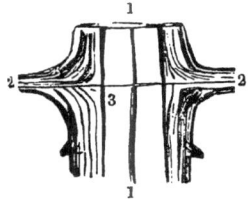

Fig. 90.

Figure 90. Magnified view of the upper surface of a segment of the spinal cord of an insect, (the spiro-streptus, from *Newport*,) to illustrate the nature of a commissure.   1, 1, The median line which divides the right side from the left.   2, 2, The nerves that are connected with the limbs.   3, The commissure, or set of nerve fibres that connect a limb of one side with a limb of the opposite side, so that an impression made on either side can communicate motion to the opposite.

DIVISION OF THE NERVOUS SYSTEM.

When treating of a complicated subject, a good general division, even if it is not quite precise, is oftentimes a great help to the understanding. The functions of the whole human constitution may be divided into those that relate to the external world, and those that relate to the internal (or vital) operations. To the external department belong the external senses, and the limbs and muscles of voluntary motion that enable us to act upon the things about us; to the internal belong all the organs concerned in the manufacture and circulation of the blood and the maintenance of mere vegetative life. The Nervous System, including all the nerves of the whole constitution, are susceptible of the same general division into those that relate to the external world, and those that relate to the internal vital organs.

Both of these systems of nerves have a common center in the oblongata, the organ of consciousness. One system, the external, is related to the intellect and the will; and the other, the internal, to the emotions alone. One system may be said to be related to the voluntary functions of the brain and the other to its involuntary. Man is so constituted that his brain cannot act upon the external without his will — his whole mind — deliberating upon and guiding the actions, but his brain acts upon his internal organs — his heart, arteries, stomach, liver and kidneys — without his will, but not without his consciousness. The reason of this distinction is that a *single* propensity can act *alone* upon the vital functions, independent of the intellect or the will, but it cannot act upon the external world without exciting consciousness, and thus giving notice of its intention.

Fig. 91 represents the main trunk of the external

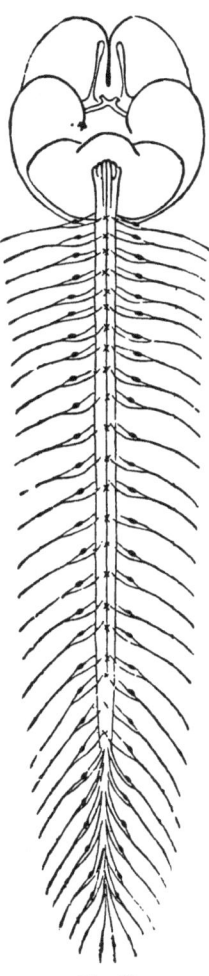

Fig. 91.

system of nerves, and Fig. 92 represents the main trunk of the internal system. Although the nerves of the two systems often intermingle, and seem confounded together, they are always perfectly distinct and independent of each other in function. I have introduced several engravings to show the positions and complications of the two systems; but the only fact that has an important bearing upon the subject of this treatise is that there is a distinct system of nerves, Fig. 92 and Fig. 93, (commonly called the sympathetic,) the office of which is to convey emotional influences from the propensities in the brain to the heart, and other vital organs in order to make them co-operate with the mind. I could not convey this idea in a satisfactory manner without giving a good general description of the whole nervous system.

Figure 91. Diagram representing an outline of an anterior view of the cranio-spinal axis.

The series of crosses in the middle line represent the spinal reflex, or aconscious centers.

There are thirty-one pairs of nerves connected with the spinal centres; each nerve has two roots—an anterior, or motor, and a posterior, or sensory root. Each posterior root has a swelling, or ganglion, upon it. The two roots unite to form a spinal nerve. Each root has fibres which connect it with the spinal cord, and which, when excited, act aconsciously; that is to say, they act independently of the mind. Beside these, each spinal nerve has other fibres that extend up and down through the spinal cord to and from the oblongata, to act in concert with the mind.

Figure 92. Side view of the intercord or sympathetic nerve, with its series of ganglia, extending from the lower part of the trunk of the body, where b, the ganglion impar, as it is called, is situated, to n, the ophthalmic ganglion, below which are o, spheno-palatine ganglion; p, otic, q, submaxillary. a, Superior cervical ganglion, remarkable for its connections with the vagus and the trigeminus, and its influence on the nutrition of the facial nerves of the senses. (See *Brown-Sequard's* Treatise.) $a\ d\ e$ These three ganglia are on the fibres that proceed from the brain to the heart and lungs, along with the vagus. The cords that proceed anteriorly from the ganglia to the semi-lunar ganglion, S, are called the splanchnic nerves. V is the situation of the stomach, and in connection with S, is the vital centre from which the whole organism is developed, and on which it depends. The nerves in the vicinity of S are called the solar plexus. m, Mesenteric plexus, an offset from S. R, Renal plexus. H, Hypogastric plexus. The mesh of fibres near the heart is called the cardiac plexus and pulmonary plexus, and relates to the heart and lungs. Between a and q are fibres of the pharyngeal plexus that relate to the vocal organs.

Figure 93. This diagram represents the intercords, or sympathetic nerves of the two sides, as drawn further apart than natural, to show the manner in which the nerves or cords, from the brain and from the ganglia converge to the middle line of the body, to form the prevertebral plexuses. No drawing that I have ever seen gives as just and clear an idea of the sympathetic system as this does; though of course the details are omitted.

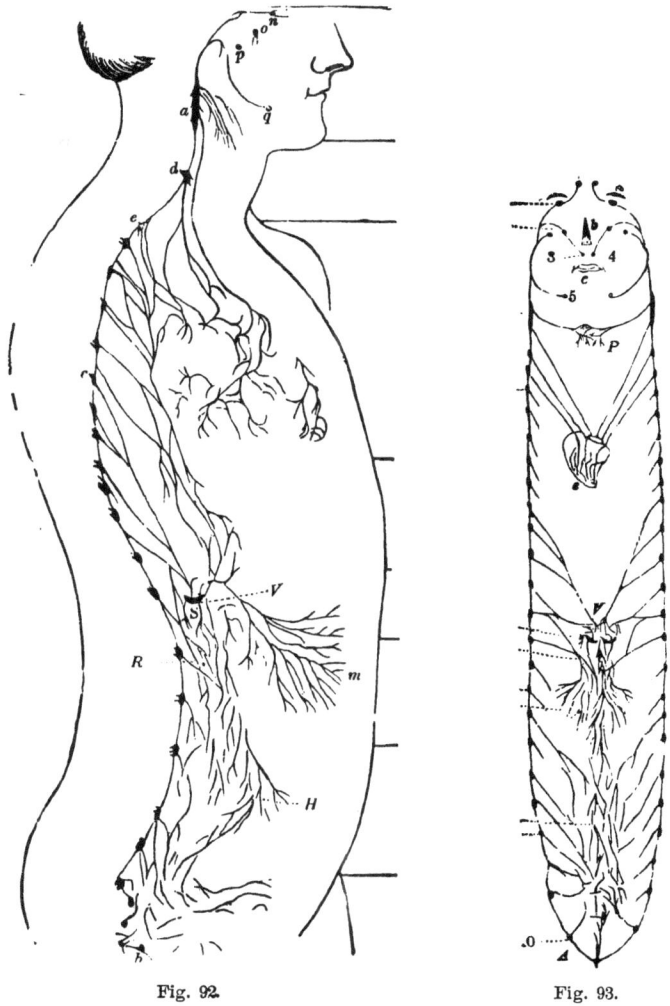

Fig. 92.   Fig. 93.

a, Place of the eye. *b*, Place of the nose. *c*, Place of the mouth. *d*, Gnnglion of Ribes, which is sometimes absent. 1, Ophthalmic ganglion. 2, Spheno-palatine ganglion. 3, Nasopalatine. 4, Otic. 5, Submaxillary. 6, Superior cervical. The two ganglia between 6 and 7 are the middle and lower cervical; and, from the three, it will be seen that branches proceed from each side to the heart, to form *e*, the cardiac plexus. Thus it can easily be understood that mental influences reach the heart through these three branches. From 7 to 8, the ganglia are called the thoracic; from 8 to 9, the lumbar; and from 9 to 10, the sacral. Below 10, in the centre, is the ganglion impar, in which the right and left intercords unite. *P* is the pharyngeal plexus, that supplies the throat. *V* Is the vital centre; and below it is *S*, the semi-lunar ganglion. *R*, The renal plexus. *m*, Mesenteric plexus. *H*, The hypo-gastric.

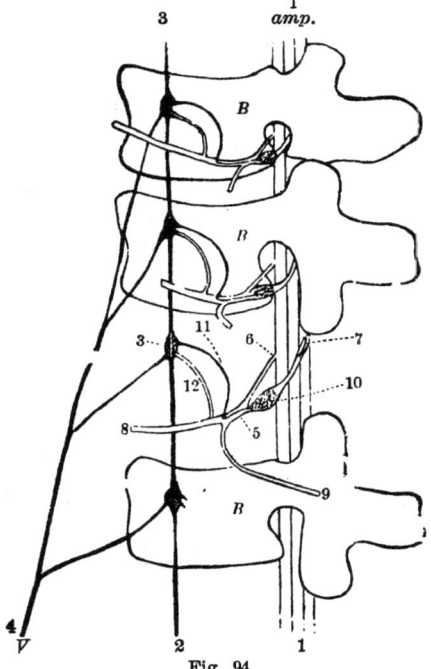

Fig. 94.

Figure 94. Diagram to show the connections of the spinal cord and its nerves, with the sympathetic intercord, and its branches. *B B B*, Three of the vertebral bones. One of the bones is left out, to show the connections of the nerves. 1, Spinal cord, extending through the vertebral canal. *a m p*, Anterior, middle, and posterior columns of the spinal cord. 2 2, Intercord. 3, One of the ganglia on the intercord. 4 *V*, Splanchnic nerves, proceeding to and from the brain, and from the series of ganglia to the viscera. 5, Short trunk of the spinal nerve. 6, Anterior, or motor, root of spinal nerve. 7, Posterior, or sensory root of spinal nerve. 8, Anterior branch of spinal nerve. 9, Posterior branch, going to be distributed to the back, without forming any connection with the intercord. 10, Ganglion on the posterior root of spinal nerve. 11 and 12, Short cords, through which the spinal and the sympathetic communicate fibres to each other.

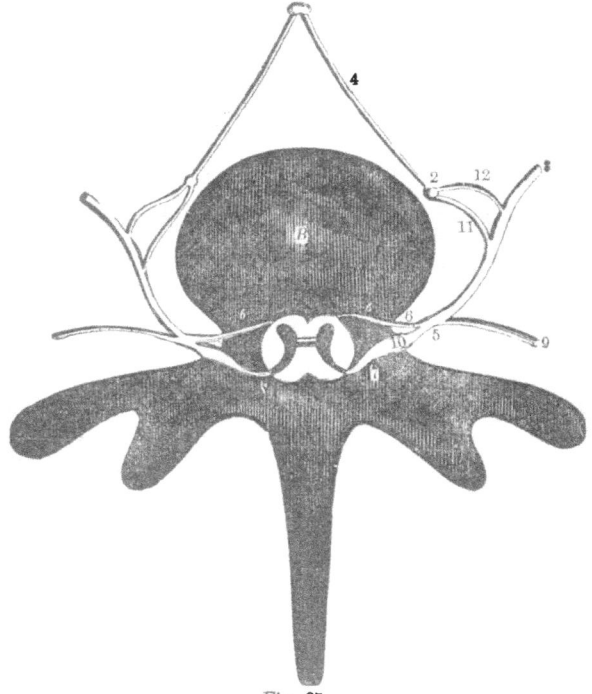

Fig. 95.

Figure 95. Ideal transverse section of the vertebra, spinal cord, intercord, vital centre, and spinal nerves, to show their connections. *B*, Bone of the vertebra. 1, Section of the spinal cord. 2, Section of the intercord. 4, Splanchnic nerve that connects the intercord with the vital centre. 5, Trunk of spinal nerve. 6, Anterior, or motor root of spinal nerve. 7, Posterior root, showing the place of its connection with the spinal cord. 10, Ganglion on posterior root. 8, Branch of spinal nerve, going to be distributed in front. 9, Posterior branch, going to be distributed to the back. 11 and 12, Short cords that connect the spinal cord with the intercord.

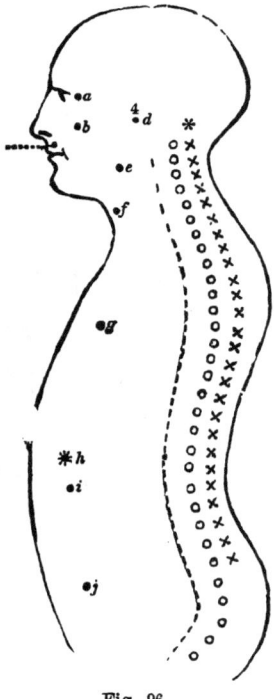

Fig. 96.

Figure 96. Diagram showing the principal nervous centres, their relative positions and arrangements. *The posterior series*— the crosses—represent the centres placed *in* the spinal cord; one centre being reckoned for each vertebra. The middle series, represented in the diagram by small circles, are the ganglia on the posterior roots of the spinal nerves. The real use of these are undetermined, but they are probably designed to act upon the capillary blood vessels, to regulate the circulation in the nerves of sensation, increasing it when the nerves have extraordinary labor to perform. I do not believe that any ganglia are found on any nerves of motion. *The anterior series*—the dashes—represent the ganglia, which are attached to the intercord, or sympathetic nerve. The star at the top of the series of crosses indicates the place of the conscious centre. The letters and dots in the face, and in the anterior part of the body, represent the ganglia which are specially related to the vital functions in their immediate vicinity. *a*, The situation of the opthalmic, or lenticular, ganglion. *b*, Spheno palatine. *c*, Naso palatine. *d*, Otic. *e*, Submaxillary. *f*, The place of the pharyngeal plexus. *g*, The cardiac. *h*, The solar plexus and vital centre. *i*, The renal plexus. *j*, The hypogastric.

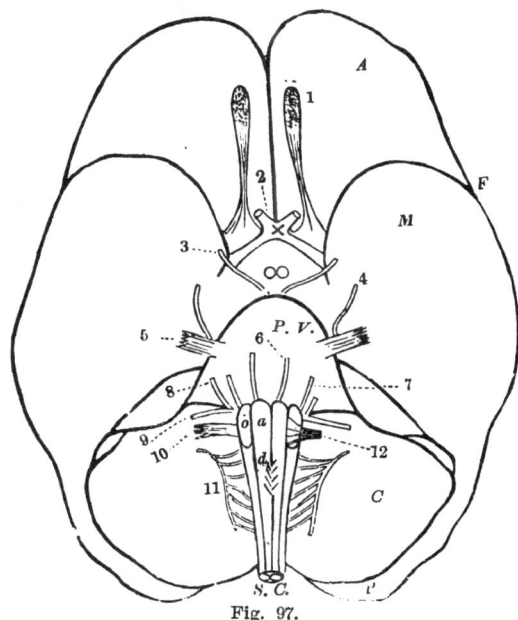

Fig. 97.

Figure 97.   Diagram of the base of the human brain, and the cranial nerves. *A*, Base of the anterior lobe, in which the lower

Directive organs are located. *M*, Base of the middle lobe, in which the lower Ipseal organs are situated. *P*, Base of the posterior lobe, in which the lower Social organs are situated. *C*, Base of the cerebellum. *S C*, Spinal cord, the upper part of which is the oblongata. *d*, Decussation, or crossing of some fibres of the lower part of the oblongata, from one side to the other, which is supposed to account for injuries in one side of the body, producing paralysis on the other side. *a*, Anterior pyramid or column of the oblongata. *o*, Olivaria, or olivary body. *P. V. Pons Varolii*, or bridge of Varolius, which connects the two halves of the cerebellum. ×, Commissure, or place of junction of the two optic nerves. *F*, Fissure of Sylvius, which divides the anterior from the middle lobe.

The numerals indicate the twelve cranial nerves, as they are enumerated in the text. 1, The Olfactory. 2, The Optic. 3, The Oculo-motor, that moves the eye upward, inward, and downward. 4, The Patheticus, that moves the eye a little inward and upward. 5, The Trigeminus, that gives sensibility to the face, moves the jaw, and gives the sense of taste to the fore part of the tongue. 6, The Abducens, that moves the eye outward. 7, The Auditory. 8, The Facial, that moves the face, in expression. 9, The Glosso-pharyngeal, that gives general sensibility to the throat, and taste to the back part of the tongue. 10, The Vagus, or Pneumo-gastric, that gives the sensations of hunger, thirst, suffocation, and pain from the nutritive viscera. 11, Accessory, that moves the lungs. 12, Hypo-glossal, that moves the tongue.

NOTE. — By irritating the sympathetic after the death of an animal, contraction may be excited in any part of the alimentary canal—in the heart, aorta * * * thoracic duct, ductus, choledoctus, uterus, fallopian tubes vas deferens and vesicular seminales. But the very same contractions may be produced by irritating the roots of the spinal nerves from which the sympathetic trunks receive their white fibers.—*Carpenter's Physiology.*

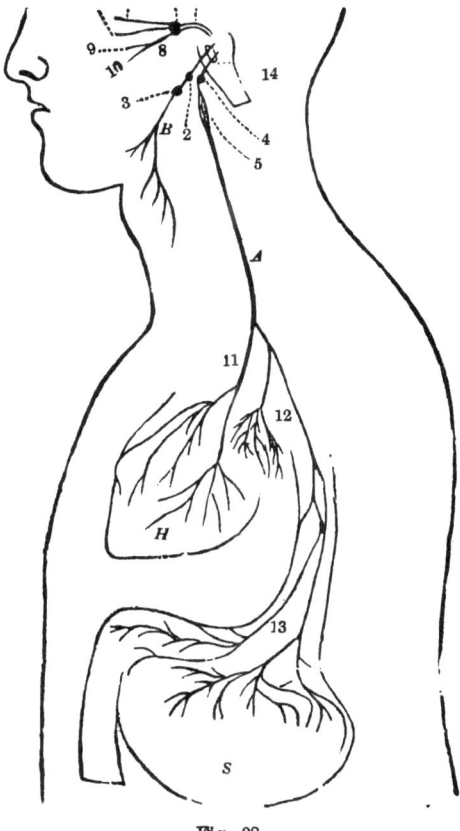

Fig. 98.

Figure 98. *A*, Vagus, or pneumo-gastric. *B*, Glosso-pharyn-geal. *C*, Trigeminus. *H*, Heart. *S*, Stomach. 1, Gasserian ganglion on the trigeminus. 2, Jugular ganglion on the glosso-pharyngeal. 3, Petrous ganglion. 4, Ganglion of the root of the vagus. 5, Ganglion of the trunk of the vagus. 6, Upper, or opthalmic branch of the trigeminus. 7, Middle, or upper maxillary branch. 8, Lower maxillary branch. 10, Nerve that moves the jaw. 11, Cardiac branch of the vagus, connected with the heart. 12, Pulmonary branch, connected with the lungs. 13, Gastric branch distributed upon the stomach. 14, The oblongata, or centre of all the sensory nerves, and phreno-organs. The diagram shows that though these nerves originate from very different and distant parts of the face and body, they all meet in the oblongata, thus demonstrating its importance.

LOCATIONS AND FUNCTIONS OF THE EMOTIONS.

The highest modern authorities are now agreed that all the mental faculties, including the emotions, are located in some part of the brain. Prof. William Hammond, of Bellevue College, N. Y., says: "The mind, under which term is included the intellect, the emotions, and the will, is ordinarily supposed to have its seat wholly in the brain.* Dr. Gall was the first to teach this fact. Brousais, the cotemporary of Gall, and one of the most distinguished physiologists of Europe, in his earlier writings opposed the doctrines of Gall. He said:

'Prof. Richerand sides with Cabanis in referring the instinctive determinations (propensities) to the viscera; and the truth of this fact seems to be no longer doubted by any one except Gall.'

Brousais afterward not only became a convert to Gall's views, but wrote a splendid work advocating and illus-

* Those physiologists who ignore phrenology, do not agree among themselves as to what part of the brain is the seat of the emotions. Some locate them in the oblongata, others in the pons varolii, and a few, including Dr. Carpenter, in the sub-cerebral ganglia. Their reasons for these locations are merely conjectural or fanciful, whereas the phrenologists found their conclusions upon positive observations. They point to the fact that temperament, health, and all else equal, the manifestations of particular emotions are proportional to the development of the phrene organs of the propensities, the excitement of which produces the emotions.

trating phrenology. Virey, another able writer, remarked:

'Dr. Gall pretends that the passions reside in the brain and not in the ganglionic (sympathetic) system, yet who does not know that the minutest reptiles, worms and insects, experience fear, desire, and love. There are then passions without the intervention of brains. The passions, properly speaking, belong therefore to animals as well as to man, because they reside in the ganglionic nervous system, and produce emotions of the heart.' "

M. Tupper, also, in his inquiries concerning Dr. Gall's system, said:

"We are far from consenting that the different organs of the affections and passions are concentrated in the brain. The opinions of the philosophers of antiquity, as well as those of our own time, supported by the testimony of consciousness, have placed in the procordial organs, or in those of internal life (which are farther distant, and which appear the most independent of the brain), the seat of our most impetuous passions."

Bichat, who is by many regarded as the greatest of modern physiologists, and who died in 1802, taught that " the ganglionic system of nerves (the sympathetic) and the abdominal viscera are the sole seats of the affections and passions."—*See Gall on the Functions of the Brain.*

The nerves commonly included under the general term sympathetic or ganglionic system (Fig. 92), undoubtedly consist of two distinct and independent systems, one of which has for its function to transmit the influences of the emotions to the heart and arteries, and other vital organs; these might with propriety be denominated *the emotional nerves.* The other system has for its office to produce co-operation among the vital organs themselves; these may be denominated the *vital system.* They are, anatomically speaking, bound up with the emotional nerves, and are distributed along with them to the various organs of the body; but they are independent of the mind and the brain; they act involuntarily and without exciting consciousness. I have no idea that the vital, or indeed any other organs, require the assistance of nerves to enable them to perform their own peculiar and separate functions, but they need nerves to enable them to co-operate. It is obviously necessary for the heart, stomach, intestines, liver, lungs and arteries to act in concert. To effect this harmonious co-operation, a complicated network of nerves is absolutely necessary. The heart can pulsate, the stomach can digest, and the liver can secrete bile without the aid of nerves; but they cannot all increase or decrease their action together without the means of inter-communication. It is not requisite that these vital nerves should be connected with the mind; they can perform their functions better without its interference. They act during sleep, when the functions of the brain are suspended, and they continue their operations during the waking hours in the same manner. The emotional system of nerves suspend their functions during sound sleep, and even during the waking hours, provided the propensities are not excited; but the instant one of these is aroused, an emotion follows, which transmits its peculiar influence to the vital organs, to bring them into co-operation and harmony with the mind.

Dr. Gall was not only the first to demonstrate that the emotions reside in the brain, but he was also the first to assert that the sympathetic nerves are the agents through which the emotional influences are transmitted to the vital organs. This opinion has since been confirmed by the experimental vivisections of Brown-Sequard and others. It will be evident, however, after reading the following quotations from the writings of eminent physiologists, that those interesting experiments did not lead them to a knowledge of what I conceive to be the real relations of the emotions to the vital organs. I have been unable to find any author who has described these relations as functional; on the contrary, the emotional influence is regarded by all of them as abnormal and deranging.

Dr. Carpenter says:

"It is difficult to speak with precision of the functions of the sympathetic; there is much reason to believe, however, that it constitutes the channel through which the passions and emotions of the mind affect the organic (vital) functions, and this especially through its power of regulating the calibre of the arteries. We have examples of the influence of these states of the mind upon circulation, in the palpitation of the heart which is produced by an agitated state of feeling; in syncope, or suspension of the heart's action which sometimes comes on from a sudden shock; in the acts of blushing and turning pale, which consists in the dilatation or contraction of the small arteries; and in the sudden increase of the salivary, lachrymal and mammary secretions under the influence of peculiar states of the mind."

Dr. Carpenter suggests, as Gall did, that probably the sympathetic brings the organic or vital into relation with the animal or mental, but neither he nor Gall has given any intimation as to what the relation is. Indeed, Dr. Carpenter, in his Mental Physiology, expressly states that "unless the emotions get the better of the will, they do not act downward upon the organic (vital) functions." Mr. Bain, in his work on "The Emotions and the Will," remarks:

" It is well known that mental excitement has an immediate influence upon all the organic functions; one set of passions, such as fear, have a deranging effect, while the exhilaration of joy, within moderate bounds, would appear to operate favorably.

"There is evidence to prove that the state of anger is associated with extensive derangement of the general secretions of organic life."

Prof. Austin Flint, Jr., of Bellevue College, New York, in his splendid work on Physiology, p. 239, says:

" *The Pneumogastric nerves undoubtedly perform the important function of regulating the force and frequency of the heart's pulsations.*"

Dr. Flint puts the above expression in italics to convey his idea of its importance; and then proceeds to argue that the *regulating* consists in preventing those irregularities which would otherwise be injurious.

If the views which I am advocating are correct, the irregularities of the heart's action (during health) are produced by the emotions, through the medium of those very nerves (branches of the emotional system), the office of which Dr. Flint supposes to be to prevent irregularities. I have an idea that the functions of the heart, and indeed all the vital functions, would be more regular if the cerebral nerves did not affect them at all. The cerebral (sympathetic) nerves communicate with the heart and the arteries on purpose to produce such irregularities as will bring the vital functions into co-operation with the excited state of the mind.

Mr. Herbert Spencer, in his " Principles of Psychology," Vol. I, says:

"There is found to exist a system of nerves which diminish action — inhibitory nerves they are called — and through one of these, it is concluded that the medulla oblongata reins in the heart when the cerebral irritation is excessive."

There is undoubtedly a system of inhibitory nerves that proceed from the brain when Cautiousness, Reverence and other inhibitory propensities are excited; and there is also another system of propulsive nerves proceeding from the brain, that instead of reining in the heart's action, transmit to it the influence of courage, hope or love, and cause it to act with redoubled energy to supply the blood to the parts of the body which those emotional faculties call into action. I cannot, for a moment, admit the doctrine sanctioned by Mr. Spencer and Dr. Flint, that the oblongata, the brain or any nervous apparatus reins in, or regulates the heart, excepting to bring it into co-operation with the mind.

Dr. William Murray, of London, in his "Treatise on Emotional Disorders," says:

"Emotion does the most mischief to the organs over which the will has the least power."

This is undoubtedly true. The will has no direct power over the vital organs. But the emotions have very great effects upon them, not only independently of the will, but against the most strenuous efforts of the will. Is it not strange that these able authors, while observing so accurately the mischievous effects of the emotions upon the vital functions, have never even inquired whether these emotional influences were not in some way necessary to the proper performance of the vital and animal functions? It is true that the vital functions would be better performed if the emotions were prevented from interfering with them; but it is also evident, to me at least, that the mental and voluntary functions would be performed in a very imperfect manner, if the emotions were deprived of their power of forcing the heart, and other vital organs, to co-operate with and assist them.

DEFINITIONS AND EXPLANATIONS.

The ideas of writers upon the mental faculties are so inconsistent with physiology and phrenology, that it is necessary to define some of the terms used in this essay, and to point out clearly the distinctions and relations which I conceive to exist between the Intellectual faculties, the propensities, the emotions and the vital organs.

1. All the powers of the mind are included under the term *mental faculties.*

2. The mental faculties are divided into two grand divisions, namely, the intellectual faculties and the propensities.

3. Any mental faculty may exist in a dormant or latent state, not only when we are asleep, but also when there is no circumstance or occasion present to call it into action.

4. When a mental faculty is excited, it produces a state of conciousness (a state of mind) which we recognize and distinguish as different from the state of mind produced by any other faculty.

5. The states of mind produced by the intellectual faculties are called perceptions, thoughts, ideas, reasonings, judgments, conceptions, imaginations and memories.

6. The states of mind produced by the propensities

are denominated emotions, passions, feelings, affections or sentiments.

7. The state of mind produced by a powerful and greatly excited propensity, is sometimes called a *passion*, while the state produced by the higher and more gentle propensities are termed *sentiments*.

8. The nerves of the external senses transmit impressions from the external world to the mind, producing states of conciousness which we term *sensations*. These sensations should properly be classed with *intellectunl* operations. The external senses are in reality the lowest species of intellectual organs. The higher cerebral intellectual faculties are superadded to these.

9. The nerves of internal and bodily sensation transmit to the mind sensations of a very different kind and for a different purpose. Their uses are to inform the mind of the conditions of the body, and to prompt the mind to make voluntary exertions to gratify the body and relieve its wants. These nerves may be regarded as organs of the lowest species of propensities, to which the higher cerebral propensities are superadded. Hunger, thirst, pain, nausea, sleepiness, weariness, faintness, amorousness, pneumor, a desire for air, and thermor, a sense of cold and heat, belong in this category. Whether these nerves act directly upon the mind, or whether each has a special representative in the brain through which it affects the mind, is a question that cannot, at present, be answered with positiveness. The probability is that each sense has the power to affect the mind directly, the instant it is impressed, but that, to keep the mind

a long time *attentive* to the impression, a cerebral organ is necessary, especially in the higher animals.

10. *Feeling* is a general term which is used to express several different ideas. We say gold feels heavy; furs have a soft, warm feeling; I feel comfortable, or I feel sorry. The passions and emotions were by Spurzheim denominated feelings. I prefer to use the word emotion in this sense. Each propensity, when excited, produces a peculiar state of the consciousness, which may be denominated an emotion. According to this definition, hunger and thirst, and several other states of mind which are usually called appetites, or bodily sensations, must be included among the emotions. But this difficulty is unavoidable, unless we coin a new word to express this idea. It will be evident to any one who adopts this theory of the emotions which I am proposing, that we must use language that will enable us to distinguish clearly between 1, the dormant faculty; 2, the state of mind that it produces when excited; and 3, the effects which it produces upon the heart and other vital organs. We must no longer speak of a feeling or an emotion as a faculty; we may as well regard a *thought* as a faculty. There is no objection to using the term emotional faculty, to signify a propensity which, when excited, produces a state of mind called an emotion. It is often convenient to use this expression. A propensity is a natural disposition to do certain kinds of things. It may, and, during much of the time, does exist in a dormant state. When excited, it instantly acts upon the consciousness and produces a state of mind called an emotion.

THE WILL.

If some of the faculties approve and others oppose, a struggle occurs between the contending forces, and the result is denominated the will. The intellectual faculties never constitute any part of the will. Their office is to furnish the knowledge which excites or allays the excitement of the propensities. They are the teachers and guides, and not the masters of the propensities; the propensities are the steam engines, the intellect is the surveyor and engineer. That the will is distinct from the intellect, is proved by the fact that the intellect is often forced by the will to think upon a particular subject, to the exclusion of others; thus, we can will to solve a problem instead of composing a discourse, although the latter would be the more agreeable task.

THE USES OF THE EMOTIONS.

What is the use of the emotions in the mind? I am not aware that this question has ever been asked before, but it seems to me well worth considering. Why do not the propensities, when excited, proceed at once to gain their objects by the aid of the intellect, without each first producing a peculiar state of the mind? I venture to answer: The use of the emotion, in the mind, is to give notice to all the other faculties, that the propensity is excited and inclined to produce certain results by getting control of the body. The other faculties, being thus fairly notified, have an opportunity to approve or oppose the proceeding.

THE INDEPENDENCE OF EACH EMOTION.

When an emotion is excited, it cannot act upon the the voluntary organs of the body without the consent of the will, but it can act upon the vital organs without the consent of any other faculty.* A single excited propensity can powerfully and specially influence the vital organs, not only without the concurrence of the will or the intellect, but against the efforts of both. When anger, or love, or fear is excited, the heart and the blood vessels are disturbed, and the circulation in the hands and cheek vary instantly, before we have time to think or will or determine anything. Even when we have time to think and will, and do so with all our power, it sometimes happens that the emotion will not down at our bidding; the heart will palpitate and the cheek redden or pale in spite of all our voluntary efforts to prevent them. So when we think of anything delicious and sour, like strawberries or lemons and sugar, the saliva flows into our mouths without the slightest regard to our will our wishes or our intellect.

Let us recapitulate some of the principal facts:

1. The fact that there are two separate and distinct sets of nerves through which the mind influences the body: one set consists of volitional nerves, through which the *will* moves the voluntary muscles, and the other set consists of the *emotional* nerves, through

*This view of the functions of the propensities and emotions, enables us to understand why the intellectual organs are so much smaller than the organs of the propensities. The intellectual organs only act upon the mind, and do not affect the body; but each of the propensities acts in two directions: it acts upon the mind and intellect, to control volition; and it also, through the emotional (sympathetic) nerves, influences the whole vital system. We can also understand why some of the propensities require larger organs than others (Cautiousness, Submissiveness and Parentiveness, for examples). It is because their frequent dominence and conservative influence is so much needed.

which a single propensity and its emotion can affect
the vital organs and vary their functional movements.

2. That while the volitional movement is voluntary,
the emotional movement is entirely involuntary.

3. That the emotional movement *precedes* the volitional. It precedes thought and anticipates will.

4. The fact that the normal effects of the emotion
upon the bodily organs are precisely such in all cases
as to qualify them for the movements which *are to be*
required, if the excited emotions get control of the
mind. Anger does not wait until the fight begins,
before it sends blood to the hands and feet and face,
and the external senses; it acts the instant the contest is suggested to the mind. The alkaline saliva
enters the mouth before the delicious sour fruit can
possibly be put into it.

5. The excited emotion not only acts *generally* upon
the vital organs as a whole, but it often acts *specially* upon a *limited set* of vital organs, as in the
case of the salivary on the mammary glands. What
is denominated emotional expression, depends, in some
degree, upon this fact, that each emotion produces its
own peculiar and distinctive effects both upon the voluntary and involuntary organs of the body.

6. The same propensity, when excited, always produces precisely the same kind of effects both upon the
mind and the vital organs; it either increases or it
diminishes vital action ; the same propensity does
not at one time increase and at another time diminish
the circulation. The law is that any propensity which,
when excited, tends to increase voluntary exertion,
produces an emotion which increases vital action also;

and, on the contrary, any propensity that restrains voluntary exertion does the same to vital action.

7. The intellectual faculties, when ever so much excited, have no effect whatever upon the *vital* organs. They neither increase nor diminish the circulation of the blood. They receive impressions through the external senses; they perceive and remember the qualities of objects, and they reason concerning them, and concerning the various emotional experiences of the mind; they also, when goaded by the will, direct and guide the limbs, and all the voluntary muscles, to the objects which will gratify the dominent propensities. The intellect, alone, has no desires and produces no emotions and no actions.

LONG-CONTINUED ACTION OF THE EMOTIONS.

It seems to be assumed by all writers upon this subject, that the emotions only affect the vital organs upon extraordinary occasions, or in times of great excitement; whereas, I conceive the truth to be that they pervade the whole body with their influences almost continually, not only while we are awake, but even during sleep, when the brain is excited by dreams. Whenever we do anything, or think of doing anything, the propensity that prompts the thought stimulates a thousand nerve fibrils to act upon innumerable distant blood-vessels, and causes them to vary their action in sympathy. It is only when a propensity is violently excited that we are able to perceive its effects upon the larger vital organs — the heart, the lungs, the stomach, or the liver. In ordinary cases the emotional influence operates imperceptibly. When ambition, avarice or anxiety predominates habitually in the mind, the morbid propensity pours an almost con-

stant stream of its own peculiar emotional influence
upon the heart, and its myriads of minute arterial
vessels — silently, unconsciously, but inevitably changing the character of the whole constitution, and bringing it into accordance with the condition and character
of the mind.

RELATION OF FAITH AND EXPECTATION TO THE EMOTIONS.

The preliminating influence of the emotions is in
no degree under the direction of the intellect or of the
will. When we imagine our hand being burned or
crushed, an emotion is excited by the thought, and
that varies the circulation in the hand without our
willing. When we think of the dentist coming to
pull out a tooth, it often stops aching, because the
emotional influence that accompanies the thought
modifies the circulation near the tooth, and as soon as
the influence ceases the aching returns. It is curious
and instructing that willing the tooth to stop aching
does not stop it, but imagining and expecting the
dentist pulling it does. The same is true in all cases
of emotional prelimination. If we will the face to
become pale and the hands to become cold, no effect
follows, but if we can imagine a situation and scene
of great danger with sufficient vividness, the preliminating paleness will follow. So if we will to shed
tears we cannot, but we can read an imaginary story
which will produce the requisite emotional state, and
the tears will follow as a natural consequence. On
this principle we can understand the *modus operandi*
by which warts are charmed away from the hand, by
the influence of the patient's own emotional state of
mind affecting the local capillary circulation. In the

same way scrofulous swellings, or king's evil, were cured by the supposed influence of the King of England, as described by Shakspeare in Macbeth:

" At his touch,
Such sanctity hath heaven given his hand,
They presently amend;
How he solicits heaven
Himself best knows; but strangely visited people
All swol'n and ulcerous, pitiful to the eye,
The mere despair of surgery, he cures."

The will and the emotions have this in common, that when the mind is put into a proper state, the appropriate effects upon the body follow without any mental direction. Thus when we will to stoop and pick a pin from off the floor, we bring more than a score of muscles into play simultaneously, balance ourselves, and make all the requisite movements, without thinking of any of them. *We only will the results*, and a complicated apparatus does the rest better without our guidance than with it. Just so the excited emotion of anger merely has to take possession of the intellect, and cause us to imagine an offense, and the blood mounts to the face and rushes into the limbs. If we *think* of acid fruits, *that* is sufficient to rouse the specific emotional influence which increases the flow of saliva. Precisely the same principle applies to the cure or the aggravation of local diseases. It is not requisite for the sufferer to understand the anatomy or physiology of the parts, the nature of the disease, or the manner in which the effects are to be produced. He has only to *imagine a result*, and all the links, between the imagination and the result are furnished by nature, without our taking any thought about it.

The influence of the mind in curing or aggravating diseases has long been known, and it has been considered a sufficient explanation to say that the results are produced by faith, by imagination, by expectation or by expectant attention. But these are only names for causes and processes, the real nature of which was unknown. It was observed that when some patients had faith in certain remedies, they were more frequently cured than when they had none, and the happy results were, therefore, very naturally attributed to their faith; it was observed that when patients confidently *expected* certain effects, they actually happened much more frequently than when they had no such expectations. In these cases the results were attributed to *expectation*, and the explanation was regarded as satisfactory. Dr. Carpenter, and other modern physiologists, seem to think that they have made an important advance by varying the expression, and calling it *expectant attention*, and declaring that this *produces* the important results which have heretofore been attributed to faith or to imagination. It is difficult to perceive that one of these expressions is better or worse than the others. The question is, what is the *physiological* change that occurs? and in what way does expectant attention produce the change? These questions I conceive that I have answered, by showing that when we contemplate a result which it requires a vital change to produce, the emotions spontaneously produce the requisite vital changes, without our conciousness or volition. The faith, expectation or imagination in such cases, is not the *cause*, but merely one of the necessary pre-conditions; just as aiming a gun correctly is one of the necessary conditions, but not the *cause*, that impels the ball to the mark.

Three links in the chain which constitutes this new theory of the emotions, have been furnished by my predecessors: 1. That the emotions are located in the brain. 2. That a distinct system of nerves connect the brain with the vital organs. 3. That through these nerves the emotions produce powerful, exciting and restraining effects upon those organs. Another link is wanting to constitute a proper theory, and I have endeavored to supply it, by showing that the emotions exert their influences upon the vital organs for a normal and useful purpose, and that the ill effects

NOTE.—The advocates of the development theory of the origin of species have insisted that the frequent use or exertion of a limb, or any other organ, in a particular direction or manner, must have resulted in the greater extension and development of that organ, and in this manner they account for the modification of a species until it becomes a new species. The opponents of this doctrine admit that many *varieties* of a species may be produced in this way, but deny that a new species has ever resulted from this or any other natural cause. Without entering into this controversy, I wish to point out the fact that the new explanation of the emotions which I am proposing, has an evident and important bearing upon the subject, by showing that the mere desire or long continued thought upon a subject, even when the limbs are not put into actual use with reference to it, by increasing the circulation in the limb, will contribute to its extension. It is not necessary for the mind to perceive the manner or direction of the needed development, but only to think upon the results desired, and the emotional nature will cause the necessary developments in the proper directions. How much more this influence is exerted upon the lower forms of animal life than the higher, and whether it is sufficient to carry modifications to the length of producing new species, I leave to be determined by those who are devoting their minds specially to this subject.

are due to the excessive, and not to the proper and normal action of the emotions.

WHY ARE MEN MORE INTELLECTUAL AND WOMEN MORE EMOTIONAL? AND WHY ARE CHILDREN MORE EMOTIONAL THAN ADULTS?

We regard those persons as emotional who give frequent and strong expression to their emotions, and we assume that they are more intellectual who suppress their emotional expressions. It is true in this sense only, that women and children are more emotional than men.

First, let us inquire what advantage there is in being free from the power of the emotions. As a general rule it is the duty and business of men to go out into the world and contend for the means of living, and for social position. In doing this they require health, courage, firmness and intellect. If one allows his feelings to be excited beyond a certain point, there are others watching him — cunning as foxes; rapacious as wolves; merciless as tigers, to take advantage of him. The amiable, sympathetic, confiding, generous-hearted man is soon ruined. In our large cities, by the law of "natural selection," the credencive, amiable and emotional characters are continually weeded out, and the entire field ultimately left to the cool-headed man, whose noblest emotions are all held in check. Women are not generally subjected to struggles of this nature. They only rival each other in dress and manners, in household skill and agreeableness of disposition. Before marriage they are protected from wrong, not only by their own shrewdness, but by the courage and power of their fathers, brothers and uncles; after marriage, by the same manly qualities in the husband, with the addition of a terrible, but perhaps dormant jealousy. Before marriage she is treated like a child, and after marriage she is still protected like one. If men were treated in this manner for a hundred generation, they would become as emotional as women. It is not in intellect that men are so much superior to women, as in the predominance of the propensities that enable them to suppress their own sympathies and take advantage of those of others. If women lack firmness and courage, men lack faith, reverence and confidingness. A man loves a woman or a child who has these qualities, but woe to the man who possesses them himself. When he goes out into the world, he goes like a sheep among wolves.

Nature makes children emotional while they are in a state of dependence, and under parental protection, but when the boy is old enough to act for himself, he "puts away childish things," and "girds up his loins like a man."

LAUGHTER AND TEARS.

Laughter and tears are neither of them intellectual operations; they are eminently emotional. Laughter belongs to the class of exalting emotional manifestations, and tears to the depressing. The theory which I am advocating enables us to give a physiological explanation of both phenomena.

When pleasing and joyous emotions are excited, the blood vessels become filled and the muscles ready and prepared for action. If at the same time there is no serious occasion to do any thing to show our joy by muscular exertion, even playfully, the surplus energy is thrown off by laughter. It is the playful exercise of the vocal and respiratory organs. We not only laugh when we see any thing ludicrous, but when we are pleased for any reason. The primary cause of laughter is in the brain, the effect is upon the respiratory and vocal organs. Submissive reverence is opposed to laughter because it belongs to the depressing class of propensities. The moment we become reverential we stop laughing, for the same reason that we stop all other kinds of playing. Crying and tears are the opposite of laughter; they are caused by a sudden suppression of the invigorating or exalting emotions and the sudden excitement of the depressing. The two most powerful depressing emotions are fear and reverence. They both, when excited, produce coldness of the extremities and the skin, check the insensible perspirations, and change them to watery secretions. When fear is greatly excited, cold sweat exudes from the skin. If the skin had maintained its warmth this sweat would have passed away in invisible vapor, but now it gathers upon the skin, just as drops gather upon a window, when the previously invisible moisture is deposited upon it from the air of a warm room that is suddenly chilled. The same moisture-gathering process goes on internally; when sudden fear invades the body and mind, the bowels and kidneys are filled with moisture and their action increased.

Tears are often produced by disappointment. When the mind is in a joyous state, and is expecting some important gratification, the face is flushed with the arterial blood; then suddenly disappointment comes and checks the genial flow of spirits, and we are unwillingly forced to submit. Disappointment is not itself a propensity; it is an negative quality, a reaction of the invigorating emotions. Just as a stream that is suddenly checked by an obstruction overflows its banks, turns back upon itself, and threatens mischief to its borders; so the emotional capillary arteries of the brain and face, that a moment before were communicating joy and energy to the mind and body, are suddenly arrested in their action; and in many cases fatal mischief would certainly follow, were it not that nature has provided an outlet at the eyes. In the act of vocal crying the same object is attained as in laughing; the surplus arterial energy is thrown off in both cases through the same channel, and relief afforded to the brain. The remark has often been made, though not by physiologists, that tears relieve the heart, and that it is a dangerous symptom when a deeply-afflicted person is unable to shed tears. Shakespeare makes Malcolm express this idea when Macduff hears of the murder of all his children:

" Give sorrow words; the grief that does not speak,
Whispers the o'erfraught heart, and bids it break."

PHYSIOLOGY OF VOCAL EXPRESSION.

INVOLUNTARY, INTELLECTUAL, AND EMOTIONAL.

It is a curious and interesting fact, that in almost every department of our nature the voluntary and the involuntary are combined together. It seems that the Creator made our functions involuntary wherever it was practicable to do so, and that he has given the mind no control or care except when it could not well be avoided; our thoughts and feelings are but slightly under the control of our will; our emotions produce powerful effects upon mind and body, whether we will or not; our power over them is limited within very narrow bounds. It is commonly supposed that our speech is entirely voluntary, but I propose to show that this is far from being the case; on the contrary, our vocal organs, which produce accent and pause, are so intimately connected with the involuntary functions of pulsation and respiration, that both the accents and pauses of speech are in a great measure involuntary also. I am not aware that any other writer has mentioned this fact, and I will therefore endeavor to explain and illustrate it as clearly as possible.

Our involuntary motions may be divided into those that are made occasionally, as circumstances render them necessary, and those that are made regularly and consecutively. The pulsations of the heart and arteries, and the movements of the respiratory apparatus, are the only regular motions. In ordinary health, when the emotions are passive, the pulsations of an adult are about seventy per minute. These pulsations are observed in all parts of the body, and in the brain. In adults the average number of pulsations to the respirations is nearly as five to one. I find that accents and pauses are remarkably coincident with pulsations and respirations in three particulars: first, accents are involuntary; second, they are regular in time; and third, the accents are to the pauses as five to one.

1. *Accent is involuntary.*—It seems to have been taken for granted that the accent of speech is like emphasis, a perfectly voluntary matter. It is true that we may place the accent on any syllables of a long word we please, but it requires a strong voluntary effort to keep from accenting any of them. Children

and savages, without instruction, accent as perfectly and regularly as cultivated people. It is sometimes said that the French language has no accents. This remark can only mean that in French the rules are less rigid than in English. Custom may determine whether the accent shall be placed on the first, the second, or any other syllable, but it cannot exclude accent altogether, any more than it can prevent respiration. To prove this let any one rapidly repeat the syllables *te-to-tum* ten or fifteen times, and he will find himself unconsciously placing the accent on one of them. By an effort of will he may avoid it for a while, but the moment his attention flags he will begin to accent. Or let any one attempt to read a sentence of a language, (the Spanish, for instance,) that he does not understand, and concerning the customary accents of which he knows nothing, and he will find it extremely difficult to repeat the words without accenting them, whether he does it correctly or not.

2. *Accent is regular in time*, and in this respect it is analogous to pulsation. When the emotions do not interfere, we make a definite number of accents in a given time. To prove this, read a few sentences of ordinary prose monotonously, without any attempt to express the meaning by variations of the voice, and you will find that you naturally, and without effort, make your accents at regular intervals of time; for example: Po*lit*ical *par*ties *fre*quently re*solve* them-*selves* into *fac*tions. Take another example, in which nearly all the words are monosylables, and are therefore commonly supposed to be incapable of accent, and we shall find the accenting impulse asserting itself instinctively, as in the following sentence: " *Take* my

yoke up*on* you and *learn* of *me*, for *I* am *meek* and *low*ly of *heart*." Accent is not a property of words, but a function of the vocal organs, to which words must conform. When we read rapidly we accent no oftener than when we read slowly. To prove this, let us read the following sentence very slowly, putting italics to represent the accented syllables:

And A*grip*pa *said un*to *Paul*, *Thou art* per*mit*ted to *speak* for thy*self;* then *Paul* stret*ch*ed *forth* his *hand* and *an*swered for him*self*, *say*ing, I *think* my_self *hap*py, *King* A*grip*pa, that *I* am per*mit*ted to *speak* be*fore thee* this *day*. Now read the same sentence rapidly. A'nd A*grip*pa said unto *Paul*, Thou art per*mit*ted to speak for thy*self;* then *Paul* stret*ch*ed forth his *hand* and *an*swered for him*self*, *say*ing, I *think* myself *hap*py, King A*grip*pa, that I am per*mit*ted to speak be*fore* thee this *day*.

In the first reading there are twenty-seven accents, and in the second sixteen. The fact is, that when we read rapidly, we crowd a greater number of syllables in between two accents than when we read slowly. If any one will use as many accents as the sense will admit, he cannot· read rapidly. Let us give another illustration:

All	*hail*	*thou*	*moon*.
We *all*	do *hail*	to *thee*	our *moon*.
We *all* of us	do *hail* to thee	and *only* thee	our *only* moon.

It seems as if our vocal organs issue sounds in a series of impulses that may be compared to waves. We can, if we choose, put as many as four syllables in between two accents, as in this example:

In*nu*merable be*fore* the *throne*.

In the dictionaries and spelling books we have many

words that are said to have two accents, a primary and secondary. The reason is now evident; if we speak slowly, we prolong the sound beyond the time required for an accentual impulse, and bring the word within the time of a second impulse, as in the following example. Read slowly:

The *dec*laration of *indepènd*ence.

Now read the same rapidly:

The declaration of inde*pend*ence.

Words of one syllable are not supposed to have the property of accentability, but if we prolong the sound of a single monosyllable, so that it occupies the time of a whole vocal impulse, we shall find that it is really accented. If the word begins or ends with a vowel, the accent is on that vowel, and if the vowel is in the middle, then the accent is in the middle. This will be seen in the following examples:

| *own* | *brow* | *throne* | *screams* |
| *owing* | *borrow* | throwing | *Iowa* |

We prolong the sounds as much in the words of the first line as in those of the second. The word *screams*, so far as accent is concerned, is equivalent to a word of three syllables, the middle one of which is accented. This may be illustrated thus:

screams im*mor*tal

3. The accents are to the pauses, on an average, as five to one. I refer only to the pauses required for respiration, and not to those required by the sense, much less to those that express emotion. Let a person repeat a single word, as — below, below, below, below, below; and he will find it most convenient and comfortable to repeat it five times, and then breathe, and again five times, and breathe, and so on. Very

young persons breathe more frequently, and they prefer to repeat the word only four times without breathing. In accordance with these facts, we find that the most popular poems are written with five accents or feet in a line. Shakespeare, Milton, Pope, Dryden, Homer, Virgil, Dante, used this measure. Poems of a more lively character, like those of Scott, are in four accents.

> Come *one*, come *all*, this *rock* shall *fly*
> From *its* firm *base* as *soon* as *I*.

The modern poets imitate the ancients. The ancient Greeks, Hebrews, and others, probably wrote their poems to be chanted in unison, by large multitudes; it was therefore necessary, as in modern music, to have the accents and the pauses occur regularly, at definite intervals of time.

I think I have established the fact of the intimate relation of pauses to lines of poetry, and to the movement of respiration; let us now remark the coincidence between pulsations and accents.

When we consider that the pulsations are to the respirations as five to one, that the accents are to pauses as five to one, and that all four are involuntary functions, we naturally suspect that the respiratory and pulsating movements are the *causes* of the accents and pauses; that, in fact, the pulsation of the heart and arteries causes the accentual impulses of the vocal organs, and the necessity of breathing causes the involuntary pauses.

The pulsations of the heart are probably more powerfully impressed upon the lungs than upon any other organs, on account of the vast quantity of blood that passes from the heart through the lungs. The air that produces vocal sound comes directly from the lungs, charged with the pulsating movement.

INFLUENCE OF THE INTELLECT UPON SPEECH.

I have described speech hitherto as if the mind had no influence over it, excepting so far as may be necessary to produce unmeaning articulate sounds. I have only spoken of the *involuntary* vocal functions. These must be carefully distinguished from the effects produced by the mind. Furthermore, the influence of the intellect and thought must be distinguished from the influence of the emotions. Intellectual reading or speaking, the object of which is merely to express thoughts without emotion, may be perfectly monotonous—at the most, it only requires pauses and stress on particular words, to make the *meaning* clear. These pauses may be of different lengths, and so may be the intervals between them, as in the following:

> To die, to sleep, no more,
> Or by a *sleep* to say we end the heart-ache.

The *ideas* expressed by the intellect are different from those expressive of mere emotion. Intellectual language is explanatory, descriptive, statemental or interrogative, and is supposed to convey or to require information; but pure emotion is exclamatory, and only conveys to the listener the idea that the speaker is under the influence of certain emotions, as in the following examples: "Oh! Absalom! my son! my son! would to God I had died for thee!" "Give me liberty or give me death!" "How dear to my heart are the scenes of my childhood!" "If thou dost slander her and torture me—never pray more!" "On horror's head horrors accumulate!"

" I know not, I ask not if guilt's in thy heart,
I but know that I love thee whatever thou art ! "

" Angels and ministers of grace defend us ! "

Emotional speaking requires variations of pitch, time, suddenness, loudness and smoothness. Each emotion produces its own peculiar effect upon the voice. The elocutionist, by watching and studying the modes in which people laboring under powerful emotions express themselves, learns to represent the passions with remarkable fidelity to nature.

The new theory of the emotions is applicable here, for it seems that those emotions that increase the energy of the conduct and of the vital action, also increase the energy of the voice. Combativeness produces violence of conduct, of circulation, and of voice; while Reverence and Kindness produce the contrary effects upon all three; Sanativeness produces crying, wailing, minor key tones; Imperativeness, loud, sudden tones; Hopefulness, high, musical, rapid, major key sounds; Amativeness and Parentiveness, cooing tones, and Firmness, decided tones.

PART THIRD.

THE HEAD AND THE HEART UNBALANCED,
PRODUCING TRANCE, MESMERISM, SPIRITISM AND HAL-
LUCINATION.

TRANCE — ITS VARIETIES AND ITS
CAUSES.

Parts First and Second of this treatise are devoted
to an explanation of the ordinary and healthful functions of the head and the heart. It is now proposed
to show that trance, mesmerism and spiritism are
produced by the excessive action of the conforming
propensities, causing vital depression, which, in turn,
reacts upon the brain.

Trances and their various attendant hallucinations,
have been matters of wonder in all ages and in almost
every community. Witchcraft, mesmerism, spiritism
and hysteria — which are some of its phases — have
always been regarded as mysteries which science was
unable to solve.

The phenomena of nature may be divided into the
ordinary or normal, and the extraordinary or abnor-

mal. The ordinary phenomena are unobtrusive and regular, and when their causes are understood, they are found to result from the operation of the regular laws of nature. The extraordinary, or abnormal phenomena, whenever their causes are ascertained, are, in all cases, found to result from some *irregularity* of the same causes that produce the ordinary. For this reason they only manifest themselves occasionally. They are exceptional, novel, striking, and calculated to excite surprise and astonishment; while the ordinary phenomena, that are produced by the very same causes, and are proceeding quietly and regularly all around and within us, are almost entirely unobserved and unappreciated.

The tremendous waves of the sea, which rise when the tempest rages, are not different in their nature from the small ripples raised by the summer zephyrs; the dreadful tornado, that sweeps over the continent like an angel of wrath, is precisely of the same character as the airy whirls that are often seen playing with the autumn leaves; the powerful human passions that have given birth to all the crimes, the vices, the insanities and the miseries of mankind, are the very same, that, in their gentler and more normal moods, constitute the most angelic virtues.

The phenomena of trance are only exhibitions of the ordinary faculties and functions in a highly magnified and somewhat distorted form.

NOTE.—Somniferousness, the phrene organ of ordinary sleep, is probably located near Alimentiveness It certainly exists somewhere in the brain, and so indeed does every propensity of the mind, whether its organ is discovered or not.

Is not sleep a want and a necessity of both body and mind?

To understand the abnormal effects of the mind upon the body, it is, therefore, absolutely necessary to acquire beforehand, a clear and correct idea of the proper and normal action of the mental organs. How many such organs are there? What is the precise function of each, under ordinary circumstances, and in ordinary health? Into what classes are they naturally divisible? Are all the organs of each class equal in rank, and if not what is the natural order of elevation, arrangement and succession? Are the organs *continually* active, or are they generally dormant and passive, unless circumstances occur to excite them?

Does it not have to be attended to and provided for nightly? Do we not suffer intensely in mind when we are forcibly prevented from sleep? Do we not spend a third of the time of our lives in sleep? Is not the feeling, the desire, the emotional condition of the mind in relation to it as strong as that of any other which we experience? Admitting then, since we must, that there is a distinct propensity of this character, the next question is, by what means does it produce the desired effect?

It is now generally understood that the *immediate* cause of sleep is the diminution of blood in the brain; but no one has before suggested any physiological process by which the quantity of blood in the brain is lessened in order to produce ordinary sleep. The explanation of the emotions contained in these pages applies to this subject. Somniferousness is a depressing propensity; it moderates the vital action in the specific manner required; it checks the circulation in the brain and the limbs just as fear does, but in a more gentle and agreeable manner. Several phrenologists have suggested an organ of a propensity to sleep, but none of them have furnished the evidence required to establish its location, and even if they had it would still be necessary to explain the manner in which it affects the circulation. I suppose that the Somniferous propensity, through the medium of the inhibitory emotional (sympathetic) nerves, produces sleep by diminishing the circulation in the brain.

When one is excited what is its ordinary and proper effect upon the mind and the body, and what is the evident utility and design of that effect? In the preceding pages I have endeavored to answer all these questions, in order to lay a foundation for the explanations that are to follow.

Trances have probably occurred in all the communities of the world. They have presented themselves under various circumstances and received various names, but they have all been produced by one cause—the depressing action of the conforming social propensities upon the vital organs. These propensities are four in number. The first, and most potent in producing the trance, is Submissiveness, which, when excited, fills the mind with the emotion of Reverence or awe; the second is Kindness, which produces the emotion of pity; the third is Imitativeness, which produces sympathy; and the fourth, Credenciveness, which produces marvelousness, wonder and belief. They all tend to a yielding and conformity of ourselves, our manners and our judgments to others.

When excited in only an ordinary degree, they act on the heart and arteries, and moderate the circulation, and at the same time produce respectful, mild and gentle conduct; but when excited in an extraordinary degree, especially in persons whose vital organs are weak, they diminish the circulation in the limbs, the face and the brain, sufficiently to produce an extraordinary species of sleep, and other abnormal effects that have been known under a great variety of names, such as trance, hypnotism, biology, mesmerism, catalepsy, hysteria, hallucination, ecstacy, witchcraft, religious power, and the mediumistic state. The immediate cause of all kinds of sleep is now understood to be a diminution of blood in the brain. There is no function of the body or the mind that does not cease when the organ of that function is deprived of blood. When a person is bled until the quantity of blood in the brain falls below a certain point he swoons, becomes unconscious. There is another peculiarity that is common to all phases of trance, and that is hallucination and dreaming, either spontaneous or suggested. The bewitched ones have an idea that a particular person is tormenting them by the aid of invisible demoniac beings; the spirit medium sees and hears spirits, and feels irresistibly controlled by them; the religiously entranced enthusiast sees heavenly visions, hears angelic voices, and utters prophecies or maledictions; the mesmerised or entranced subject sees what is described or suggested to him, and is "fooled to the very top of his bent." His condition of mind is, in some respects, like that of one dreaming in ordinary sleep, and still more like that of a common somnambulist. But there is an important difference; the trance is not like an ordinary sleep, nor is the hallucination of one entranced an ordinary dream. . They resemble each other in some of their effects, but they differ in the manner of their production and in the facility with which the one is managed by an operator while the other is utterly unconformable; they differ, also, in the fact that the somnambulist is not, in most instances, susceptible to the peculiar emotional influences that produce the mesmeric trance. The mind of the somnambule is occupied by an ordinary dream, but the entranced person is not, he is a conforming dreamer. His sleep is not produced by his somnifer-

ous propensity acting normally, but by his conforming propensities acting abnormally.

When any one is exposed to cold severe enough to
check vital action and the manufacture of blood, sleep
is induced, the precursor of death; when fear is greatly
excited, it checks and depresses vital action and cerebral circulation so as to produce, in some weak constitutions, faintness and swooning, which, physiologically,
is nearly the same as sleep.   On the same principle,
when Submissiveness is greatly excited, as it frequently is in religious meetings, some persons fall
down and are said to "lose their strength," or to be
"stricken down by the power."   In reality their own
excited conforming propensities constitutes the power
that entrances them.

When sincere spiritists assemble and "form a circle," and sing, and wait for the spirit to come and
"control" one or more of the company, those who are
the most conformable and vitally susceptible, will be
the very first "controlled."   All their symptoms are
such as a diminished circulation and a conforming
state of mind would naturally produce.

In the different phases of trance that I have enumerated, it is worthy of especial remark that there
are certain attendant symptoms that are in some
measure common to them all; these are paleness, coldness, tremulousness of the limbs and of the respirations, rapidity and feebleness of the pulse, and rolling
upward and inward of the eyes.   If we compare the
accounts in the books, of persons mesmerised, biolo-
gised, hypnotised, mediumised, cataleptic, or religiously entranced, we find them generally agreeing in

regard to their vital conditions, and all indicating a greater or less tendency to sleep.

WHY SOME PERSONS ARE MORE EASILY ENTRANCED THAN OTHERS.

When this theory is first presented, it will be natural for the reader to presume that persons with the conforming organs large will be found more suscep tible than others; but this is not necessarily true. Uncommon susceptibility to the emotional influence seems to depend upon a peculiar weakness of the vital organs. I have found many persons with all the conforming organs large, who could not be entranced in any degree; and, on the other hand, I have found many with the conforming organs small, who were very susceptible. If a dozen persons are tried at once, and all submit passively and sincerely to the experiment, the susceptibility will generally be manifested without much reference to the proportions of the head. But those who have Submissiveness small, are seldom disposed to try it fairly; and when really affected they take no pleasure in the operation, and are inclined to return very soon to their normal condition; those, on the contrary, who have the conforming organs large, give themselves up more readily, and have less antipathy to performances which require so great a degree of self-abnegation. I have met several persons who could not be entranced by any one else, but, after repeated trials, succeeded in putting themselves into the trance state, and making speeches and singing songs; and what is quite curious, they go through with the programme that they have previously agreed upon, come out of the trance precisely at the time designated, and have no recollection of what occurred during the trance.

The *extreme* cases of susceptibility are found among persons in whom the vital energies are somewhat deficient; whose flesh is soft and the complexion light, with what the doctors denominate "a scrofulous temperament." But I have frequently tried persons who gave every external indication of susceptibility, and yet could not be affected, while others, who seemed to be utterly unpromising, were readily entranced. I have finally come to the conclusion that it is better to try all who offer, without venturing any opinion beforehand concerning the probable results. Seers and religious enthusiasts, in all ages, have regarded the trance state as a superior condition, in which they enjoyed the companionship of supernatural beings, and received important communications from them. It is worthy of remark that they all agree in regarding fasting and solitude as favorable to the development of trance. This harmonizes with the fact that trance, or the mesmeric state, is induced by exciting the depressing instead of the invigorating emotions. The probability is that the low vital condition produced by fasting and solitude is favorable to the excitement of the depressing emotions, and therefore to trance; while genial society and good living have the contrary effect. Persons suffering from delirium tremens have exhausted their vital power, and are laboring under extreme mental as well as vital depression, when they see their terrible visions. As soon as the stomach resumes its functions, and the good blood returns to the brain, the visions cease to appear. People who have depressed their vital powers by opium, generally become visionaries and waking dreamers. Dying persons are often ecstatic on the same principle. In some persons the susceptibility amounts to a positive disease; perhaps it would be more correct to say that it is *indicative* of a diseased condition of the vital organs, the precise nature of which is unknown. A young woman who lived in the family of Mr. Wing Russell, in Syracuse, N. Y., could not hear the subject talked about, or even mentioned at the dining table, without instantly becoming entranced. I have known scores of men whom I could stop in the street by a sign, when they were a hundred rods off; or, if I wrote a note saying that on reading it at the dining table, they could eat no more, or could not speak without lisping, or could not use tobacco, or would be intoxicated, the experiment succeeded. A young man named Porter, clerk and cashier for Judge Marvin, proprietor of the great United States Hotel, at Saratoga, was entranced one evening in a public hall, and the next day, in concert with the Judge, I went to the office and presented a piece of brown paper, and told Porter that it was a fifty dollar note, and that I wanted to pay my bill, which was ten dollars. He took the note, looked at it carefully on both sides, put it into the money drawer, and gave me forty dollars in change; the Judge all the time, with several friends, was watching behind a screen. In this case, and hundreds like it that I have seen, there was no "dominant idea" ruling the mind; but there was a remarkable susceptibility — a predisposition to *conforming monomania*. Porter *seemed* to be in his normal condition; he transacted Judge Marvin's business correctly in dealing with any one else besides me.

He had, the night before, had his conforming propensities greatly excited, and when he saw me again the conformity almost instantly returned and conquered his self-will and individuality -- in other words, his governing propensities. It cannot be said that it was anything peculiar in me, for Judge Marvin himself, or any other person in whom Porter had confidence, could have acquired the same influence over him in a few minutes, by proceeding in the manner I have already described.

It is a curious and interesting fact that persons in the conforming trance are unusually sensitive on moral subjects, and manifest an aversion to indecencies or improprieties. If the operator uses his influence to make them do very improper things, which they are not in the habit of doing, his influence begins to wane — the subject either recovers himself or becomes stupid, and afterwards manifests an unwillingness to submit to be experimented with again, although he cannot give any reason for his aversion, and has no recollection of the past occurrences.

Coarse-minded operators do not succeed well in experiments upon highly refined and moral subjects. It would seem that entranced persons have a keen and almost clairvoyant perception of the characters and motives of those with whom they are in communication. They submit and conform to the commands and suggestions of the operator, but they appear to do so with the implied understanding that he shall be worthy of their full and implicit confidence. When a subject is entranced, if the operator extorts from him a promise that no one else shall entrance him, the promise will generally be kept for a long time. The conforming propensities are the natural sources of loyalty; and when a subject is entranced by one, he is indifferent to the commands, the suggestions or even the voices of others, unless permission is first given or implied by the operator. This *fact* has always been well known to experimenters, but the *reason* of it has not been understood. How could it be when phrenology was ignored, and the natural classification of the phrene organs, together with the peculiar functions of the conforming propensities, unknown? The old mesmerizers supposed that it was because a magnetic connection existed between the operator and his subject, and that the magnetism or electricity was controlled by the will of the operator. The truth is that the loyal conforming organs of the subject held him in bondage to his superior. His operator was his sovereign, without whose consent his allegiance could not be transferred to another. I have met several cases of persons who were very susceptible after having suffered severe sickness or great domestic afflictions, but who had previously been tried repeatedly without being affected at all. I have observed that printers, students and those who have reduced their vital energies by sedentary employments, are more susceptible than the average of other people. I seldom find good subjects among those who are in positions of authority, or in the habit of controlling others. Of forty United States officers at West Point, I did not succeed with one; but on the opposite side of the Hudson river, among the foundrymen and mechanics, I entranced on an average one in six of those that were tried. But I have met some notable exceptions to this rule. On one occasion, in a public hall, the governor of the State (I omit his name for obvious reasons) was present, and when several ladies and gentlemen volunteered to try the experiment, the governor endeavored to persuade his niece to try it with the others. She at length said that she would if he would stand up with her. "Oh," he replied, "there is no use of my standing up; he cannot affect me." But to encourage her he stood up, closed his eyes and put his hands together as the others did. His niece was not affected at all, but the governor was entranced in three minutes to an extraordinary degree; wrote communications from spirits; saw visions, and pardoned all the criminals in the State. His whole performance did not last twenty minutes, and when, at the request of his astonished niece, I told him that he was "all right," he denied all recollection and all belief of what he had done.

The various phases of spiritism confirm and illustrate these views. The medium fancies himself *possessed* by the spirit of a distinguished character, and, accordingly, surrendering his own individuality and self-hood, he conforms all his powers of body and mind to those of the character he assumes. His manners, language, tone and ideas are so utterly inconsistent with his own normal character, that I have not wondered when ill-informed spectators were half converted to the belief that a spirit really did possess the medium. It would not seem strange if a trained actor performed in this manner, but it is not uncommon that the medium is an uneducated person, who never was in a theatre and never read a play. While this work has been going through the press, I have had the privilege, at the house of a friend, one of the most respect-

able business men of Chicago, of witnessing very
interesting manifestations of this character. The
medium is a young lady, a native of Sweden, who
speaks English fluently and properly, but has not yet
learned to read it, and never enjoyed the advantages
of an education in her own mother tongue. Her situation is now such that she is under no necessity of
earning money, and no motive can be conceived for
deception. This lady was induced, in opposition to
her own skepticism and prejudices, to attend a spirit
"circle." In the midst of the performance, she suddenly became cold, tremulous and faint, so that she
was obliged to leave the house and return home. Her
family, though decided spiritists, had no desire for her
to become a medium. Without any apparent reason
or preparation, she commenced personating the characters of deceased members of the family; and, in addition to these, the spirit of a Winnebago half-breed
Indian, of a semi-civilized and superior character,
became her chief controller. She had then never seen
an Indian, though she had heard accounts and descriptions of them. She possesses a very superior brain,
and is endowed with great natural sagacity and
ingenuity, but is totally ignorant of chemistry, anatomy and physiology. She frequently goes into trances,
and prescribes for diseases, and has actually produced
— so I am told, on good authority — several remarkable cures. While under the control of her Indian
spirit, her manner and language change instantly, and
become strikingly different from her ordinary style.
I listened and watched her for more than an hour, on
one occasion, and several times for shorter periods;
and not in a single instance did she say or do anything

inconsistent with her Indian character. She spoke of
herself in the third person, and called herself "the
medium." Charlotte Cushman could not enact the
character more perfectly. There was no hesitation;
her answers were shrewd, sharp, and often caustic;
but, running through all her speech was a disposition
to do good, and to inculcate the strictest morality.
While I was visiting at the house, some venison was
sent home — a kind of meat she never willing ate; but
the Indian took possession of her, and insisted on
cooking it in the Indian fashion, by roasting, and then
she, or he, ate several pieces in a ravenous manner.

Medical philosophers all admit that there is a mystery connected with hysteria, that they have hitherto
been unable to fathom. Bringing this new philosophy
of the emotions to bear upon the subject, I should say
that the disease consists in the alternate excitement of
the exalting and depressing propensities of the brain,
and that the changes in the vital organs are the legitimate effects of the cerebral excitement; the attending
hallucinations are closely allied to those of mesmerised
subjects and mediums.

WILL AND SELF-WILL.

I have defined the will as the resultant of the action
of all the mental faculties that are interested in the
matter under consideration. This is what the will
should be, and what it is when the mind is in the normal condition, and all the faculties have had time to
bring their influences to bear upon the subject. It
must be evident that the will of a dreaming man,
many of whose faculties are asleep, will be likely to
differ from the will of the same man awake. The

dreamer's will is like the decision of a small faction of a legislature — it may or may not coincide with the decision of the whole assembly.   Something analogous occurs when a person is under the dominion of a passion, that sweeps before it the opposition of the other propensities. The suggestions of prudence, of self-interest, of conscience, of reason, are of no avail; it strides onward to its own gratification, regardless of the consequences.   If a single passion thus usurps all the power, it may become the will *de facto*, but it is not the will *de jure* — the legitimate will.   Richelieu said, " *I am the state*," and with quite as good a reason a tyrant passion can proclaim, *I am the will*.   A similar usurpation takes place in monomaniacs, when, in consequence of a disease of the organ of a single faculty, perhaps one that normally has but little influence over the mind — it becomes influenced and irritated, it spurns the control of the other faculties, distorts the reason, and becomes the most potent element of the temporary will.

SELF-WILL.

Self-will results from the dominance of Imperativeness, or Self-Esteem and Firmness. When, on comparing ourselves with other people, we determine to do as we think proper, without reference to their will or wishes, it is said that we are self-willed.   This must not be, (as it generally is,) confounded with *ordinary* will.   It is only one distinct species of will. The dominance of Combativeness may make us will to fight, of Alimentiveness to eat, of Constructiveness to work, and of Acquisitiveness to acquire property; but in these instances there is no necessity of comparing ourselves with others; these are not examples of *self*-will. But when it is proposed for us to abandon our freedom of action, and submit to the control and dictation of another, the proposition involves our *self*-will.

One of the most remarkable peculiarities of the mesmeric and conforming trance, and one that has never before received a rational explanation, is the total surrender of the subject's self-will. But this abnegation, or abeyance of the self-will, is the necessary consequence of the supremacy of the conforming propensities. There are some persons in whom they are so largely developed, and the governing organs, (Imperativeness and Firmness,) so small, that it requires no trance to make them habitually subordinate to the will and wishes of others. Strictly speaking, any propensities that predominate for the time determine the will, and those that predominate habitually determine the character. In the dealings of social beings with each other, while there is a great deal of subordination and conformity to society in general, and to certain individuals in particular, there is also, even in the humblest and least assuming persons, a certain degree of reserve and self-will, and more or less of a disposition to maintain their own distinctive individuality and independence. There is a point beyond which they will not yield without compulsion. They feel that it is not only unjust and unreasonable, but absurd; the idea is too ridiculous and preposterous to be entertained for a moment. Now, phrenologically speaking, what propensity is it that is specially offended by these requirements, and that thus instinctively resists them. It is not Combativeness, for there is no suggestion that force will be used. It is Imperativeness and Firmness. These are the organs of self-will and individual sovereignty. When any one is in the conforming trance *this* self-will is in abeyance. The reason is that the trance is the *effect* of the victory of the conforming organs over those of self-will. The conforming organs, when dominant, constitute the *will*, but not the *self*-will; it is a conforming will; a will to obey and believe and enact what is required or suggested by others. The evidence that the trance depends upon the conforming organs is, 1. That they are depressing propensities, and therefore check the circulation, and thus tend to produce sleep, especially when greatly excited. 2. When large, the subjects remain in the trance longer and more willingly. 3. In somnambulism, although the ordinary will is in abeyance, the subject is not conforming nor amenable to suggestions. 4. Dr. Carpenter says the Mesmerized subject is like a child, in whom the will is not yet formed; but the child has a self-will, and oftentimes a stubborn one, which the trance subject has not. 5. It is also said that the entranced are like monomaniacs, who have lost the controlling will-power; but the monomaniac has a will, and cannot be controlled, though it is not his ordinary will. The truth is that the conforming trance is unlike any other form of monomania somnambulism, or sleep, in the fact that it *is* conforming. The conforming propensities, when excited to a certain pitch, become what lawyers would term the *quasi* will: that is, they act *as though* they were the actual and normal will. In cases of monomania, we say that the patient is not *himself.* By this expression they mean that the faculties, which in health constitute the will, are pushed aside, and their places filled with other faculties, which, in the normal and healthy state of the brain, are habitually subordinate. St. Paul said, " I have a law (a power,) in my members, warring against the law (the power,) of my mind, (my will.") When the power in these members overcome, they enact the part of the will, until, in turn, they are dethroned by the higher powers of the mind.

Every person is occasionally conscious of a struggle going on in his mind between his different propensities. He may, and frequently does, change his mind— his will—several times in a day, or even in an hour. In some instances the scale is so nearly balanced that he really has no mind—will—of his own; the slightest circumstance may decide him one way or another. If his conforming organs predominate over his governing organs, he does not change his will himself, but he allows it to be changed by the influences of others, he is then said to be deficient in self-will.

HISTORY AND THEORIES OF MESMERISM.

The ancients attributed trance, as they did insanity and a thousand other things, to the agency of supernatural beings. In 1784, during the reign of Louis the XVI, Mesmer, a Swiss physician, appeared in Paris, and by his experiments, produced so much excitement that the government appointed a commission, of which Dr. Franklin was one, to examine the subject and report upon its merits. This was the first attempt at a scientific investigation of these phenomena; and it is perhaps not far from the truth to assert that Mesmer's theory, and the report of the commission contain, essentially, all that has been advanced by scientists since that time. Mesmer maintained that the human brain generates a peculiar species of magnetic fluid, which the will can project to indefinite distances, into the brains and bodies of certain susceptible persons, curing their diseases, putting them to sleep, and producing various other remarkable effects. This theory is still believed in by a majority of the people of this country, and is assumed as the basis of reasoning by nearly or quite all the Spiritists. Dr. Franklin and his associates reported that the theory of a magnetic, or fluid of any kind, was unproved and untenable, and that most of the extraordinary phenomena exhibited by the subjects could be accounted for by the effects of expectation and imagination. This is the sum and substance of the theories now maintained by Dr. Carpenter and other prominent British physiologists. Mesmerism did not attract public attention in this country until 1837, when Dr. Hartshorn first performed some experiments in the city of Providence, notices of which, in the New York papers, induced amateurs in all parts of the country to procure " Déleuze's book on Mesmerism," and try their own powers. In 1841 a new impulse was given to the subject by the announcement of Dr. J. R. Buchanan, of Cincinnati, and Leroy Sunderland, of New York, that the phrene organs could be separately excited in susceptible subjects. Dr. Buchanan found, as he thought, that those effects could be produced upon persons who were not asleep, or in a trance, though they had a tendency to go into that condition.

In 1838, while I was publishing my new system (classification) of phrenology, in Buffalo, N. Y., Mr. Wing Russel, a highly respectable citizen, introduced Mesmerism into that city, and among others, taught me to practice it. When, in 1841, Dr. Buchanan announced his success in exciting separate phrene organs, by touching the heads of susceptible persons, I took up the subject in earnest, and made a series of careful experiments, the results of which I stated in numerous public lectures, and embodied in a volume of about four hundred pages, published in Boston by James Munroe & Co., and in London, Strand, Edward T. Whitfield, 1845. I did not then understand the physiology of the emotions, as explained in these pages, and had no idea of the depressing effects of the conforming propensities upon the vital functions. This was a subsequent discovery; but the following extract will show that even then I repudiated the practices of Mesmerists, and clearly perceived that the conforming propensities of the subject were the principal sources of the power that subdued his will and made him subservient to the operator.

CREDENCIVE INDUCTION.

"While engaged in performing various experiments, I made a very important discovery, which I have never before communicated to the public, in writing, though I have frequently mentioned it privately to my friends, and publicly in my lectures. It is this: that, when a subject is but slightly affected, and when any of the operators in Mesmerism, or neurology, or pathetism would send him away as unprofitable — merely by the application of a very simple stimulus, which every one has always at hand, the subject may be brought perfectly under your control. Do you ask me what this simple and powerful stimulus is? I answer, that it is *an assertion*.

"Assert to the subject, in a decided tone, for instance: ' *You cannot open your eyes*,' and if his eyes were shut when you made the assertion, he cannot open them afterwards, until you again say, ' *Now you can open them*,' or something to that effect. Again, say to the subject, '*Put your hands together, and you cannot separate them*.' If, now, he puts his hands together, he will try in vain to separate them until you reverse your assertion. Say, 'The floor is hot,' and instantly, to him, it seems hot.

"In order to explain these experiments, we must first understand the nature of the organ of *Credenciveness* — the impulse to act upon testimony or assertion. It is a *conforming social impulse, and its natural stimulus is an* ASSERTION.

"When greatly excited by any extraordinary stimulus, it governs the individual, and produces such uncontrollable tendencies to gratify itself, as to constitute a peculiar species of monomania.

"It is generally supposed by those who see experiments of this kind performed, that the operator accompanies his assertion by an effort of his will. This, however, is not the case. If the operator makes an assertion, it will have nearly as much effect, though he wills that it shall have no effect whatever. This proves, that it is the assertion and not the will. We are so constituted, that we take the assertions of our fellow-beings as the true expressions of their wills, and we sometimes believe them, in spite of all our efforts to resist the belief.

"If the process of induction did not operate as a stimulus to the conforming Socials in particular, if it stimulated the governing equally with the conforming Socials, the experiments which depend upon the influence of assertion could not be performed at all.

"Strange as it may seem, however, it is a fact, that a person of intelligence and education, with whom I am acquainted, although I have explained to him the nature of the influence which I have obtained over him — although he knows as well as I do that it is his own Credenciveness that paralyzes his muscles, yet when I assert that he cannot open his eyes, he instantly loses all control over them."

Although I had then made an important advance, I

had discovered but half the truth. There were many phenomena still unexplained. What produces the Mesmeric sleep — the trance? Why, when subjects are Mesmerized, do their hands become cold and clammy with prespiration? Why does the breathing become tremulous, and why do the limbs tremble? Do the conforming propensities produce *these* effects, and, if so, what is the physiological explanation? After many experiments, I became satisfied that nearly all the symptoms were produced by the unusual excitement of the single organ of Submissiveness or Reverence, and that most of its effects were precisely like those produced by fear. After Submissiveness had produced the trance, the other conforming propensities manifested themselves in an extraordinary manner. Here is the key to all the phenomena. The upper front region of the brain is the spirit land, in which all the fairies, witches, superstitions and wonders of the world are born. I do not mean to say that such are the *legitimate* fruits of those high and noble faculties; they are its abnormal productions; wild and monstrous weeds and tares that, in the absence of proper care and cultivation, spring up here, and find congenial soil. Submissiveness or Reverence is the natural impulse to submit to proper authority, and obey its laws. In ignorance it prompts to slavish submission to usurped authority, and to the worship of myths and senseless idols. Kindness is the impulse to do good to all, even to the enemies of God and man. In ignorance, it prompts men to send relief to the poor with one hand, while they light the fires of persecution with the other. Imitativeness is the impulse to surrender our habits and manners, and adopt the habits and manners of others, good or bad. Credenciveness is the impulse to believe what others say — to give up our own opinions, and even to disbelieve our own senses, if opposed to the assertions of others. It is easy to understand that when those four impulses are dominant in the mind, it requires but little Mesmerism to make it perfectly subordinate. When we consider that the success of the Mesmeric experiments depend upon the sovereignty of the conforming propensities, it will be evident that any circumstances that are calculated to interfere with that sovereignty, will tend to prevent success. Among those opposing or unfavorable circumstances may be enumerated: 1. The excitement of the pride, or vanity, or combativeness of the subject; or, indeed, his unwillingness, from any cause to give the experiment a fair trial. 2. A want of respect for the operator, or a want of confidence in his ability or integrity. 3. An ignorant fear that the experiment, if successful, may injure the health or the social position of the subject. 4. A disbelief in the whole matter, and a consequent want of reverence for all engaged in it. 5. A disposition to act with levity or contempt on the part of the company.

The favoring circumstances are: 1. The manifest ability and fairness of the operator, and the confidence of all concerned in him. 2. A perfect willingness on the part of the subject to treat the matter seriously, sincerely and respectfully; for this reason it is generally pleasanter to perform the experiments with religious persons, who are in the habit of behaving reverentially. 3. To have a company present who are either favorable to the experiment or passive and quiet. 4. The experiment is much more likely to be successful, after those who propose to try it have witnessed it successfully performed upon others whom they know and esteem. 5. It is more likely to succeed if the persons who try it are confident that they will not be made to do anything ridiculous or unbecoming, but that, on the contrary, they will behave admirably.

PRACTICAL INSTRUCTIONS,

CONCERNING THE MANNER OF INDUCING THE TRANCE IN THE PRESENCE OF AN AUDIENCE.

We are so much in the habit of requiring silence and privacy when going to sleep, that it is difficult to make people understand that we can produce the trance sleep more readily in a public assembly, with a thousand eyes upon us, than we can in private. But the mystery disappears when we understand that the trance sleep is produced by the excitement of Submissiveness, or reverence, and that a public audience is itself an object of reverence, and even of awe, to those not accustomed to it. I frequently meet a small company of jovial friends who urge me to entrance them privately, just for the fun of the thing, and under circumstances where scarcely any one can keep from talking, and all are ready to scream with laughter upon the first excuse. The principal difficulty of the operator in such cases is to produce a serious and respectful frame of mind on the part of the whole company. I never fail to have successful experiments in public audiences when the mental "conditions" are sufficiently serious and respectful, and there is a general willingness on the part of volunteers to try the experiment in good faith. It is not necessary for the subjects to believe anything in particular in relation to the matter, provided they are willing to assume a passive, respectful attitude, and are sincere in their professions of willingness to be affected, provided they have the requisite susceptibility. I have often put persons into the trance in a few minutes who only tried the experiment in the spirit of fun. But such persons were naturally very susceptible, though they had no idea of it. There are many people who can only be entranced when they voluntarily surrender themselves, and, as it were, *invite* the influence by their perfect conformity of body and mind. It is frequently asserted that only one in fifteen can be affected; some say one in ten; the highest number that I have heard mentioned is one in six; yet I have frequently seen a large audience so "wrought up" that when eight or ten came upon the platform, *all* were so much affected in three minutes that they could not open their eyes, or speak, and afterwards another equal number were affected in the same manner. At other times, when the "conditions" were unfavorable, all experiments failed. I have, on such occasions, been much amused to hear men who pretended to very profound knowledge on this subject, attribute the failures to the peculiar electric state of the atmosphere, while I knew very well that the difficulty was in the mental state of the audience.

I find, by reading the treatise of Dr. Tuke, that Mr. Braid, of Manchester, England, induces the trance (which he denominates hypnotism) by taking "a bright object between the thumb and fore and middle fingers of the left hand and holding it from about eight to fifteen inches from the eyes at such a distance above the forehead as may be necessary to produce the greatest possible strain upon the eyes and eyelids, and enable the patient to maintain a steady, fixed stare at the object." Mr. Braid then proceeds to exhibit the same phenomena as other operators do. It is only necessary for me to remark that I obtain precisely similar results by allowing the subjects to sit or to stand with their eyes closed, that Mr. Braid does by his method. I have not the slightest idea, therefore, that there is any causal connection between the staring at the bright object and the trance which results; no effects will follow the staring if the subject is not constitutionally susceptible, and if he is so, almost any ceremony, seriously performed, will answer the same purpose, provided the mind of the subject is in the right condition.

Dr. Carpenter, after describing some of the wonderful effects produced upon biologized or Mesmerized subjects, adds: "The chief marvel lies in the discovery that a continued, steady gaze at a fixed object will *induce* this peculiar state in certain individuals — chiefly such as are constitutionally predisposed to abstraction and reverie, or who possess that kind of imaginative power which transports them without efforts into scenes and circumstances altogether different from those which usually surround them. The proportion of those who are susceptible are from one in twelve to one in twenty.

Dr. Carpenter regards the trance of hypnotized or Mesmerized subjects as ordinary sleep. He says, in his "Mental Physiology," "One of the most remarkable phenomena of this (hypnotic or trance) condition is the superinduction of genuine sleep." And the doctor proceeds to argue that it is induced by the same kind of monotony and mental inactivity that tends to produce ordinary sleep. In this last remark Dr. Carpenter is mistaken. The fact is that a really very susceptible person can be put into a trance or sleep amid noise and confusion, and cannot be wakened by any ordinary means except by the command of the operator. He is also mistaken in his supposition that persons inclined to reverie and abstraction are more susceptible than others. The causes of susceptibility are to be found in the bodily and not the mental organs.

ASCERTAINING SUSCEPTIBILITY.

Let from four to eight persons stand in a row facing the company, all present preserving the utmost seriousness, each subject placing the palms of the hands together and closing the eyes. These circumstances are calculated to excite reverence, and do excite it at once. If the operator will pass along the line of subjects and listen to their respirations, he will generally hear one or more of them breathing in an unusual manner — a kind of short, spasmodic or trembling movement of the lungs. Now let him take hold of the fingers (see Engraving) and he will find the very extremities of them cold, the coldness gradually extending up toward the middle of the hand. The pulse will be about a third more rapid but weaker than usual. The subject will occasionally swallow, as if saliva or mucus is accumulating in his throat, as it probably is; the limbs are more or less tremulous, and the expression of the countenance serious and reverential. If you see one of the set smiling, you may know that his reverence does not yet predominate, for, if it did, it would manifest itself in his countenance. A beautiful woman, when entranced, has an expression of the face that seems almost holy, "like one inspired."

I have described the symptoms as they are generally exhibited, but in some cases the manifestations are much more decided and extreme; the trembling is almost violent and even spasmodic; or the sleep becomes profound; occasionally the subject turns extremely pale, and becomes faint, especially if his health is delicate. The operator should be looking for this, and as soon as he perceives it he should speak to the subject and tell him to go to his seat, and that he will feel well presently. Sometimes the subjects act hysterically, and the spectators and friends begin to be alarmed, but there is no danger. Let the operator be calm and self-possessed. If the subject is really under the Mesmeric influence only, he will presently recover. If he does not, you may be sure that some other cause produces the effects. I once had a subject, a student at Williamstown College, suddenly exhibit violent insanity, but I afterwards learned that he frequently suffered from such attacks. People who are subject to hysterical affections are liable to manifest some of the symptoms when Mesmerized, especially if by doing so they can become objects of interest and attention. Occasionally you will find a subject in whom the bodily symptoms are manifested, but whose mind is unsubdued. In other instances the mind yields, and the subject is perfectly conforming, without manifesting the usual bodily symptoms. This proves that the circulation in the brain may be diminished without affecting that of the body. and the con-

TRYING AN EXPERIMENT IN MESMERISM.

Which is susceptible?

trary. Those who are in the habit of going into the trance are affected but slightly in the body, while the brain is perfectly conforming.

MANNER OF INDUCING THE STATE OF DREAMING AND HALLUCINATION IN PERSONS WHO ARE FOUND TO BE SUSCEPTIBLE.

Mesmerism is a species of sleep and a species of dreaming. I have sufficiently explained the sleep, its causes and the manner of producing it. I will now describe the manner of evolving the dreams after the trance sleep has been developed. It is somewhat analogous to that of ordinary sleep and dreaming. It is a mistake to suppose that in common sleep we dream most when sound asleep. The truth is that we dream most when the least asleep, if we are asleep at all. I do not doubt that in some instances the whole brain is awake and dreaming, while only the external senses are perfectly asleep. In other instances the external senses and some parts of the brain appear to be perfectly awake while other parts are evidently asleep. This seems to be the case with sleep-walkers. Many persons, during ordinary sleep, will answer questions put to them by a familiar acquaintance, and their minds can thus be directed to any subject that the questioner desires; afterwards, when fully awake, they do not always recollect the conversation. Sometimes, while asleep, the sound of distant music starts a dreaming train of thoughts and emotions relating to a dancing party, or to a religious meeting, in which we recognize old friends; a rumbling noise overhead may cause a dream concerning a thunder storm; lying under a heavy load of bedclothes may suggest a dream that we are being crushed beneath a falling building. It is not unusual for people, especially children, to talk in their sleep, or to act as if embracing or fighting. These manifestations belong in the same category as sleep-walking. In performing experiments in Mesmerism, or in developing the so-called spirit mediums, we proceed on the same principle. When a number of persons stand before an audience with their eyes closed, and all present are serious, in less than a minute the operator will discover evidence that the circulation of one or more is becoming diminished. He will at once elect the one that appears to be the most affected, make him step a little forward and thus separate him from the others, and proceed to make him dream. Put a pencil into his hand and place his arm in a position as if he were going to write, and whisper to him and say, "Now your hand will move just as if you were writing; it will make large letters and write a long line." Then take hold of his hand and commence the desired movement. If the subject is in the requisite dreaming condition, his hand will move as if writing. Now bring his hand back to the first position and say, "Now your hand will move again and will write the name of a dear friend who is dead. Take notice of the name and tell me what it is." His hand will then move and appear to write in the air, and if you ask him what name it wrote, he will generally say, "It is the name of my father," or mother, or sister, or of some other departed friend. Now ask him if he moved his hand intentionally, and if he by his will wrote the name, and he will answer that he did not. I believe it was Judge Edmonds who remarked, when he held a pencil, "The

DEVELOPING A WRITING MEDIUM.

Q. What does it write?
A. The name of my mother.
Q. Do you write intentionally.
A. I do not.

spirit moved my hand, but did not move my mind; for what I wrote did not pass through my mind." Now say to the subject, "Your hand will move again and your departed friend will write a communication to you." If he is in the proper condition, his hand will move in the air as if writing a communication. Ask the subject and he will generally, if he is an intelligent person, tell you what the spirit writes. When you are satisfied that the subject is sufficiently *conforming,* you can tell him to open his eyes, and take the pencil and sit at the table, and ask the spirit to move his hand and write communications on paper, and the spirit will do it. Of course the communication of the "spirit" is the offspring of your suggestions begotten upon his dreaming brain.

After a few trials, there are many persons who can put themselves into the trance, and write or talk or see visions without the aid of an operator. They are what the spiritists denominate *mediums;* in reality they are emotional dreamers.

In the city of Detroit a society was organized, one object of which was to perform experiments in trance and Mesmerism. One gentleman, Mr. Hawley, a member of the legislature, after having repeatedly stood up with others in the usual manner to try to get entranced, succeeded at one of the meetings of the society in going into a trance by standing up, putting his hands together, and seriously endeavoring to bring upon himself the right condition of mind. He had previously declared that if he did get entranced he hoped that he should make a political speech. Accordingly, while in the trance, he actually made a violent democratic harangue. When he awoke,

he declared upon his honor that he did not recollect
speaking at all. Several of the members of the
society who were known to be susceptible, and who
had been Mesmerized before, demonstrated, by repeated
experiments, that they could lay down a programme
of proceedings beforehand, and go into the trance and
perform it, neither more nor less, and then, when
awake, have no recollection of what they had done.
They could also awake at a time previously agreed
upon. One young gentleman named Davis, who was
a good subject, on one occasion when I was present,
said to the company, " I will try to go into the trance,
hop all around the room on one foot, sing a comic song,
and in ten minutes awake and not recollect anything
that I have done." To the great amusement of his
friends, he carried out the programme, and when he
awoke he turned and asked, " Did I really do it all? "
He then solemnly declared that he had no recollection
of it. He then tried the experiment again, with a
determination expressed beforehand that he would
recollect it, and he did so.

Some individuals, in consequence of constitutional
disease or weakness, go into the trance state spontaneously, and become ecstatics, visionaries and prophets.
If they live in a superstitious community, they will
be regarded as possessing " more than mortal knowledge "; and even in the most cultivated social centres
there is a class of apparently superior persons — poets,
metaphysicians and myth-loving scientists — who seem
to be incapable of taking physiological views of the
subject. They puzzle themselves with psychic and
odylic forces, and auras and electric and magnetic

analogies, and a score of other myths, that only exist in their own "heat-oppressed brains."

To make a vision-seeing medium, you have only to say to the subject, while his eyes are closed, "See, yonder in the sky is a beautiful rainbow; there it is! Do you not see it?" He will point to it and say yes. Tell him that the river Jordan is rolling beneath the rainbow, and that on the other side of the river is the beautiful spirit land. He will declare that he sees them. Now tell him to look and he will see the forms of the spirits, and that among them he can recognize one of his own departed friends, and he will instantly do so. Now ask him to listen and he will hear the spirits sing something that he knows, and that he must join and sing with them, and if a good singer he will do it. In the same manner he can be made to converse or shake hands with the spirit of any departed friend you suggest. These scenes can be, and sometimes are, made exceedingly solemn, and even pathetic; so much so that it is difficult for one unacquainted with the subject to believe that it is all a mere dream. If the subject has an active mind and a cultivated poetical taste, he will sometimes proceed spontaneously and without further suggestions to point out the beautiful things of which he is dreaming.

The engraving represents one of these who on being asked by the operator to look into the distance and describe what he saw, seemed delighted with the vision, and exclaimed, "I see a beautiful rainbow, and beyond, beneath the arch, I see the spirit land, and I hear the spirits sing." He then listened and beat the time of the music with his hand. I asked him if he knew the tune; he said, "No; but it surpasses all the music I ever heard." I then requested the spirits to sing something that he knew, and after listening a moment he joined with them to sing:

ARIEL.

> " O, could I speak the matchless worth,
>   O, could I sound the glories forth
>   That in my Saviour shine,
>   I'd soar and touch the heavenly strings,
>   And vie with Gabriel while he sings
>   In notes almost divine."

As soon as he began to sing, several other entranced persons who were on the stage joined and sang with him, to the infinite delight of the audience.

Now let the operator suggest something that is absurd, ridiculous and impossible, that the spirit land is full of buffoons and monkeys, or that on the rainbow sits his sweetheart eating peanuts and throwing the shells at him, and hitting him in the eyes; he will instantly dream this, and act and suffer accordingly. There is a strong temptation to amuse a company of spectators with these grotesque and laughable experiments, but they should never be performed except with the previous consent of the subject, and the unanimous approbation of his friends. They are useful, however, in demonstrating that all the other mental manifestations, including those of the "spirit mediums," are mere dreams suggested by the operator, or pre-existing in the mind of the subject. Persons who voluntarily put themselves into the reverential dreaming state, can proceed to speak or write or perform in any manner which they had previously resolved that they would. The speaking mediums, among the spiritists, often perform the same feat. In some instances, I presume that they really believe that they are actually inspired by spirits.

TWO OPPOSING WILLS.

We are now prepared to understand another class of experiments, to which I have not before alluded. Say to the subject, " You cannot put your hat on." He takes the hat and tries to put it on, but his hand moves the hat to one side and then to the other side, but will not obey his will. He seems to make great efforts and nearly succeed, and then repeats his efforts, but in vain. Tell him that he cannot sit-down, or get up, or open his eyes, or speak, and he tries and fails in the same manner. The modern spiritists, and some others, assert that there are two wills contending; that one is the will of the operator, and the other that of the subject; but it is easy to prove that this is not true. Any one who will perform the experiment, will find that the mere unexpressed will of the operator is ineffectual. The truth is, that both the contending forces are in the brain of the subject himself — one force is his own proper and normal will, and this is rendered abortive by the superior force of the conforming faculties.

In Judge Edmonds' book on Spiritualism, he gives an account of a performance with a table, which several men could not hold still. In spite of their efforts, the spirits pushed it over and held it down until the spirits were requested to allow it to be raised, when it was lifted with great ease. In this case, one force was supposed to be the wills of the men who had hold of the table, and the other force to be exerted by some invisible spirit. In reality, both forces resided in the brains of the distinguished operators themselves.

I often perform an experiment involving the same principles, in the presence of large audiences. After a person is found to be susceptible and conforming, I ask him to take hold of a table and hold it still if he can; I then ask the spirit to push it over toward him. He will take hold of the table, and while he seems to be holding it up, an unseen power appears to be pushing it over. He is, in reality, holding it up with one hand and pulling it over with the other. If his conforming organs are sufficiently excited, the experiment will succeed perfectly; the table will go over, and he will be unable to raise it again until I request the spirit to allow him to do so.

I usually call on the spirit of Sampson to push the table over, and at the same time urge the young man, the subject, to hold it up. If the audience are unacquainted with Mesmerism, and inclined to believe in spiritism, they generally regard me as a wonderful medium, and suppose that a spirit is really moving the table. To give greater effect to the performance, I use encouraging language to both parties. I say: "Push, young man! push, spirit! push, both of you!" (See the engraving.) Sometimes I have two or three subjects take hold of the table, and in trying to hold it they occasionally demolish it.

HOW TO WAKE A SUBJECT AND THROW OFF THE INFLUENCE.

The old Mesmerizers made passes with their hands over the subject, from his head downwards, and at the same time exerted their wills to produce the Mesmeric sleep. In order to wake and restore him, they reversed the movement, and commanded him to wake. Now, that we understand the matter more perfectly, we know that the passes and the exertions of the will are useless. The only thing necessary is to make the subject understand that you wish him to wake and resume his normal state. It is generally sufficient to speak to him decidedly and tell him that he is awake and may go to his seat as usual; but if he has an idea that some particular ceremony is necessary to restore him, it will be well to indulge him. A man was brought to Boston, from Danvers (about fifteen miles), who had been Mesmerized, and who had been unable to open his eyes for six weeks. The person who Mesmerized him had not the power to restore him. His friends had heard that I was a very powerful magnetizer, and that I could perform wonders by my *magnetic power!* Of course this was all delusion; I had no more power than any one else; but when the man was brought before me, accompanied by his weeping wife and several friends, I saw that it was necessary for me to pretend that I was possessed of all the power that had been ascribed to me. I therefore performed several apparently mysterious ceremonies, and then commanded him to open his eyes, which he did. The subject, in this case, was in the same condition that hysterical patients often are. He believed that the power which had shut his eyes was very wonderful, and that they would never open again. He submitted to his fate like a conforming monomaniac. He had lost confidence in the man who had Mesmerized him; but, as the Boston newspapers represented me as possessing tremendous magnetic power, he conformed to that opinion and returned home confirmed in it, declaring that he felt a shock and a thrill all over him, the moment I touched him.

INFLUENCE OF IMITATIVENESS AND CREDENCIVENESS IN TRANCE MANIFESTATIONS.

I have stated that Mesmerism depends upon the dominance of the conforming socials, but I have hitherto only described the abnormal influence of one of them. I am convinced that Submissiveness or Reverence is the principal, and perhaps the only agent, in producing the trance sleep, but every one who has had much experience in the practice of trance experiments is aware of the remarkable tendency of subjects to oblige, to imitate, and to believe. Suggest to one of them that he is an orator, an elephant, a lion, a drummer, or a singer, and he will proceed to enact the character according to the best of his abilities. If he has a natural, and especially if he has a cultivated talent for any particular art, he will frequently delight and surprise the spectators by his performances. The speaking mediums among the spiritists sometimes produce a powerful impression upon an audience by their beautiful 'dramatic manner of speaking. The fact that they surpass their ordinary and normal performances, convinces some people that they are actually under spirit influence. But any one who is familiar with camp-meetings of religious people, and has seen women religiously entranced, and heard them pray and exhort, can bear testimony that, under the influence of religious emotions, they surpass their normal selves in the same extraordinary manner.

In regard to Credenciveness, it requires no argument to convince any one who has witnessed many Mesmeric experiments, that the believing propensity is greatly excited in the subjects. They believe, and instantly act upon the belief of the most incredible, absurd and impossible things. It is worthy of especial remark, that entranced persons never spontaneously manifest any propensity in a decided manner except the four conforming propensities. They never exhibit anger or pride, or stubbornness. They are never vulgar or indecorous, or even jocular, unless the ideas are suggested to them by the operator. They are in a condition to *receive* impressions, and not to make them upon others unless incited to do so by the operator.

RELATION OF TRANCE TO POETIC GENIUS.

The conforming social propensities have so large a share of influence in producing mental phenomena, that it is important to acquire correct ideas concerning their proper, and also their abnormal manifestations, we should contrast the conduct of those in whom they are deficient with those in whom they are uncommonly developed; we should also observe the different manner in which they are exhibited by the ignorant and by the educated; by the profound thinkers, and by the superficial; we shall then be prepared to understand the extravagances of persons under the influence of Mesmerism, trance, and spiritism.

When we clearly understand and fully appreciate the fact that persons who are entranced have the conforming organs greatly excited, we shall expect to see them manifesting some sparks of the genius that distinguishes those writers and speakers in whom those

organs are very large. Nearly all great poets belong
to this class. The tendency of such minds is to conceive of the existence of unreal beings, ideal creations,
spirits of the mind, "false creations, proceeding from
the heat-oppressed brain," "such bodiless creations,
ecstacy (trance,) is very cunning in." With this basis
for reasoning, we are prepared to understand the
extemporaneous ideal rhapsodies of speaking mediums, some of whom, with very little education or
social refinement, pour forth a copious stream of poetical prose language, which, in their ordinary condition, they could not possibly have uttered. They are
denominated inspirational speakers, and it is believed
by some of their friends that they are actually inspired
by spirits. The truth is, they are inspired by their
own excited conforming propensities. We never see
them spontaneously expressing rage, pride, stubbornness, amorousness, avarice, or fear; these propensities are not excited. They are gentle, kind, liberal,
respectful, poetical, and dramatic. The Italian im-
provvisatores exhibit the same extraordinary abilities.
I have seen mediums, in private families, go into the
trance state and converse with great beauty and skill,
and guess the characters, motives, and diseases of different persons in the company, with such acuteness
that inexperienced people could not resist the convic-
tion that they possessed "more than mortal knowledge."

The common opinion of Phrenologists is that
poetical talent depends principally upon the organ of
Ideality or Perfectiveness. Dr. Gall discovered what
he supposed was the organ of poetry. I have made a
great many observations of this organ, and find that

Credenciveness is much more intimately related to literature, and especially to poetry, than Ideality is. The latter is more especially related to the fine arts, and the former to romance and the exaggerations in which poetry abounds.

Persons with the conforming social propensities large, when in the normal state, are more desirous than others to acquire historical, biographical, literary and traditional knowledge. In the absence of this kind of knowledge, or of the ability to appreciate it, they indulge in romances and myths. This being the normal tendency of these faculties, we can readily understand that when they are abnormally excited by the Mesmeric, or any analogous process, they would incline strongly in the same direction. They are hungry for impressions of some extraordinary kind. If there is any such thing as a clairvoyant faculty they are certainly in a condition to exercise it. If there is no such faculty, they are still capable of appearing to possess it, and of sincerely believing that they do so. Their minds are often so acute, active, and shrewd, that it requires a cool, clear head on the part of the observer to keep from being misled into the belief that they really do perceive things that are supposed to be " beyond the reaches of our souls."

THE RELATION OF THE IMAGINATION TO THE EMOTIONS.

The emotions may be excited in a variety of modes. 1. By the presentation to the senses of objects that are directly related to them. The sight or sound or smell of prey excites the destructive propensity of a ferocious animal; the sight of gold excites the acquisitive propensity; certain sensations from the body excite the related propensities and appetites.

2. Hearing or reading descriptions of the objects that gratify the propensities frequently excites the emotions.

3. The propensities and emotions are oftentimes excited by the operations of the imagination alone. A man may imagine a scene in which he is grossly insulted until he finds his face reddening with anger, his fists clenched, and his teeth firmly set. He can also imagine a scene of danger and horror, until his cheek is blanched, his limbs tremble, and the cold sweat exudes from his skin. Some persons possess this imagining art in a wonderful degree. It was said that Garrick could turn deathly pale, while playing the part of Hamlet, the moment he saw the ghost of his father. I have heard that Madame Rachelle possessed this power, and I certainly saw Miss Herron turn suddenly and appropriately pale, while performing in Cincinnati, on hearing of or imagining a dreadful calamity. In these cases the voice, the expression, the language, the ideas and the gestures all conspire to produce a powerful effect upon the audience. Some persons insist that there is a species of magnetic communication in these instances, whereas it is merely the legitimate effect of the natural language of the emotions on the part of the speaker, causing similar emotions in the imitative mind of the hearers. When I was a boy, in passing through the Boston museum, I suddenly saw near me the painting of a maniac, who seemed ready to spring upon me from the canvass. I started back with the utmost terror but the *magnetism* was all in my own eye. **An**

orator whose ideas interest an audience, and who has the natural gift, well cultivated, of expressing the emotions, is always magnetic.

THE RELATION OF THE EMOTIONS TO DISEASES.

When we consider that a great number of diseases are produced by some derangement of the circulation of the blood, and when we also take into the account the great influence of the emotions upon the circulation, we can readily conceive that the emotions must exercise a powerful influence in mitigating or in aggravating disease. The emotions only produce their effects by increasing or by diminishing the vital action. They may increase or diminish the circulation, the secretions, the digestion, the action of the liver, the kidneys, the intestines, and the skin. In fact there is no part of the constitution but can be affected in an instant by the emotions; and if a particular emotional condition becomes chronic, the emotional influence upon the body, whatever it is, becomes chronic also, and varies for good or evil the state of the health. Physicians, without being acquainted with the true physiology of the emotions, have long been well acquainted with the fact that they exert a powerful influence upon their patients. In describing many diseases they refer to certain conditions of the mind as attendants and symptoms. They have learned by experience that some symptoms of bodily disease have their origin in the emotions of disappointed love, ambition or avarice, and they can suggest no better remedy than a change of society and of scenery. They can seldom minister with mere drugs to "a mind diseased."

When it is known that one particular disease requires for its cure the excitement of those emotions
that increase the vigor of the circulation, and another
of those that diminish it, the case is quite simple.
But there are many cases of local disease which require
more skillful mental engineering than any mortal possesses, and yet such diseases are sometimes alleviated,
and perhaps cured, by the mysterious power of the
imagination when excited by the charlatanism of an
ignorant quack.

This theory of the emotions enables us to understand how anxiety of mind produces diseases of the
vital organs, especially in persons who are constitutionally predisposed to such diseases. From this point
of view we can also perceive how a person may be *har-
rassed* to death; or fall into a *decline*, from disappointed love; and how the secretions of a cow's milk may
become unhealthy, if she has been chased and worried
by dogs.   Prof. E. N. Horsford, of Cambridge, Mass.,
in a very interesting lecture given at Chicago, during
the meeting of the American Association for the
Advancement of Science in that city, stated that when
beef cattle were conveyed in railroad cars, under circumstances calculated to excite fear and anxiety, their
meat was not as good as that of animals that had not
been subjected to such annoyances.

A gentleman who has had a good deal of experience
in fishing, assures me that the fishes that are killed as
soon as caught, are much firmer and better flavored
than those that are allowed to suffer long and die
gradually.

MANIFESTATIONS OF GREAT STRENGTH AND INSENSIBILITY.

The manifestations of wonderful strength by Mesmerized persons, and also by the insane, have never
been explained upon any reasonable hypothesis; but
emotional prelimination evidently affords the long
desired clue to this mystery. A person who, in the
the normal state, could not lift a hundred pounds,
when in a Mesmeric state has been known to raise a
chair with a man in it who weighed nearly three hundred pounds, without appearing to make any extraordinary effort. Insane patients, who had normally
less than common strength, could not be held without
the united efforts of two or three stout men.

This wonder does not entirely cease, but it becomes
much less, when we know that, in addition to ordinary
volition, the brain has, through separate and distinct
nerves, the power of turning all the energies of the
heart and arteries upon one set of muscles. The
patient only wills the result, and the diseased emotional brain does the rest. Similar reasoning applies
to the faculty which the Mesmerized subject often
manifests, of becoming insensible to the pain of surgi-
cal operations. The brain has the preliminating
power of checking the arterial circulation in the nerves
that supply the parts wounded. The subject thinks of
the result, and nature does the rest. These phenomena
manifested by the insane, the hysterical and the Mesmerized, differ from those of ordinary healthful persons, not so much in kind as in degree.

MIND READING.

The attention of the public has lately been aroused

by an apparently wonderful phenomenon denominated
mind reading. The principal performer, who however has many imitators, is a young gentleman named
Brown. His mode of proceeding is as follows: A
person in a company goes out of the room, while
Brown is blindfolded, and hides an article, no one but
himself knows what or where. He then returns to the
room and gives his hand to Brown, who places it
against his — Brown's — forehead, and immediately
begins to move about, but at length proceeds to the
right place and discovers the hidden article. In some
cases he fails, but in a large majority of instances he
succeeds. He declares that he can give no explanation of his peculiar faculty; he, however, states that a
bright light seems to emanate from his forehead that
guides him on his way. One of the conditions upon
which he insists, and without which he declares that
success cannot be expected, is that the person whose
hand he holds, and whom we will denominate his
guide, must keep the hiding place and the thing hidden continually in his mind.

Two theories have been proposed to account for these
" mind reading " performances: one is, that the guide,
by fixing his mind intently on the hiding place, unconsciously exerts upon his hand a slight degree of imperceptible volition, which the mind reader perceives, and
by which he is guided to the place; and this is the reason why the experiment fails when thoughtless or
unfairly skeptical persons act as guides. This explanation is perfectly physiological, and, if true, it would
seem to be sufficient. Dr. G. M. Beard, a highly
respectable physician of New York, declares that, after
carefully and repeatedly trying the experiment with

Brown, he had no doubt that the explanation just given is essentially the true one. But, in justice to Mr. Brown, it must be stated that hundreds of persons, of all professions and grades of intelligence, who have had the same opportunities of investigation that Dr. Beard has, regard his theory as untenable, and as more incredible than the phenomena which it professes to explain. They declare that the promptness, rapidity and confidence with which Brown moves, when his guides act fairly, excludes all possibilty of such unconscious guidance as Dr. Beard suggests.

I never saw Brown perform; but a few evenings ago I was invited to the house of a friend, a well known citizen of Chicago, to witness some experiments in mind reading. I very gladly accepted the invitation, but with a mental reservation of unbelief. When the company had assembled, the gentleman sent his daughter into another room, where she blindfolded herself and remained in waiting. The gentleman took a paper weight, about half as large as his hand, and in the presence of the company placed it in a small drawer of a library table, at the same time stating that he would will his daughter to find the weight. The young lady was then led blindfolded into the room and the gentleman placed three fingers of his right hand upon her left shoulder. See illustration. She at once moved quickly around the room, taking the precise course that had been previously indicated to the company, and concluded by laying her hand upon the drawer, opening it, and taking out the paper weight. Other experiments were performed, with unimportant variations of detail, and with perfect success.

At the request of the company, the same young lady

was again sent from the room and blindfolded as on previous occasions. The gentleman requested the company to suggest anything they desired the subject should be willed to do, thus removing any possibility of a secret agreement to deceive, between the parties. It was suggested that the young lady should be brought into the room and placed in a position with her face toward the north; that the gentleman should then place his fingers upon her shoulder, as before; that she should turn immediately to the *right*, facing the south, and proceed to a certain figure in the parlor carpet; then turning to the west, she was to approach a sofa in a remote corner of the room, from which she should remove a small tidy, which she should take to the opposite side of the room and place upon the head of a certain young gentleman in the company; she was then to proceed to the extreme end of the parlor, and take a coin from the *right* vest-pocket of a gentleman, and return to the opposite side of the room, and place the coin in the *left* vest-pocket of another gentleman named; she was then to remove the tidy from the head of the gentleman upon whom it had been placed, and return it to the *tête-à-tête* where she originally found it.

I must confess to no little surprise when I saw the young lady perform, with the most perfect precision, every minute detail, as above described, and with the most surprising alacrity; in fact, so quick were her motions that it was with the greatest difficulty that the gentleman could keep pace with the young lady's movements.

When I was called upon for an explanation of the phenomenon which I had just witnessed, I suggested

Dr. Beard's theory. This was earnestly repudiated, and after some pleasant discussion, it was proposed for me to be blindfolded in place of the young lady. I consented, and very conscientiously rendered myself as passive as possible. Immediately up... being brought into the room, and placed under the gentleman's influence, I walked along without the slightest idea where I was going, but putting out my hand, like a blind man, to prevent hitting against the furniture, or hurting myself, until at length I felt my hand lying upon the paper weight which had been hidden in another drawer, and heard the merry shouts of the whole company. Thinking that it might be a mere accident, I repeated the experiment successfully again and again; and I can truly affirm, that if my friend's fingers on my shoulder communicated any pressure by which I might guess in what direction to move, I did not perceive it; I did not see any such light as Brown describes, but I experienced a slight dizziness. My friend afterwards declared, and I believe with perfect truth, that he did not intentionally indicate by the pressure of his fingers which way I was to move. He may have done so unconsciously, but even if he did, it is scarcely conceivable that I should receive the direction in that manner unconsciously, unless, indeed, my conforming socials partially entranced me, which is very unlikely.

The other theory of mind-reading, is that it is a species of sympathetic clairvoyance, or imperfect magnetic communication of impressions from one brain to another. Thirty years ago all the Mesmerisers believed in clairvoyance, but at the present time the belief is mostly confined to spiritists, and the self-

styled and interested magnetic doctors. Carefully
conducted experiments, during the last fifteen years,
have led me to doubt the possibility of clairvoyance,
and to look upon all persons who pretend to the art as
impostors; perhaps, however, it would be more just
and philosophical to suspend judgment upon the
subject for the present, and give mind-reading a more
thorough investigation before we pronounce a final
sentence.

In a conversation with a distinguished medical jour-
nalist, a few days ago, he suggested a modification of
the theory of clairvoyance in its application to mind-
reading. His idea is, that when two persons bring
their limbs into contact, the nervous system of one
being active and positive, while that of the other is
passive, the brain of the latter may unconsciously
receive slight mental impressions from that of the
former. This hypothesis has at least the recommend-
ation of being within the possibilities of physiology.
When I was a boy, I recollect very well the excitement produced in Springfield, Mass., by the first case
of clairvoyance that ever attracted public attention in
America. A girl named Jane Rider became a somnambulist, and when carefully tested by such persons
as the Hon. W. B. Calhoun, the Rev. W. B. O. Pea-
body, and nearly all the physicians in the county, she
satisfied them that she could read a closed book, and
do various other things that to ordinary persons
seemed impossible. Dr. Belden, who was a careful
scientific physician, and who had special charge of the
case, gave a public lecture, and also published a small
book upon the subject, in which he attempted to
account for the phenomena by the abnormal exaltation

of the nerves of sensation produced by disease. He made no attempt to deny or evade the fact that she actually possessed the marvelous perceptive powers ascribed to her, though he assented to it with great reluctance. Dr. Belden's theory is in some degree sustained by the performances of dogs in following, unerringly, the footsteps of their masters, over ground where scores of people have since passed; by the fact that sharks are said to follow a vessel for several days if a sick person is on board; and the fact that some fishes possess the power of communicating, (and probably of also receiving,) electric currents through a large body of water. Possibly Brown, and some other persons, may possess a peculiar gift of susceptibility in their particular way, analogous in some respects to that of blind Tom for music, or Zerah Colburn for arithmetic. Who would believe, if we did not know it to be true, that blind people can read as readily and rapidly as they do, by feeling of the raised letters on their blocks; or that telegraphers could interpret so easily the sounds made upon their instruments? I have heard of a blind man who could tell the color of the hair of a person, or of a certain kind of goods, by feeling of them.

That people betray the state of their minds unconsciously by slight motions, has been often demonstrated. The power of the so-called divining rod, by means of which some persons pretend to find hidden springs or minerals, depends upon the fact that the holder of the rod unconsciously turns it in accordance with his own mind. When a person fixes his mind upon a result which he knows that he *may* accomplish by volition, but does not intend to, he really exerts a slight degree of imperceptible volition, which tends to produce the result. Persons who are naturally susceptible to the Mesmeric influence, are peculiarly liable to exert imperceptible volition; it may be said that their volition "leaks out," or "runs over," and escapes imperceptibly, and produces unconscious movements. It should be considered that when we do anything voluntarily, we only will the *results;* all the bodily organs conspire and move in the manner required, without our attention or thought. In mind-reading, we are required to fix the mind intently on the desired results, while in contact with the mind-reader, and there are certainly many persons who cannot do this without betraying what is in their thoughts. Every one who is Mesmerically suscepti-ble, will manifest imperceptible volition much more decidedly than those who are not so. If both parties, the mind-reader and the one whose mind is supposed to be read, are susceptible, the experiment will be certain of success; but if neither are susceptible in the slightest degree, possibly the experiment will, in every such instance, be a failure. In making these remarks, I may be wrong in assuming that there is no truth whatever in clairvoyance or magnetic communi-cation; I can only say that I have been unable to find the requisite evidence of its reality, though I have sought diligently for it during several years. The mind-reading experiments just described approach nearer to it than any other that I have witnessed.

EMOTIONAL INSANITY.

Phrenology may be made useful in determining whether a person is insane or not, in those cases in which the form of the head indicates a character the reverse of that exhibited by the patient. In Wheeling, Virginia, I was once requested by the county judge to examine a young married woman who had killed her child. The question was whether or not she was insane. Her head was one of the most beautiful I ever saw, and of course it furnished some evidence of her insanity, by showing that the crime of child-murder, which is always unnatural, was particularly so in her case. I have known many people who were not supposed to be insane, but whose conduct could not be explained phrenologically, except on the supposition that they were partially deranged. Insanity is so shocking that people are generally unwilling to admit that a friend is insane as long as they can avoid it. They require the most positive proofs, and suggest all kinds of excuses and explanations, before they will pronounce the unpleasant verdict. Besides, the evidence is of such a metaphysical and equivocal character, that it is often impossible to distinguish between caprice and eccentricity on the one hand and real insanity on the other. The evidence consists of peculiar acts or speeches, which, in most cases, differ from mere eccentricity in degree rather than in kind.

Some people, when a little unwell, will manifest ill-humor or melancholy. If the health is soon restored the mind resumes its wonted cheerfulness; if not, the patient, in some instances, becomes permanently insane. When this happens we do not hesitate to trace the disease back to the time when the first symptoms were manifested, and declare that the patient was really insane at that time. Had he recovered before the insanity became manifest beyond doubt, we should not have called it insanity.

When a person suffers from a slight cold, we do not call it an inflammation of the lungs, provided it is soon removed; but if it continues until it produces death, we do not hesitate to say that the cold was a slight degree of the same disease which terminated fatally. I have met hundreds of people supposed to be sane, whose conduct was so peculiar that there seemed to be no theory by which it could be explained except that of cerebral disease. I have seen persons who were noted for suavity and patience under very annoying circumstances, become suddenly irritated, and use the most offensive language without any adequate cause that could be perceived. When afterwards the disease of their brains became known, the explanation of their former conduct was obvious.

These remarks apply with considerable force to two distinguished public men lately deceased — the Hon. Horace Greeley and Prof. Louis Agassiz. The marked contrast between the latest insane manifestations of those two patients is highly illustrative of the distinction between the governing and the conforming propensities and of their effects when diseased. In Greeley the exalting or sthenic emotions were excited, and manifested themselves by impelling him to furious conduct; in the brain of Agassiz, on the contrary, it was the conforming group that were dominant, and caused him to kneel in the midst of his astonished and afflicted pupils and pray. The careful and scientific examination of the brain of Agassiz, after his death, revealed the most positive evidence that it had been diseased for many years; and I have no doubt that a similar examination of the brain of Greeley would have afforded evidence of the same fact.

In the course of this treatise I have illustrated, at considerable length, the effects of the depressing propensities both upon the body and the mind. They are represented as producing coldness, tremulousness, weakness, paleness, sleepiness and dreaming. The dreams are such as those propensities would naturally produce; generally mild, gentle, spiritual and poetical, except in cases of tremens, when they doubtless proceed from fear and marvelousness combined; and except also in cases of hysteria, when Secretiveness often predominates and prompts to the most absurd deceptions. In Mesmerism the dreams assume any character that the operator chooses to suggest.

I have hitherto barely alluded to the effects produced upon body and mind by an extreme and abnormal excitement of the exalting or sthenic propensities, and their attendant emotions, such as pride, anger, sexual love and hope.

The question will be likely to arise in the mind of the reader, if the abnormal excitement of the depressing propensities produces such remarkable effects as have been described in these pages, why do not the abnormal excitements of the exalting or sthenic propensities produce equally strange manifestations? The answer is that in reality they do so, and these extreme effects are generally denominated insanities. Besides, when the depressing propensities prevail, they check the circulation in the brain, and thus produce a species of partial sleep, some of the mental faculties being asleep and others awake and dreaming; but when the exalting propensities prevail, the cerebral circulation is increased, and therefore the whole brain and *all* its faculties are excited; the conduct is positive, egotistical, energetic, aggressive, and even furious. The first effects of alcoholic liquors are exalting, and are manifested in eloquence, vivacity, singing, boasting, egotism, quarrelling — the subject is hopeful, cheerful, rich, and confident of success — in a word, he is in a condition of mind just the reverse of that of one entranced. When the effects of the alcohol have passed away, and the reaction follows, the depressing propensities predominate — Reverence, Credenciveness, Cautiousness and Secretiveness — the subject is now afflicted with horrid dreams and visions; he is suspicious, fearful, superstitious, remorseful. When a person is in a Mesmeric state or trance, the only depressing propensities that are excited are the conforming socials, but in tremens the depressing propensities of the Ipseal or self-relative class are excited also, namely, Cautiousness and Secretiveness.

MODERN SPIRITISM.

The philosophical student of human nature, when called upon to explain the phenomena of modern spiritism, naturally calls to mind the analogous instances of remarkable superstitions and impositions that are recorded in history — Mohammedanism, Mormonism, Shakerism, the deceptions practiced by monks in the middle ages, and by the priests and pretended virgins in the ancient Grecian temples. These all naturally rise in his mind and prompt him to scrutinize the phenomena with an expectation of detecting the evidence that " history is merely repeating itself," and that the key to the whole mystery is that a few shrewd knaves have imposed upon a large number of dupes. Assuming this to be true, as I have no doubt that in some degree at least it is, he would also suppose that the dupes were in all cases men and women of inferior minds, or that they had enjoyed less than the average share of educational advantages. This, however, is far from being the case.

As a public lecturer, and an opponent of modern spiritism from its very birth, I have had occasion to meet and converse with its believers in all parts of the Union, and I have found them to be persons of much more than ordinary intelligence. Indeed, I do not recollect a single instance of a very ignorant or uneducated man who was a professed spiritist. I have just been looking over a book entitled "A Defence of Modern Spiritualism," by Alfred Wallace, F. R. S., one of the most scientific men of the age, who divides with Darwin the honor of having revolutionized — or rather evolutionized — natural history.

The following passage from his book gives an account that is probably not much exaggerated:

No amount of education, of legal, medical or scientific training, was proof against the overwhelming force of the facts, whenever these facts were systematically and perseveringly inquired into. The number of Spiritualists in the Union is, according to those who have the best means of judging, from eight to eleven millions. This is the estimate of Judge Edmonds, who has had extensive correspondence on the subject with every part of the United States. The Hon. R. D. Owen, who has also had great opportunities of knowing the facts, considers it to be approximately correct; and it is affirmed by the editors of the "Year-Book of Spiritualism" for 1871. These numbers have been held to be absurdly exaggerated by persons having less information, especially by strangers who have made superficial

inquiries in America; but it must be remembered that the Spiritualists are to a very limited extent an organized body, and that
the mass of them make no public profession of their belief, but
still remain members of some denominational church — circumstances that would greatly deceive an outsider. Nevertheless,
the organization is of considerable extent. There were in America, in 1870, 20 State Associations and 105 Societies of Spiritualists, 207 lecturers, and about the same number of public mediums.

In other parts of the world the movement has progressed more
or less rapidly. Several of the more celebrated American mediums have visited this country, and not only made converts in all
classes of society, but led to the formation of private circles and
the discovery of mediumistic power in hundreds of families.
There is scarcely a city or a considerable town in Continental
Europe at the present moment where Spiritualists are not reckoned by hundreds, if not by thousands. There are said, on good
authority, to be fifty thousand avowed Spiritualists in Paris and
ten thousand in Lyons; and the numbers in England may be
roughly estimated by the fact that there are four exclusively
spiritual periodicals, one of which has a circulation of five
thousand weekly.

The question naturally arises — Why should so
many intelligent persons believe in a doctrine which
is so extremely absurd? 1. We must take into consideration the fact that the early teaching of all Christians
has been such as to prepare them to believe in spirit
communication.* The Bible, especially the New Tes-
tament, sanctions this doctrine, and the churches go
still further. The Roman Catholic Church, from
which all Protestant churches have been derived, has ·
always taught that legions of good and of evil spirits
are hovering about us continually and influencing our

---

* There is not a single instance in the whole Bible of a deceased
human being using the brain or mouth or hand of a living one
as a medium of communication. This method is a modern invention. Does not this fact indicate that it is a *mere* invention?

conduct. They believe in not only mental, but physical manifestations. I heard Bishop Timon, in Buffalo, declare, before a large audience, that the picture of the Holy Virgin, in Washington, shed tears while more than a thousand people were present. They invoke a large number of saints to intercede for them, and to protect them from danger and from evil spirits. I met a Catholic clergyman lately, who assured me that he had exorcised an evil spirit that had taken possession of a young man, a member of his church, who had been attending spiritual seances. The lad had become a medium, and the pious father sprinkled him with holy water, and commanded the spirit to leave him. The ceremony had to be repeated three times before the sp'rit was expelled. It will readily be perceived that it requires but little evidence to convince such persons of the reality of the modern spirit communications and manifestations. None of the Protestant churches deny the probability that spirits influence human conduct.

The witchcraft mania that prevailed throughout christendom during the last century, was founded upon the teachings of the churches. The historian Barrington is quoted by Judge Edmonds as asserting that thirty thousand people were publicly executed in England alone, during one hundred and fifty years, for witchcraft.

What was that witchcraft? It was a compound of Mesmerism (or rather emotionalism) and superstition. No sensible people now believe that spirits had any agency in producing the manifestations. The phenomena of trance explained by the church was witchcraft; explained by science, it is emotionalism; explained by Prof. Wallace and Mr. Owen, it is spiritism.

The believers in witchcraft could boast of quite as respectable names as the modern spiritists. Lord Chief Justice Hale was one of the most learned, just and pious magistrates that ever England produced, yet he sat on the bench and condemned scores of old women to be burned to death for witchcraft. King James the 1st, the same monarch who ordered the present translation of the English Bible, published a treatise on witchcraft, in which he endorsed its absurdities, and threatened with the severest possible punishments all who should be found guilty of the offense. None of the churches have ever opposed the belief, and none of the laws against it have ever been repealed, though the courts have refused to execute them. I remember well that in New England, fifty years ago, the belief in witchcraft was universal. No one doubted it except those who doubted the Bible itself. Even now the belief in ghosts, omens and warnings is common among religious people. Our children are taught in the nursery to believe in fairies, dragons and giants. The groups that gather round the hearths of our country homes on winter evenings, are entertained with ghost stories oftener than any other.

Another fact that deserves consideration is, that nearly all those who pretend to be skeptical concerning the Bible, still retain, though perhaps unconsciously, their superstitious belief in ghosts and myths. There are few of them who can go through a graveyard at night without listening, and looking around, and starting at every sight and sound, half expecting to see a ghost glide near them. When we are called upon to account for the rapid spread of the belief in modern spiritism, this fact, that all christendom is educated to believe in the most marvellous part of it, must not be overlooked. If we ask almost any sincere Christian the question, " Do you believe that the spirits of the departed ever visit this earth?" he may hesitate, but the chances are that he will finally suggest that the Bible warrants an answer in the affirmative. He will doubtless protest, however, that he does not believe in modern spiritism. If you question him closely, you will find that his principal objection will be that the communications received are not in accordance with his religious views.

There is probably no religious sect that would oppose spiritism, if its manifestations and communications were confirmatory of their own peculiar teachings. The Roman and Greek churches have had thousands of miraculous manifestations of saints and devils, which, instead of repudiating, they solemnly affirm to be true. Indeed, the Romanists do not deny

NOTE.—As an evidence of the tendency of the spiritists to extreme credulity, it may be observed by any one who will look over the books of their ablest authors, that they gather up almost all the marvellous stories that have any relation to their theme, many of which have been repudiated and discarded by all sensible writers, and publish them as cumulative evidences of spiritism. Men who have been notoriously skeptical in regard to the Christian religion, since they have become spiritists, believe that all the Roman Catholic legends concerning miracles and saints, had a basis in reality. They reject everything in regard to religion, excepting its most incredible portions. According to their view, witchcraft, instead of being a delusion, consisted of realities that were not understood. The spirits, it seems, had power enough to do infinite mischief, but not enough to do any good.

the phenomena of modern spiritism; on the contrary, they admit their genuineness, but declare they proceed from devils, and prohibit their converts from having anything to do with them. It is clear, then, that modern spiritists are not under the necessity of proving that spirits exists, visit the earth, and manifest themselves in various ways. The people already believe it; the highest church authorities teach it, and the Bible is supposed to sanction it. Prof. Wallace, Mr. Peebles, and Mr. Owen, in boasting of the great number of distinguished characters who believe in spiritism, may with perfect truth add the whole Roman Catholic church, and nine-tenths of all other Christian churches. The only question with Christians is concerning the *character* of the spirits that communicate.

From this view of the subject, it appears that the so-called *converts* to spiritism were, in most cases, believers from their youth up. They are converted and confirmed in what they believed before. When Prof. Wallace and Judge Edmonds estimate the believers at fifteen millions, they fall far short of the reality. Its believers may be reckoned by hundreds of millions; indeed, there are probably few doubters in the civilized world.

ANTI-CHRISTIAN SPIRITISTS.

From the foregoing, it is evidently necessary to distinguish between Christian and anti-Christian spiritists. The modern spiritists, *as a sect*, probably do not number one million, and perhaps not half a million; but they are far from being contemptible on that account, for a majority of them are active, proselyting, enthusiastic, and withal, intelligent people, full of moral courage, enterprise and shrewdness. Why are they not Christians? Andrew Jackson Davis was the real founder of the sect, and he was nominally a Universalist, and so also were all, or nearly all, of the first dozen of his converts and associates. Gibson Smith, Partridge, Newton, Brittan and Fishbough, were, I believe, all Universalist clergymen, and accordingly the first communications were opposed to evangelical orthodoxy. The consequence was that many members of the *liberal* Christian denominations favored them, and the orthodox opposed them. But it was soon ascertained that the spiritists had an element which was necessarily fatal to any Christian church. They professed to receive communications directly from Christ and the apostles, which contradicted the Bible. At one of the seances they pretended that Christ himself came and tipped the table, so as to make it keep time to the tune of Yankee Doodle. The Universalists are strict believers of the Bible, and they, as well as all other Christian denominations, were obliged to disband or repudiate the spiritists. The Swedenborgians, at first, sympathized with Davis, and doubtless supposed that he and his friends would prove valuable auxiliaries, but they were soon undeceived. They believe every word of the Bible, and regard Christ as very God. I have said that the founders of spiritism were nominally Universalists, but there is abundant evidence that they were really unbelievers. The theological scheme which they adopted, and to which they still, as a sect, adhere, may be denominated Swedenborgianism with the Bible left out. One important consequence of their anti-Christian doctrines is, that they have the opposition of all Christian sects, and a great deal of the sympathy of skeptics. If you attend their meetings, you will generally find there the leading irreligious men and women of the vicinity, whether they are spiritists or not, and you will hear discourses that abound with severe criticism of what they style the " popular theology." Another circumstance that must be taken into consideration and explained is, that many of the leading disbelievers in the Bible have become spiritists. The reason of this, after a little reflection, is obvious. They hunger and thirst after religion of some kind, and having abandoned that of their fathers', they are like the prodigal son, left out in the cold, destitute and starving. Under these circumstances a new religion is presented, one that is much better suited to their ideas of freedom from restraint than the old one; the natural desire to live another life, and the desire to meet once more those that have gone before them, is powerful; and when to this is added the evidence which the mediums furnish of actual communications from their departed friends, their skepticism gives way before the strong natural feelings that are aroused within them.

EVIDENCE.

There are certain rules of evidence by which all scientific and all legal minds are guided in the investigation of doubtful and difficult matters. These rules should be constantly borne in mind when considering the nature of the evidence in favor of spiritism.

1. One rule is that those who assert anything new or extraordinary must prove it; and they have no right to demand of skeptics to prove the contrary.

2. Another rule is that they must prove it by the *best* evidence that the case admits of. If the thing in dispute can be inspected, it must be submitted to inspection on all sides, and by every light that can be brought to bear upon it. If it has a history, that must be fairly stated and proved, and the credibility of the witnesses thoroughly tested by cross-examinations, and by inquiries into their capabilities and their previous habits and characters.

3. If the question can be settled by an experiment, that must be tried and repeated under every variety of circumstances, and with every modification that will be likely to exclude error and reveal the truth. If the thing examined is a machine that produces a mysterious effect, the machine should be taken apart and tested in every way calculated to detect deception. I once saw a machine, that it was pretended was endowed with perpetual motion, examined in this manner, and a secret spring discovered. I also saw a complicated contrivance by which it was pretended that illuminating gas could be made from pure water; and in the midst of a shaft a reservoir of petroleum was found concealed. Smugglers, spies, jugglers and detectives are acquainted with a hundred ways in which ordinary investigators can be deceived. A gentleman of great experience declared to me, a few days ago, that not one person in a thousand possesses the proper qualifications for the investigation of the pretended spiritual phenomena, although very few doubt their capability.

4. The spiritists frequently challenge skeptics to debate before public audiences the question whether spiritism is true or false; but on such occasions the

only evidence offered is the mere *ipse dixit* of the spiritists. The skeptic is solemnly called upon to disprove their bold assertions. The most that the skeptic can do on such occasions is to insist upon the production of the proper evidence, and in its absence demand a popular verdict in his favor. The spiritists will relate wonderful things that *they* have witnessed, and declare that they would not have believed if they had not seen them, and yet they expect others to believe without seeing them.

Let us now examine the evidence upon which modern spiritism is founded.

1. Prof. Wallace assumes that those who have examined and reported against spiritism would, in all cases, have made a different report if they had examined longer. In reply to this assumption I will state that modern spiritism grew out of my lectures in Poughkeepsie, in 1843; I was the first to report adversely to the pretensions of the Fox girls; and have continued to investigate the subject ever since, and yet have failed to find a single iota of proper evidence in its favor; on the contrary, there is an overwhelming mass of evidence against it. I have not the slightest doubt that all the so-called spirit phenomena have been produced by Mesmerism (emotionalism), or by jugglery, and I am not alone in this opinion; scores can be produced who saw all the manifestations of the Fox girls in their own home in Hydesville, and who agree with me in regarding them as false.

Prof. Wallace seems to think that because Crookes and Varley, of London, were convinced, therefore spiritism must be true. Might we not, with much more reason, say that the fact that out of the hundreds of scientists in London so few were convinced, with the same evidence before them, proves that it is false? Were Faraday and Carpenter, Huxley and Tyndall less capable of forming a correct judgment than Crookes and Varley? If the evidence were so positive and perfect as Prof. Wallace regards it, surely there should be no skeptics among such capable, truth-seeking men. One would think that the very fact that there were such wide differences among competent judges, ought at least to have induced Prof. Wallace to regard the question as a doubtful one. But Prof. Wallace says that Carpenter, and other scientific opponents, did not investigate long enough — hardly attended five seances while the believers attended fifty, and some were several years engaged in constant investigation before they were convinced. Does not Prof. Wallace perceive that he is proving too much? If the evidence is so clear, positive and abundant, why does it require such a long time and such a repetition of seances? Why is it necessary to winnow out such an immense amount of chaff to obtain a single grain of truth?

In presenting his "Defense of Spiritualism" before the public, Prof. Wallace, in order to make out a clear case, represents the Fox girls as having been tested and examined by committees and skeptics, and as in every instance coming out of the ordeal triumphantly. His statements are all what the lawyers call *exparte*, or one-sided. It is no more than just to presume that he never heard the following adverse evidence:

THE FOX GIRLS.

In the very small village of Hydesville, in Wayne county, N. Y., about five miles from Palmyra, lived an unpretending family, the principal of which was *Mrs. Fox*, the mother of three daughters, the eldest of which, *Mrs. Fish*, was a young widow, and resided in Rochester, while the two younger daughters resided with their mother.

One evening, as the story goes, the attention of the old lady was attracted to an unusual knocking near the feet of one of the girls, and, supposing, of course, that the girl herself made the raps, requested her to stop them; but the girl assured her mother, most solemnly, that she did not make the noises, and was utterly ignorant of the cause of them. It was next observed that the raps seemed to reply to the language of the old lady. Questions were then asked, and a certain specified number of raps requested in reply. Immediately the number of raps mentioned were given, just as if some intelligent person was rapping. The whole village was soon in commotion, and two parties were formed, one of which, judging by the past, contended that the whole thing was a trick of the girls to gain notoriety; while the other party inclined to the opinion that the noises were made by super-natural beings, who had just discovered this method of communicating with mortals. One of the girls soon after made a visit to her sister in Rochester, and the knockings not only followed her, but soon after manifested themselves near or through the sister, *Mrs. Fish*. Accounts of these wonderful communi-cations found their way into the public prints, and were discussed all over the country, under the name of the "Rochester rappings:" thus the fame of the *Fox Girls* soon began to rival that of the Pough-keepsie seer.

The *Foxes*, evidently, it would appear, did not set out with any settled plan of operations. They had no theological system to build up, nor any philosophical theories to maintain or promulgate. They were simple country girls, who woke up suddenly one morning, and found themselves famous. They began, in girlish sport, to make raps upon the floor and the furniture of their rural home, at the same time that they roguishly denied all knowledge of the causes of the raps which they made. None were more astonished than they, at the result; though the cause of their astonishment was very different from that of their dupes. They must have been perfectly amazed at the avidity with which their rude marvels were swallowed, and the hungry eagerness with which more were demanded.

When, however, they found that they were attracting public attention, and were regarded as spiritual mediums, they were not ignorant of the best mode of proceeding to make the most of their pretended gifts.

The following is *Mrs. Fox's* account, as published by *Mr. Ch. W. Elliott:*

" 'T was in December, of the year 1847, that she moved from Rochester into this hired house. Very soon they were disturbed, after going to bed, by various noises, which, however, did not attract much attention, as they supposed them to be made by the rats, which do sometimes, of themselves, have strange doings. It is a pity, that the age and condition of the house are not stated in either account. They were, however, disturbed, and, indeed, kept awake some, until they began to suspect that mischievous persons might be playing tricks. Examination, however, did not show any such explanation, and they were obliged to content themselves with the rats, until, after a space of nearly four months, when, on the last day of March, year 1848, they determined to go to bed early, so as to get a good night's rest, in spite of all noise; but this was not permitted. The thought *then* struck *Mrs. Fox* whose bed was in the same room with that of her two daughters, *Margaretta*, aged fifteen, and *Katy*, aged twelve, that she would question the noise.

"'Who makes the noise?'

"'Is it made by any person living?'

"'Is it made by any one dead?' Rap.

"'If by an injured spirit?' Rap.

"'If injured by her or her family?'

"'If by various other names?'

"Getting no further reply, she arose, somewhat excited, and called her husband, and some of the neighbors, who were yet up.

"The two girls, so *Mrs. Fox* states, were not apparently as much excited as she was, but entered, with some spirit, into the doings of the other spirit, one of them snapping her fingers, and asking the spirit to do as they did, which it did do.

"One of the neighbors followed up the injured spirit, asking, when the injury was done? Five raps, indicating, as they supposed, five years.

"'What name did the injury?' Rap, at the name mentioned of a man who lived there some five years before.

"'Is the body here, then, in the cellar?' A rap was heard, and they determined to dig, but somehow learned that they must delay it some four months, and, of course, did so.

"*Mrs. F.* stated, that, upon digging at the time mentioned, her son, and two others, found some pieces of bone, but whether or not those of a man, does not seem to have been ascertained. The person accused by the spirit, she said, was much outraged, but took no very efficient steps to remove so questionable an accusation. *Mrs. Fox* stated that she left the house, and lived with some friends, as the excitement for, or against them, was so considerable; but, strange to say, the sounds followed her two girls, and, in the course of the summer, the alphabet was revealed to the son, when alone, in the wonderful house.

"The son's wife, also, for a time, she stated, was a 'medium,' for such is the title now used, but has, somehow, lost the gift."

I was informed, in Palmyra, that very few, if any, in that vicinity, believed in the pretensions of the *Fox* girls; even their relatives, who knew them the most intimately, were the most ready to testify against them, as will appear from the following affidavit of *Mrs. Culver.* When *Dr. Boynton* gave a lecture against spiritualism in Palmyra, *Mrs. Culver* exposed, publicly, the manner of producing the raps, and performed, in the presence of the audience, precisely as the *Fox* girls did.

DEPOSITION OF MRS. NORMAN CULVER.

"I am, by marriage, a connection of the *Fox* girls; their brother married my husband's sister. The girls have been a great deal at my house, and, for about two years, I was a very sincere believer in the rappings; but some things which I saw, when I was visiting the girls at Rochester, made me suspect that they were deceiving. I resolved to satisfy myself, in some way; and, some time afterwards, I made a proposition to *Catharine* to assist her in producing the manifestations. I had a cousin visiting me from Michigan, who was going to consult the spirits, and I told *Catharine* that if they intended to go to Detroit, it would be a great thing for them to convince him; I also told her, that, if I could do any thing to help her, I would do it cheerfully—that I would probably be able to answer all the questions he would ask, and I would do it if she would show me how to make the raps. She said, that, as *Margaretta* was absent, she wanted somebody to help her, and that, if I would become a medium, she would explain it all to me. She said that when my cousin consulted the spirits, I must sit next to her, and touch her arm when the right letter was called. I did so, and was able to answer nearly all the questions correctly. After I had helped her in this way, a few times, she revealed to me the secret. The raps are produced with the toes. All the toes are used. After nearly a week's practice, with *Catharine* showing me how, I could produce them perfectly, myself. At first, it was very hard work to do it. *Catharine* told me to warm my feet, or put them in warm water, and it would then be easier work to rap; she said that she sometimes had to warm her feet three or four times in the course of an evening. I found that heating my feet did enable me to rap a great deal easier. I have sometimes produced a hundred and fifty raps in succession. I can rap with all the toes on both feet—it is most difficult to rap with the great toe.

" *Catharine* told me how to manage to answer the questions. She said it was generally easy enough to answer right, if the one who asked the questions called the alphabet. She said, the reason why they asked people to write down several names on paper, and then point to them, till the spirit rapped at the right one, was to give them a chance to watch the countenance and motions of the person; and that, in that way, they could nearly always guess right. She also explained how they held down and moved the tables. (*Mrs. Culver* gave us some illustrations of the tricks.) She told me, that all I should have to do to make the raps heard on the table, would be to put my foot on the bottom of the table when I rapped, and then, when I wished to make the raps sound distinct on the wall, I must make them louder, and direct my own eyes earnestly to the spot where I wished them to be heard. She said, if I could put my foot against the bottom of the door, the raps would be heard on the top of the door. *Catharine* told me, that, when the committee held their ankles, in Rochester, the Dutch servant-girl rapped with her knuckles, under the floor, from the cellar. The girl was instructed to rap whenever she heard their voices calling the spirits. *Catharine* also showed me how they made the sounds of sawing and planing boards. (The whole trick was explained to us.) When I was at Rochester last January, *Margaretta* told me that when people insisted on seeing her feet and toes, she could produce a few raps with her knee and ankle.

" *Elizabeth Fish*, (*Mrs. Fish's* daughter,) who now lives with her father, was the first one who produced these raps. She accidentally discovered the way to make them, by playing with her toes against the foot-board, while in bed. *Catharine* told me that the reason why *Elizabeth* went away west to live with her father, was, because she was too conscientious to become a medium. The whole secret was revealed to me, with the understanding, that I should practice as a medium, when the girls were away. *Catharine* said, that, whenever I practiced, I had better have my little girl at the table with me, and make folks believe that she was the medium, for she said that they would not suspect so young a child of any tricks. After I had obtained the whole secret, I plainly told *Catharine* that my only object was to find out how the tricks were done, and that I should never go any further in this imposition. She was very much frightened, and said she believed that I meant to tell of it, and expose them; and if I did, she would swear it was a lie. She was so nervous and excited that I had to sleep with her that night. When she was instructing me how to be a medium, she told me how frightened they used to get in New York, for fear somebody would detect them; and gave me the whole history of all the tricks they played upon the people there. She said that once *Margaretta* spoke aloud, and the whole party believed it was a spirit.

"Mrs. Norman Culver."

" We hereby certify that *Mrs. Culver* is one of the most reputable and intelligent ladies in the town of Arcadia. We were present when she made the disclosures contained in the above paper; we had heard the same from her before, and we cheerfully bear testimony, that there can not be the slightest doubt of the truth of the whole statement.

"C. G. Pomeroy, M. D.
"Rev. D. S. Chase."

Prof. Flint, Sen., of the Bellevue Medical College, one of the ablest medical authors in America, and Prof. Lee, of the Buffalo University, investigated the subject, and found a lady in Buffalo who could perform precisely what the Fox girls did, and make raps by a peculiar movement of the bones of the knees. The following extracts from Prof. Lee's letter gives the account of their experiences:

" *To the Editors of the Tribune:*

" *Mrs. Fish* and *Miss Fox* were requested to be seated on chairs, their limbs extended, and their heels resting on cushions. The reasons for placing them in this position were stated — viz., that we believed, in order that the raps should be heard, that the feet should have some solid support, serving as a *fulcrum;* else the contraction of the muscles of the leg would not throw the bone, (head of tibia,) out of place; or if so, no sound would be heard, unless the concussion, or vibration, which would be thus produced, could be communicated to some sonorous, or vibrating body. While thus seated, more than fifty minutes elapsed, during which no 'raps' were heard, though the 'spirits' were urged, and called upon, by *Mrs. F.*, to 'manifest' themselves. A part of this time, *Miss Fox* was allowed to seat herself on the sofa — her limbs and feet resting on the cushions of the same. No sounds having been heard, it was suggested, that the ladies be allowed to take any position they pleased, and see if any 'raps' were then heard. Accordingly, they seated themselves on the sofa, their feet resting on the floor, when, immediately, a loud succession of 'raps' followed, and continued for several minutes. We then proposed to try another test; so, seating ourselves before the ladies, we grasped each of their knees firmly, so as to prevent any lateral movement of the bones; the 'raps' immediately ceased, and were not heard while the knees were thus held, except near the close of the experiment, which continued, once, forty minutes, when two slight sounds were heard, on slightly relaxing my grasp, while, at the same time, I distinctly felt the heads of the bones grating on each other, and the muscles contracting, which, though a very positive kind of evidence to me, I am aware, is not so satisfactory to bystanders.

"I should state, that our hands were removed several times from the knees, during the trial, and 'raps' were always heard, during the interval of removal. At the close of the sitting, which continued till past eleven o'clock, *Miss Fox* was much affected, and shed many tears, which excited much sympathy on the part of some of the gentlemen present. I need not add that our position was triumphantly sustained, and that public opinion here, is, now, almost universally, on our side.

*   *   *   *   *   *   *   *

"You may, very naturally, ask, why has not this physiological phenomenon been known to physicians before? I answer, that it has, so far as the smaller joints are concerned. Every person, almost, can snap their finger-joints; many, also, as *Mr. Burr*, can snap their toe-joints, and some their ankles, producing a pretty loud 'rap,' when placed in contact with some sonorous body; but the same phenomenon is very seldom met with in the larger joints, as the knees; and when it is, it has escaped particular observation, and not been made known to physicians, as it neither requires, perhaps, nor admits, of medical aid.

"But it may be said by some, that the above explanation is

not altogether satisfactory, inasmuch as these 'rappings' are heard in different parts of the room, at the same time; or, sometimes, on the table, then the door, then the walls of the room, and at a distance from the 'rappers,' etc. After spending several hours a day, for three days, with *Mrs. Fish* and *Miss F.*, during which the 'raps' were invariably heard, whenever called for, without, as I recollect, a single exception, I found, that, in no one instance, did the sounds seem to proceed from the door, unless *Miss F.* was near enough to touch it with her heel; nor did the sounds seem to proceed from the table, unless she was near enough to the leg of the table to touch it with her foot; but, generally, they proceeded from the floor, apparently, in her vicinity, although the floor could be felt to vibrate, at the same distance from her, just as the whole table would vibrate, when she placed her foot against one of its legs. Much of the confusion and error on this subject, arises, doubtless, from an ignorance of the laws which regulate the propagation of sounds."

Since the detection of the *Fox* girls in Buffalo, I have not learned that they have submitted to another personal examination; but they have, I understand, thrown themselves upon their dignity, and refused.

I received the following statement from such a source, that I have no doubt that it is substantially correct:

When the *Fox* girls visited the city of Washington, *Prof. Page*, the distinguished electro-motive inventor, formerly an examiner in the patent office, tested them, by making them stand upon pillows; but this did not prevent them from rapping. He noticed, however, that they *lowered* themselves a little when they rapped, and, upon reflection, he suspected, that they did this to step off the pillow, and get one foot in contact with the floor; accordingly, at the next interview, he arranged a mat so extensive that they could not step off, and then amused himself by hearing them call in vain upon the spirits to rap. They gradually, and with apparent indifference, got so near the edge of the mat, that they could get a foot over its edge without its being seen, and then, sure enough, the raps were heard. The professor was satisfied that the whole was a deception, and so reported to the public. The spiritualists — that is, *Mr. Fishbough* and the *Fox* girls — claim, that electricity is the agent by means of which the spirits make the raps. No man in the world understands the principles and practicable application of electricity better than *Prof. Page;* but he found that electricity had nothing to do with it, and was forced to the conclusion, that the raps are made by rogues.

The history of physical spirit manifestations would fill several volumes larger than this, but it may be safely asserted that those which have been regarded as the most remarkable, and which have been verified by the most authentic proofs, have been *proved* to be impositions. A memorable instance was that of the Cock Lane ghost in London, in which the chief imposter was a girl, who was at length detected and imprisoned. Another case was that of Angelique Cottin, a girl in France, fourteen years old, who, under the management of one Cholet, deceived the great philosopher Arago, and induced him to have a committee of distinguished scientists appointed, to investigate and ascertain if articles of furniture were moved in a wonderful manner in her presence. After investigation they reported "that certain habitual manoeuvres hidden in the feet and hands, could have produced the observed fact." (*See Popular Science Monthly, March,* 1875.)

Dr. Bell, President of the Massachusetts Medical Society, in 1857, published an account of the movements of a heavy table under the mysterious influence of a young woman near Boston. The authority, talents and character of this gentleman were such that thousands believed without further investigation. I went two hundred miles, called on the doctor, saw the manifestations and satisfied myself that the girl produced them by "manœuvres of her hands and feet." One condition was that no one must look under the table. I demonstrated that, under the same conditions, I could do the same things that she did. A full account of this interview was published by me at the time.

There is, however, no case on record better authenticated, or vouched for on higher authority, than that of Katie King, in Philadelphia. The Hon. Robert Dale Owen, a gentleman of unsurpassed learning, experience and integrity, and author of a remarkable work in favor of these spiritual manifestations, witnessed the pretended materializations of spirits at the house of a Mr. Holmes. He had unrestricted opportunities for examining the rooms, the walls and the furniture. Dr. Child, a reliable gentleman and eminent physician, assisted him. There appeared to be no possible chance for deception. When all was ready, a beautiful woman appeared! Where did she come from? There was no place where she could have entered! She walked about the room, conversed with Mr. Owen, allowed her hands to be felt and kissed, and then disappeared as mysteriously as she came! In an article published in the *Atlantic Monthly*, Mr. Owen fully committed himself in regard to the spir-

itual character of Katie King, and produced a great
sensation by his glowing description of the lovely
vision. A few days afterwards he created a much
greater sensation, by his frank and manly confession
to the public that he had been grossly imposed upon.
It seems that Katie was a young widow who lived in
the neighborhood, and who, when the rooms and bed
were searched, lay concealed in the bolster! If gen--
tlemen of such abilities, experience and learning as
the Hon. Robert Dale Owen and Dr. Child can be
deceived and duped by such people as the Holmes
family and their pretended Katie King, what assur--
ance have we that Professor Crookes or Wallace, or,
indeed, any one else, has been more shrewd or more
fortunate?

Prof. Wallace next introduces and endorses the
tricks of the Davenport brothers, and the Fays, all
of whom are now repudiated by a majority of the
spiritists themselves in their own country. They
have been exposed and imitated again and again by
Dr. Van Vleck, Dr. Phillips, and several other
experts.

A lady in Chicago, named Blair, astonishes her
patrons by painting beautiful flowers in public, while
blindfolded; but Dr. Phillips, a highly respectable citi--
zen of Belvidere, Illinois, allowed himself to be blindfolded in the same manner, by the same committee,
and proved that he could see, notwithstanding, well
enough to draw and paint as well as usual. But
neither he nor Mrs. Blair can perform the same feat,
if a card is interposed between the eyes and the paper
— *this* interferes with the *conditions!* Dr. Slade, Dr.
Van Vleck, and Dr. Phillips can each hold a slate under

a table, while the spirit writes upon it, provided no one looks under or attempts to detect the trick. Dr. Slade declares that a spirit does the writing, but the other two doctors admit that they do it by slight of hand.

When the Fox girls were in Troy, N. Y., the Hon. L. Chandler Ball was astonished, when pointing to the letters of the alphabet on a large card, to find that the Fox girls rapped every time he pointed at the particular letter that he was thinking of; but his wife, a lady of extraordinary sagacity, detected the trick and surprised and amused him, the next day, at home, by proving experimentally that his own face betrayed him in each instance, by indicating when he came to the right letter.

> " Your face, my Thane, is like a book in
> Which man may read strange matters."—*Shakspeare.*

Prof. Wallace, like all other spiritists, insists upon certain " conditions " as necessary to the manifestations. He says:

" Scientific men almost invariable assume that, in this inquiry, they should be permitted, at the very outset, to impose conditions; and if, under such conditions, nothing happens, they consider it a proof of imposture or delusion. But they well know that, in all other branches of research, Nature, not they, determines the essential conditions, without a compliance with which no experiment will succeed. These conditions have to be learnt by a patient questioning of Nature, and they are different for each branch of science. How much more may they be expected to differ in an inquiry which deals with subtle forces of the nature of which the physicist is wholly and absolutely ignorant! To ask to be allowed to deal with these unknown phenomena as he has hitherto dealt with known phenomena, is practically to prejudge the question, since it assumes that both are governed by the same laws."

According to the established laws of evidence, if a performer insists upon a condition which is of such a nature as to favor concealment, or prevent a thorough investigation, his experiment is tainted with a suspicion of fraud, and self-respect requires us to treat it accordingly. It is not incumbent upon the investigator, in such a case, to show that there is actual fraud, nor to point out in what precise way the condition or restriction insisted upon favors fraud, the fact that a restriction is imposed is sufficient of itself to convict the exhibitor of fraud.

It is no answer to this assertion, that "nothing can be done in nature nor in art without conditions;" that is a self-evident fact — nothing can exist without conditions. But concealment, restriction of investigation, is *not* one of the conditions of nature nor of art; it is only required by jugglers, gamblers, confidence-men, swindlers, imposters and cheats. Falsehood can only be effective while the truth is concealed. A very significant fact, which is at the same time a proof that the pretended necessary conditions is a mere blind, is that the writing and speaking mediums perform openly in the presence of large audiences, just as well as in darkness. The truth is, that if the writing or speaking medium is an imposter, you cannot by means of sunlight look into the brain and see the deceit working there. Mr. A. J. Davis, Mr. Jameison, Mr. Loveland, and Mr. Peebles, the very leaders of spiritism, have declared publicly that more than three-fourths of the pretended physical manifestations are deceptive. When so much is admitted, shall we skeptics not be forgiven if we respectfully suggest that the other fourth belongs in the same category? What should we think of a Rt. Reverend minister, who should say to his congregation: "Dearly beloved, three-fourths of the Bible is deception and fraud, but you can make your calling and election sure by believing the remaining fourth!"

MENTAL MANIFESTATIONS.

Under the head of mental manifestations are included the phenomena of trance speakers, seers, healing mediums, vision-seeing mediums, table-tipping and planchette and other writing mediums. There is one important distinction to be made between the mental and the physical manifestations, and that is that nearly all of the former, and none of the latter, can be explained on the assumption that the medium is honest. I have explained the causes of trance, and the manner in which it is induced. The prevailing opinion that one person can Mesmerize or magnetise another is utterly groundless. No one possesses any such power. There is no proper evidence that the will of one person can put another into a trance or a Mesmeric sleep. The power that Mesmerizes or entrances a subject is in the subject's own brain. All that the operator does is to arrange the circumstances and manage the conditions. The spiritists having adopted the erroneous notion that the mere will of the Mesmeric operator entrances his subjects, have *inferred* that there must be an invisible spirit, whose will entrances the mediums. When I demonstrate that the operator's will has no effect, and that the conforming propensities of the subject are the real sources of the power, I take the foundation from under them. Any person who can be entranced by an operator, can also entrance himself without the aid of any operator. This has been proved by hundreds of experiments. I developed the first trance speaker that ever addressed an American audience. It was in Poughkeepsie, New York, in 1843, during the course of lectures that led to the public advent of Andrew Jackson Davis, the first modern spirit medium. A young gentleman named Potter, a nephew of Bishop Potter, was Mesmerized or entranced, and was found to be exceedingly susceptible and versatile. I lectured to very large audiences every evening for several weeks. Young Potter was a graduate of Union College, and a beautiful speaker. One evening he came upon the platform, and after he became entranced, I made him believe that he was Henry Clay, and he at once assumed the character, and astonished all present by imitating the manner and using the very language that many of the audience had heard Clay use. I then told him that he was Daniel Webster, and instantly he changed his manner, and imitated him also. I recollect one sentence of the great orator that he repeated with decided effect:

"I thank God, Mr. President, that my lot has been cast in this country, and in this age; for it is the land of liberty; it is the age of improvement."

The next day after this performance he called at my room in the hotel, and I entranced him, and as a mere amusing experiment I showed him several drawings of the brain and nerves, and explained them to him, and asked him to repeat the lesson, which he did. I then told him not to recollect that he had been to my room when he awoke, but to recollect in the evening, on the platform, that in his own room, at home, the spirit of Dr. Spurzheim had appeared to him and taught him this lesson, and directed him to repeat it to the audience. In the evening he walked forward and repeated the lesson, explaining the structure of the brain and the functions of the nerves in such a manner as to surprise the audience, who all knew him well. One gentleman arose and said, " I know Potter very well — he and I were room-mates in college — and I know that he knows nothing of the nerves and brain; and I wish to ask if we are to understand by this experiment that you stand by Mr. Potter's side and *will* him to use the language and express the ideas that he does?" I replied that as he was an intimate friend, it would be proper for him to ask Mr. Potter himself to give an explanation. He did so, and Potter said, "To-day, in my own room, the spirit of Dr. Spurzheim came, and showed me some drawings, very much like these, and explained them to me, and commanded me to come here to-night and repeat what he taught me." The gentleman turned to me and asked, " Is this story true?" Said I, "Don't you believe your friend and class-mate, Mr. Potter?" " Well, yes, I believe that he would not utter a falsehood; but this is very wonderful." After Potter had returned to his seat in the audience, and the " influence " had apparently passed off, his friends gathered around him and questioned and cross-questioned him; but he adhered to his statement, that, while the doors and windows of his room were fastened, Spurzheim entered and instructed him. At a subsequent lecture I explained to the audience the manner in which I performed the experiment.

It was *after* this performance that Andrew Jackson

Davis was developed as a wonderful speaking and writing medium by some of the persons who had attended my lectures; and when it was reported that he knew things in the trance state of which he was ignorant in the waking state, instead of supposing that it was in consequence of spiritual influence, I very naturally inferred that he had been manipulated and influenced by his friends privately, in a manner similar to that in which I had influenced Mr. Potter, the only essential difference being that I explained to the public the manner in which the feat was performed, whereas the friends of Davis only revealed enough to excite wonder and a belief in spirit agency, thus affording another illustration of the truth that "a little learning is a dangerous thing."*

The motives that actuated the Davis clique will be more apparent when it is further stated that they expected to make a large sum of money out of a book, " Divine Revelations of Nature," that he was dictating under spirit influence. As I was present at the very birth of modern spiritism, and was in some sense accidentally the very father of it, and knew that it had a purely Mesmeric or emotional origin, the reader will readily understand why I have been skeptical concerning all the succeeding manifestations. When, about

* In several histories which I have seen of modern spiritism, it is stated that it began with the advent of the Fox girls, in 1848. This is only true of the physical manifestations. Andrew Jackson Davis commenced his public career in 1843. He and his friends published the first spiritual book, and started the first spiritual newspaper. Among his converts before 1848 were no less than ten clergymen, including Mr. Sprague, Mr. Newton, Mr. Partridge, Mr. Brittan, Mr. Gibson Smith, Mr. Fishbough, and Prof. Bush of the New York University.

five years afterwards, the Fox girls exhibited themselves at Barnum's hotel in New York city, the Davis
clique welcomed them and defended them against the
attacks of the skeptics, particularly Dr. Flint, Dr. Cov-
entry, Dr. Lee, and myself.

Prof. Wallace says, p. 16:

" By explaining table-turning or table-tilting, or raps, you do
not influence a man who was never convinced by them, but who,
in broad daylight sees objects move without contact, and behave
as if guided by intelligent beings, and who sees this in a variety
of forms, in a variety of places, and under such varied and
stringent conditions as to make the fact to him just as real as
the movement of iron to the magnet."

" Dr. J. Lockhart Robertson, long one of the editors of the
Journal of Mental Science — a physician who, having made
mental disease his special study, would not be easily taken in
by any psychological delusions. The phenomena he witnessed
fourteen years ago were of a violent character; a very strong
table being, at his own request and in his own house, broken to
pieces while he held the medium's hands. He afterwards himself tried to break a remaining leg of the table, but failed to do
so after exerting all his strength. Another table was tilted over
while all the party sat on it. He subsequently had a sitting with
Mr. Hume, and witnessed the usual phenomena occurring with
that extraordinary medium — such as the accordion playing
' most wonderful music without any human agency,' ' a shadow
hand, not that of any one present, which lifts a pencil and writes
with it,' etc., etc.; and he says that he can ' no more doubt the
physical manifestations of (so-called) spiritualism than he would
any other fact — as, for example, the fall of an apple to the
ground of which his senses informed him.' His record of these
phenomena, with the confirmation by a friend who was present,
is published in the ' Dialectical Society's Report on Spiritualism,' p. 247; and, at a meeting of spiritualists in 1870, he re-as-
serted the facts, but denied their spiritual origin. To such a
man the *Quarterly Reviewer's* explanations are worthless; yet it
may be safely said, that every advanced spiritualist has seen
more remarkable, more varied, and even more inexplicable
phenomena than those recorded by Dr. Robertson, and is there-

fore still further out of reach of the arguments referred to, which are indeed only calculated to convince those who know little or nothing of the matter."

Prof. Wallace is perfectly right in saying, in substance, that men who think that they have seen impossible things, cannot be convinced by any but impossible arguments. I have not the slightest degree of belief that a pencil, a table, or anything else ever did really rise and write or move about in the manner asserted. It is much more probable that any number of men should dream, with their eyes open, and believe afterwards, that what they saw in their dreams was real, than that such things should actually happen; it is even a thousand times more likely that all the witnesses to these pretended phenomena are guilty of falsehood than that their statements are true. A great many respectable persons have been known to lie in almost every community, but furniture has not been known to move about without any physical agency. The thing is so uncommon as to be incredible, and therefore to require the strongest possible proofs. I agree with Prof. Wallace that a man who has actually seen such things cannot be convinced by any arguments that have been presented, or, I will add, by any that can be. Such a man is beyond the reach of argument or of evidence.

THE TRANCE SPEAKERS.

There has probably been no age or nation of the world in which trance speakers have been unknown; and like all other things that were not understood, the trance has generally been attributed to spirit influence. The ancient Hebrews had their prophets and seers; the Assyrians their soothsayers; the Greeks their oracles, and the Italians their improvisitoires. The Grecian poem-singers, or minstrels, were supposed to be inspired by a special class of spirits called muses. The poetic fervor or inspiration was regarded as a kind of "Divine madness." Even in modern times poets are *licensed* to fly on wings of imagination beyond the boundaries of common sense, on the supposition that there is something etherial, spiritual or semi-angelic in their mental natures which cannot be confined down to the realities of practical life. There is a character or condition of mind that is common to the poetic and to the entranced; the true poet has a larger development of the organs at the upper latteral part of the forehead, and to this is generally added a sensitive and excitable temperament of body. He is also deficient in Acquisitiveness, and indifferent to ordinary business; but he has a large intellect which enables him to enrich the brilliant productions of his fancy with the valuable gems of truth.

If the intellect is shallow, there may be the same poetic disposition, the same glowing fancy, but the productions are all "sound and fury, signifying nothing"; in nautical phrase, there is "more sail than ballast;" we admire it one moment, and then despise or pity the next.

I have explained in another place that trance is produced by the *excitement* of some of the same organs that, when large, produce poetic genius; but, though excited, they may not be large; or, if large, and excited, they may not have the required cultivation, or be accompanied with the requisite perceptive and reflective ability to enable them to produce superior results. Spirit mediums, when entranced, almost always manifest a poetic fancy, and a tendency to use exalted and refined language; so much so, that it seems as if they are not the same persons as in the normal state. But the very same thing is observable in those who are entranced by the common Mesmeric process, especially when refined people are Mesmerized, and their minds turned exclusively to high moral and religious subjects. It is not true, as some spiritists pretend that it is, that entranced mediums of any kind know more than in the normal state; that they speak languages which they never heard before—French, Latin, Spanish or German — it is absolutely false. I have read in books and newspapers that they do so, and I have heard it asserted on the public platform, by persons who seemed to believe it; but again and again, after careful inquiry, I have found it to be untrue.

Almost every week for the last twenty years, I have heard assertions like the following: that the contents of sealed letters were read by mediums; that the names of deceased relatives were written or spoken by a medium who never had heard, or read, or in any way known of them before; that deceased persons were described minutely and accurately, and the circumstances of the last sickness and death related correctly; that the medium painted a correct portrait of a person long since dead, whom he had never seen, nor his photograph, nor even heard him described; that a medium who was utterly ignorant of music, and never played upon a piano before, surpassed all mortal players by her performances while in the trance, but could not play at all when in the normal state. I speak from a large experience, when I pronounce all these stories and pretensions unqualifiedly false. By the accepted and universal rules of evidence, the spiritists have no right to complain of this accusation which I make. If they really can do these things, they can convince the whole world in spite of my denial. I have in vain sought, most diligently, for a single instance in which one of these things could be proved, except by secondary evidence; that is, the evidence of persons who declare that *they* know it, that *they* have had the evidence, and that Crookes, and Owen, and Wallace, and Peebles believe it, and therefore I must not question it. Such evidence I have had in abundance; but if you go into a court of justice with your case, this evidence would not even be heard, much less believed. The court would require the experiments to be repeated and verified, and all the witnessed to be cross-examined, and other witnesses introduced to impeach them, or to show that they were biased, or interested. You cannot deprive a citizen of life, liberty, nor even one dollar's worth of property, without going through the ordeal just mentioned, and yet you ask us to surrender what is infinitely more valuable than anything on earth, upon evidence which every court of justice would reject.

I have conceded that the trance speakers *may* be honest; while I make this concession, I know very well that many of them are not. Some of them were sincere when they were first entranced, and poured forth spontaneously and extemporaneously what was in their minds, but as soon as they began to speak in public, they found it necessasy to cultivate their intellectual faculties, like other people — their knowledge of grammar, rhetoric, history, logic, elocution, theology and science is accumulated in the usual manner. Still there is an activity and acuteness of the mind manifested in the trance, together with a loyalty to the laws of social propriety and refinement, that invests the speaker with a peculiar charm. Prof. Wallace, who evidently understands natural history better than he does mental physiology, on page 44 of his Defense of Modern Spiritism, seems to regard the peculiar excellences of the trance speakers as evidences of their inspiration. He says:

Those who helped most to spread the belief were, perhaps, the trance speakers, who, in eloquent and powerful language, developed the principles and the uses of spiritualism, answered objections, spread abroad a knowledge of the phenomena, and thus induced skeptics to inquire into the facts; and inquiry was almost invariably followed by conversion. Having repeatedly listened to three of these speakers who have visited this country, I can bear witness that they fully equal, and not unfrequently surpass our best orators and preachers; whether in finished eloquence, in close and logical argument, or in the readiness with which appropriate and convincing replies are made to all objectors. They are also remarkable for the perfect courtesy and and sauvity of their manner, and for the extreme patience and gentleness with which they meet the most violent opposition and the most unjust accusations.

Trance speaking.—The medium goes into a more or less unconscious state, and then speaks, often on matters and in a style far beyond his own capacities. Thus, Serjeant Cox — no mean judge on a matter of literary style — says, " I have heard an uneducated bar-man, when in a state of trance, maintain a dialogue with a party of philosophers on 'Reason and Foreknowledge, Will and Fate,' and hold his own against them. I have put to him the most difficult questions in psychology, and received answers, always thoughtful, often full of wisdom, and invariably conveyed in choice and elegant language. Nevertheless a quarter of an hour afterwards, when released from the trance, he was unable to answer the simplest query on a philosophical subject, and was even at a loss for sufficient language to express a commonplace idea." That this is not overstated, I can myself testify, from repeated observation of the same medium. And from other trance speakers — such as Mrs. Hardinge, Mrs. Tappan, and Mr. Peebles — I have heard discourses which, for high and sustained eloquence, noble thoughts, and high moral purpose, surpassed the best efforts of any preacher or lecturer within my experience.

In regard to Mrs. Hardinge, to whom Prof. Wallace refers as a trance speaker — although in her book she does me gross injustice — I confess that I am one of her admirers. It is true that she has been trained in the very best of schools, and taught the art of elocution and the uses of poetical rhetoric; but thousands who have enjoyed equal advantages have failed as speakers. Mrs. Hardinge, though apparently awake when declaiming, is probably under an " influence " which she does not fully understand, and probably believes to be a spirit. However that may be, it is certain that she is one of the most accomplished public speakers I ever heard. Her elocution, her rhetoric, her manner, her voice, are perfect; even her logic — if you admit her premises — is faultless. I felt a deep regret, when I heard her, that such splendid talents could not be devoted to more useful purposes.

Prof. Wallace also refers in a complimentary manner to the Hon. J. M. Peebles. What I have said of Mrs. Hardinge applies in a good degree to him. He is a highly cultivated gentleman, of large experience as a public speaker, thoroughly acquainted with the arts of social life, and more than sincere — almost fanatical — in his belief of what he advocates. He very much resembles Prof. Wallace in his enthusiastic endorsement of the extravagancies of spiritism. With all this he mingles a knowledge of the world, of philosophy, of theology, of history, that to my mind seems to be utterly inconsistent with his unbounded credulity in regard to his special and favorite theme. It is easy for me to understand that such a man, when in a trance, even partially, can become a fascinating speaker. Mr. Peebles differs from all the so-called inspirational speakers that I have heard in the fact that he makes his discourses instructive. He does not deal, as the other trance speakers do, in mere beautiful nothings, but seems to have some pity for the ignorance of a large number of his co-believers and marvel-loving auditors.

PERSONATION.

I can also endorse all that Prof. Wallace says of Impersonation, except their speaking foreign languages never heard in the normal state; and I notice that Prof. Wallace does not profess to know the fact himself, except by report.

He says:

Impersonation.—This occurs during trance. The medium seems taken possession of by another being; speaks, looks and acts the character in a most marvelous manner; in some cases speaks foreign languages never even heard in the normal state; as in the case of Miss Edmonds, already given. When the influence is violent or painful, the effects are such as have been in all ages imputed to possession by evil spirits.

In another place I have referred to the dramatic effects produced by the excitement of the conforming social organs, particularly Imitativeness — those very organs that are large in dramatic authors, and that are the sources of their inspiration, are excited in trance mediums and Mesmerized subjects.

Whoever has had much experience in Mesmerism, and has seen six or eight persons all entranced at once, must have observed a strange and often ridiculous disposition to imitate. If one does a thing, another is very likely to begin to do the same; or if the operator wishes to amuse his audience, he cannot do it more effectually than by telling a subject that he is some one else, who is known to the audience, and who has some striking peculiarities of voice or gait or manner; not only so, but if you tell him that he is a lion, a horse, or a locomotive, he will not merely imitate those things, but he will show by his manner and speech that he has no doubt, at the time, that he *is* just what he is personating. He not only enters into the spirit of it, but the spirit of it enters into him. If he is a natural actor, his performances surpass in ludicrousness anything ever seen in a theatre.

When these facts in regard to Mesmeric trances are understood, the mystery of the personifications of spirit mediums disappears, or is merged into that of Mesmerism. It is common for entranced mediums to believe or assume that they are *possessed* by the spirit of a deceased Indian. In that case the medium enacts the character and imitates the broken English that he has heard Indians use or been told that they use. It is often asserted that they speak the native Indian language; but there is no truth in the assertion. They merely represent the character as they understand it, and they do this with a degree of acuteness and *abandon* that is admirable. The same medium is sometimes supposed to be controlled by several different deceased persons — one at a time, however; and I have seen a delicate young woman go into a trance and enact the part of an Indian chief for half an hour, and then "switch off" onto an old lady, and then change again and enact the part of a docto ; and though we know very well that the whole performance is merely dramatic, it is sometimes done so admirably that we are strongly tempted to surrender our better judgment, and admit that it is real. This is especially true where the medium is an interesting young lady, in whose sincerity we have implicit confidence.

The personification sometimes assumes another form. The medium describes the disease, or perhaps the death, of some person—not by words, but by imitating the supposed patient. If the medium has proper information, this is done with painful accuracy. It is often pretended that the spirit of the deceased takes possession of the medium, and repeats the death scene under circumstances in which there could have been no knowledge of the case on the part of the medium. This is not true.

DEGREES AND MODES OF TRANCE AND CONFORMITY.

I have described the effects of extreme conformity upon the mental and vital functions, but there are many degrees of conformity. In trying the trance experiments, the operator will find on an average about one in a company of ten who will become a perfect dreamer, and who can be put, temporarily, into any mental condition that, with his abilities, he is capable of assuming. But though the remaining nine may none of them be fully entranced, a careful examination will enable the operator to discover that a majority of them are affected to a greater or less degree. Perhaps one will be unable to open his eyes when told that he cannot, or he opens them with difficulty, but all other experiments with him may fail; another will move his hand involuntarily, as if writing, and yet will not write anything intelligible; a third, when told that a pencil or anything else is hot, will be unable to hold it, yet he cannot be influenced otherwise. A majority of persons can be relieved of the headache, or any other slight ailment that can be affected by a change in the circulation of the blood. It is common to find subjects that can be controlled in their movements, but not in their sensations; some can become writing mediums, but not vision-seeing mediums. These differences in subjects depend upon the peculiar conditions of their minds, their opinions, beliefs, prejudices and caprices, many of which may be unknown to the subjects themselves.

It frequently happens that one of those who are experimented with, pretends to be affected when he is not, and performs all the feats suggested, to the satisfaction of the operator and the whole company. The question is often asked, can we detect the imposition in such cases, and distinguish between the genuine and the counterfeit? If the person tried is not affected in the slightest degree — if his pulse, his breathing, and the temperature of his fingers do not vary, he is certainly not affected, whatever he may pretend. But a subject may manifest all the bodily symptoms, and yet his mind be unaffected, or but slightly affected. In such a case he may counterfeit the trance, and perform in such a manner as to deceive any one, however experienced. The only evidence we have in many cases that the subject is really entranced, and is not deceiving, is his own word of honor. I know of no person who has had half the experience in these matters that I have, and yet I am often unable to distinguish the true from the false. I never perform an experiment, even with the most respectable people, without guarding against false pretences, by asking them such questions that they cannot deceive without disgracing themselves, by adding falsehood to treachery.

From the preceding explanations, the reader will be prepared to believe that the conforming trance furnishes the key to many of the otherwise unaccountable transactions of both men and women. In matters relating to sickness, to love, to business, to religion, to crime, we often see a person of at least ordinary intelligence, surrendering his own interest, judgment, person, property, character, in a manner that indicates a kind of infatuation nearly akin to insanity. In many of these cases, I have no doubt that the victim is actually in a condition nearly analogous to that of those who are in the Mesmeric trance.

HALLUCINATION.

When a person appears to be perfectly awake, and yet believes that he perceives things that do not really exist, except in his own dreaming imagination, he is said to be laboring under an hallucination. The common Mesmeric conforming experiments are very instructive on this subject. They prove that at least one person in ten will, under certain circumstances that are easily arranged, seem to see visions of persons and things near him, that only exist in his own mind. He can be made to hear voices and experience cold, heat, pain, or any other sensation whatever — in a word, to dream anything that can be imagined, while to all appearance he is awake and actively engaged in his ordinary business.

This fact being fully understood and appreciated, enables us to understand how some honest and truthful people come to relate such incredible stories as they do concerning their experiences and observations in regard to modern spiritism. They assert, in the most solemn manner, that they have seen tables, chairs, pianos and stoves move about without physical agency; that a man was raised by invisible forces — not physical — and conveyed out of one window and in through another; that a beautiful painting, which an ordinary artist could only produce in a week, they have seen executed in half an hour; that photographs are taken of deceased persons; that they have often conversed with people who have been dead many years. There is, of course, not a shadow of truth in any of these statements, but neither is there necessarily any *intentional* falsehood. If we gently intimate that they were in a dreaming state of mind, they indignantly reject this charitable hypothesis and leave us no alternative but silence or rudeness.

The works of Shakspeare give some some fine illustrations of this species of hallucination. He lived in the times when witchcraft abounded in Europe. So keen an observer of human nature was not likely to let the extraordinary phenomena which attended that remarkable delusion escape his notice. There is nothing in his writings that I have admired more than

the wonderful accuracy with which he describes some
of the curious phases of hallucination. He must have
seen persons in what we should now call a trance. He
denominates it *ecstacy*. Macbeth is represented as subject to it.   If he lived at the present day he would
be regarded as a vision-seeing medium. He was a
nobleman, a military commander, and a Roman Catholic, fully imbued with the superstitions of his age
and nation. On his way homeward from a successful
expedition against the Norwegians, he met a band of
gypsies, who prophesied that he would ultimately
become king. He was convinced, as he wrote to his
wife, that they "had in them more than mortal knowledge." Prompted by his wife, and goaded on by his
ambition, he resolved to murder the venerable monarch who was his guest. Arming himself with a dagger, at the hour of midnight, he is stealthily crossing
the great hall of his castle of Iverness, listening fear-
fully to each noise. "Thou sure and firm set earth
hear not my steps." His mind filled with superstitious dread, yet firmly resolved. Ah! he sees a vision
of a dagger in the air. He sees it so plainly, and so
near, that he reaches forth his hand — "Come let me
clutch thee"; but he only clutches the air. "I have
thee not, and yet I see thee still. Art thou not, fatal
vision, sensible to feeling as to sight?" And thus
reason combats the delusion: "Art thou but a dagger
of the mind, a false creation proceeding from the heat-
oppressed brain?" He looks again, and finally comes
to a conclusion that our spiritual friends might well
adopt: " *Tis no such thing.*"

In the banquet scene, the ruffians whom he employed
to kill Banquo come and inform him that " Deep in a

ditch he lies, with forty mortal murders on his crown."
With this idea in his mind, he commences the banquet by proposing Banquo's health, when, in the very
place where Banquo would have sat had he been present, there was his pale and bloody ghost, staring him
in the face. No one else saw anything strange, but
Macbeth, supposing that others saw what he did,
exclaims: " Can such things be and overcome us like
a summer cloud, without our special wonder?" " You
can keep the natural ruby of your cheeks, while mine
are blanched with fear." And when his wife, fearing
that he would betray himself, said: " After all, you
look but on a stool!" He exclaims: If " I stand here
I saw *him*." I have heard many spiritists make similar exclamations, with equal sincerity and with equal
truth.

Hamlet is another of Shakspeare's mediums. In
the scene where he upbraids his mother, he suddenly
sees the spirit of his father, and hears his voice commanding him to forbear. His mother asks:

Queen.—Alas! how is't with you,
          That you do bend your eye on vacancy,
          And with the incorporeal air do hold discourse.
          Whereon do you look ?
Hamlet.—On him! on him!
          Look you how pale he glares!
Queen.—To whom do you speak this ?
Hamlet.—Do you see nothing there?
Queen.—Nothing at all; yet all that is I see
Hamlet.—Nor do you nothing hear?
Queen.—No; nothing but ourselves.
Hamlet.—Why, look you there! Look how it steals away!
          My father in his habit as he lived!
          Look, where he goes even now out at the portal!

Queen.—This is the very coinage of your brain,
      This bodiless creation ecstacy
      Is very cunning in.
Hamlet.—Ecstacy! my pulse
      As yours doth temperately keep time,
      And makes as excellent music.

Shakspeare is the only author that I know of who has remarked that ecstacy or trance is accompanied by a change in the pulse.

APPENDIX.

___

PHRENO-CHART OF

EXPLANATION OF THE MARKS USED IN EXAMINATION.

If a head is perfectly balanced, every organ will be marked 4. If an organ is marked more than 4, it is above the average of the organs of the same head; if it is marked less than 4, it is below the average. An interrogation point (?) signifies that the examiner is in doubt about the organ.

APPENDIX.

APPENDIX.

OPINIONS.

When Prof. Grimes' system was first published, the Phreno-logical societies of Buffalo, Albany, Hartford and London, appointed committees who, in each instance, reported in its favor, and regarded it as a great improvement upon the systems of his predecessors. The following is an extract from the report of the Albany society, of which Thomas W. Olcott was president and Rufus Peckham (afterwards attorney general) vice-president. Among the members were Prof. Amos Dean, Prof. E. N. Hors-ford, and Mr. Wm. Combe, brother of Geo. Combe, the phreno-logical author:

" While the division of the powers into three classes, and their subdivision into ranges and groups, may be considered import-ant and useful, the distinguishing feature, and that which to the committee constitutes the highest merit of the new classification consists in this, that it traces the chain of functional relation-ship, from the lowest organ to the highest of each class.

" If Mr. Grimes' classification is founded in nature, the follow-ing are some of the advantages which may be expected from its adoption:

" 1. It will facilitate the application of phrenological princi-ples in deciding upon character from an examination of the head. Upon noticing the predominance of one class of organs. it may be said of the individual thus marked, he is Ipseal, Social, or Intellectual; or, upon observing two classes prevailing over the third, it may be said, he is Ipseal and Intellectual, or Social and Intellectual, or both Ipseal and Social. The same principle will be applicable in speaking of the development of one group, or of two groups of the Socials, and also of the ranges of Ipseals and Intellectuals. The effects of a combined development of particular groups in the different classes will be more readily understood.

" 2. It will aid analysis, in ascertaining the ultimate function of each organ. Upon knowing its position, and the relation it sustains to others — with what organ it would probably act, and whether in the centre of a class, or joined to organs of other classes, its manifestations will be more readily perceived, and more clearly comprehended.

" 3. It will aid in discovery, by directing the eyes of all phrenologists to limited regions of the brain, when in search for the seat of a faculty, in whose existence they have been induced to believe. For example, if the seat of a supposed power related to corporeal wants be sought, the attention will be directed to developments and deficiencies in the corporeal range. If the function of the organ occupying the region marked upon the bust of Mr. Combe as unknown, be the object of discovery, several aids will be afforded. It must, in the first place, be either Ipseal or Social; and in the second place, it must be either a Social of the conforming group, or an Ipseal of the human range.

" 4. It will furnish phrenology with new claims to the characted of an established science; and by its simplicity and consistency, will induce the student to pursue its investigation with the same kind of satisfaction that now attends his study of the older sciences.

" In conclusion, the committee state, that distrusting their own abilities to discharge the duties assigned them, they entered into correspondence upon the question to be determined with several phrenological writers. They have also examined all the published works relating to the subject which they could command. And with these materials before them, after weighing the whole matter, the result is the opinion, that the classification of Mr. Grimes is a decided improvement, as it arranges the powers of the mind more nearly in accordance with the laws of natural relationship than any of the systems which have preceded it.

" E. N. HORSFORD, *Chairman
of Committe on Grimes' Classification.*"

———

" At the close of Mr. Grimes' lectures, delivered in the Chapel of the Albany Female Academy, the class organized by appointing Charles D. Townsend, M. D., Chairman, and Thomas W. Olcott, Esq., Secretary. Whereupon Henry Green, M. D., introduced the following resolutions, which were unanimously adopted:

"*Resolved*, That we have listened with exciting interest to the lectures of Mr. Grimes, President of the Phrenological Society of Buffalo, on the science of Phrenology.

"*Resolved*, That we believe Mr. Grimes has made new and important discoveries in Phrenology; that his arrangement of the brain into three classes of organs, viz.: — the Ipseal, Social and Intellectual, together with their subdivisions into ranges or groups, is founded in nature, the anatomy of the brain, and the natural gradation of animals as they rise in the scale of being.

"*Resolved*, That we are forced to believe that Phrenology, as taught by Mr. Grimes, may be learned by persons of ordinary intelligence and observation, so as to be useful to them in their every day intercourse with society — that it is destined to improve our race, remodel the present mode of education, become useful in legislation, and in the government of children in families and in schools.

"*Resolved*, That we not only esteem it a duty, but regard it a pleasure, to encourage talents, genius and enterprise, wherever we discover them, and in whatever pursuit, if the object and effect is the improvement of mankind — that we regard Mr. Grimes as possessing the highest order of intellect, as original in his observations and deductions, and as destined to fill a distinguished place in the scientific world.

"*Resolved*, That we confidently recommend Mr. Grimes to the attention of our fellow-citizens in different sections of our extended country, believing they will find him an accomplished lecturer, a close, accurate, forcible reasoner, and inimitable in his illustrations of the science he so triumphantly advocates.

"*Resolved*, That Henry Green, M. D., and Professor McKee, of the Albany Academy, be a committee to present a copy of these resolutions to Mr. Grimes, and request their publication in the daily papers of the city.

"C. D. TOWNSEND, M. D., *Chairman.*
"T. W. OLCOTT, *Secretary.*"

"Professor Grimes, the phrenologian, whose original and ingenious views on phrenological science have caused his lectures to be very much followed in our western cities, has arrived here, and puts up at the Astor. He brings with him most flatter-

356

ing testimonials, from his Excellency the Governor and others of Albany, where his last course was delivered. He proposes, we are pleased to hear, to give an opportunity to the citizens of New York to judge of the merits of his discoveries and deductions, in what he justly terms the science of phreno-physiognomy, embracing all the phenomena developed in the brain, features, and whole organization, and character and habits of the individual, as divided into three great orders of mammalia, viz.:—the *carnivoræ*, the *graminivoræ* and the *rodentia*—corroborated by illustrations from every tribe of animated nature—the only true and exact base of this interesting science."—*N. Y. Star.*

" *Lecture on Phrenology.*— Professor Grimes, we are happy to hear, has consented to repeat his introductory lecture on Phrenology this evening, at the rooms of the American Institute, rear of the City Hall. The views on the science of Phrenology, presented by Professor Grimes on Monday evening, were entirely new, and elicited a universal request from the audience for a repetition on this evening, and we trust all who feel an interest in the subject will attend."—*N. Y. Times.*

" We understand, the lectures of Mr. Grimes, at the Crosby street Institute, before the Mechanics' and Tradesmen's Library Association, are so crowded that it is next to impossible to obtain admission. Last night a great number had to go away. We felt sure that when this gifted and luminous expounder of the only true laws of phrenological science should have a hearing, he would daily gain more and more converts to his views on this interesting subject."—*N. Y. Star.*

" *Phrenology.*.—This science, which seems strongly based upon truth, however erroneous may be some of the theories deducted from it, and however mistaken some of its professors may be in its application, nevertheless appears to be slowly gaining a strong hold upon the faith of the multitude. A new and popular lecturer on this subject is now in this city, and will deliver a course, . as will be seen by the advertisement. Mr. Grimes gave an introductory lecture last evening. His first regular lecture will commence this evening. His mode of illustration is exceedingly happy and forcible. Possessing a great fund of humor, he tickles his audience into a roar while conveying much important information—so, his hearers are both instructed and exceedingly amused at the same time. We cannot tell, of course, how the

357

lectures will wear; but he seems to have made a decided hit in the beginning. We understand that he has made some practical experiments of his theory at the College, with great success, hitting the characters even of those who attempted to mislead him. We perceive that Mr. Grimes brings with him flattering testimonials from a number of well known individuals in the larger cities, and the Phrenological Society of Albany have published resolutions highly commendatory of him and his system."—*New Haven Palladium.*

" Mr. Grimes' Phrenological Lectures have been exceedingly well received in this city, by the class in attendance. As he progressed with his course, his hearers increased, and those who were in constant attendance were apparently more and more interested with every succeeding lecture, to the close of the series. We do not believe Mr. Combe is his superior, in any sense, as a lecturer on this science, and we know he is altogether his inferior in many particulars. The following resolutions express the opinions of most if not all of Mr. Grimes' hearers in this city."— *New Haven Palladium.*

" *Professor Grimes.*—This gentleman is slowly, but surely gaining a merited popularity among our citizens, without resorting to any of the usual means to acquire notoriety; hardly advertising in the public prints to inform our people that he is present with us, his audiences are nightly increasing, and are of a class which neither humbugs nor mediocrity could satisfy. His great merit is quaint and hearty originality. He appears to be a close observer of human nature, the foibles of which he illustrates with infinite fancy and sarcasm. His manner of discourse is peculiar; he is exceedingly impressive in depicting the different emotions of the mind, a capital mimic, when relating the droll anecdotes in which he abounds, and yet sober and serious when treating of the more profound themes of his discourse.

" The basis of his lecture is Phrenology, being a modification of the systems of Spurzheim and Combe. He does not confine himself to the brain alone, but to the whole structure and constitution of the frame, to judge of the tendencies and capabilities of the individual.

" Mr. Grimes, we understand, is a lawyer of some eminence in the State of New York. Having had much success as a lecturer, he employs the vacant time between the sessions of the court, in promulgating his peculiar views on men and things. This is his first visit to our city in this capacity, although originally a Boston boy, where at school, we have heard it hinted, he was chiefly remarkable for the fact that he could thrash every boy in it. He seems disposed to come off victorious even now with any one, either physically or mentally, who is inclined to grapple with him, or is anxious to feel the weight of his calibre. His lecture this evening is on Hope, at the Tremont Temple."—*Boston Daily Whig*.

A VISION SEEING MEDIUM.

" I see a beautiful rainbow, and beyond, beneath the arch, I see the spirit land, and I hear the spirits sing."

A TABLE TIPPING MEDIUM.

Push, young man! Push, Spirit! Push, both of you!

MIND READING.

362